THE BEST OF The MAILBOX® Magazine

The Best of The MAILBOX® Book 4

Grades 4–6

Table of Contents

Since the first book was published in 1988, ***The Best of* The Mailbox®** books have become the most popular titles available to teachers of grades 4–6 today. Now we're proud to present the newest ***The Best of* The Mailbox®** book for intermediate teachers, ***The Best of* The Mailbox®—*Book 4.*** Inside these covers, you'll find many of the best teacher-tested ideas published in the 1997–2001 issues of *The* Intermediate *Mailbox®* magazine. Our editors selected these practical ideas from those sent to us by teachers across the United States. We've included many of our regularly featured sections of the magazine plus special teaching units and reproducibles.

www.themailbox.com

Project Managers: Becky Andrews, Peggy Hambright
Copy Editors: Sylvan Allen, Gina Farago, Karen Brewer Grossman, Karen L. Huffman, Amy Kirtley-Hill, Debbie Shoffner
Cover Artist: Clevell Harris
Art Coordinator: Theresa Lewis Goode
Typesetters: Lynette Dickerson, Mark Rainey

President, The Mailbox Book Company™: Joseph C. Bucci
Director of Book Planning and Development: Chris Poindexter
Book Development Managers: Stephen Levy, Elizabeth H. Lindsay, Thad McLaurin, Susan Walker
Curriculum Director: Karen P. Shelton
Traffic Manager: Lisa K. Pitts
Librarian: Dorothy C. McKinney
Editorial and Freelance Management: Karen A. Brudnak
Editorial Training: Irving P. Crump
Editorial Assistants: Terrie Head, Hope Rodgers, Jan E. Witcher

ISBN# 1-56234-488-9

Manufactured in the United States
10 9 8 7 6 5 4 3 2 1

CLASSROOM DISPLAYS

CLASSROOM

Lock up a sensational school year with this student-made display! Post an enlarged copy of the locker character shown. Have each student fill in the rim of a lock pattern (page 22) with her own combination for unlocking a great year. Then have her label the lock with her name and lightly color it. All locked up!

Michelle Trubitz—Grs. 5–6, Brookside Upper Elementary, Westwood, NJ

For a year that's sure to shape up nicely, "tri" this motivational display! Give each student a large equilateral triangle cut from colorful paper. Have the child decorate his cutout to illustrate a way he can "tri" to succeed this year. Mount the drawings on a bulletin board as shown to create one giant triangle. Not enough student triangles to complete the large one? Just ask several kids to decorate more than one triangle. Or if you have more student triangles than you need, use the extras to decorate the corners of the display.

Andrea Troisi
LaSalle Middle School
Niagara Falls, NY

DISPLAYS

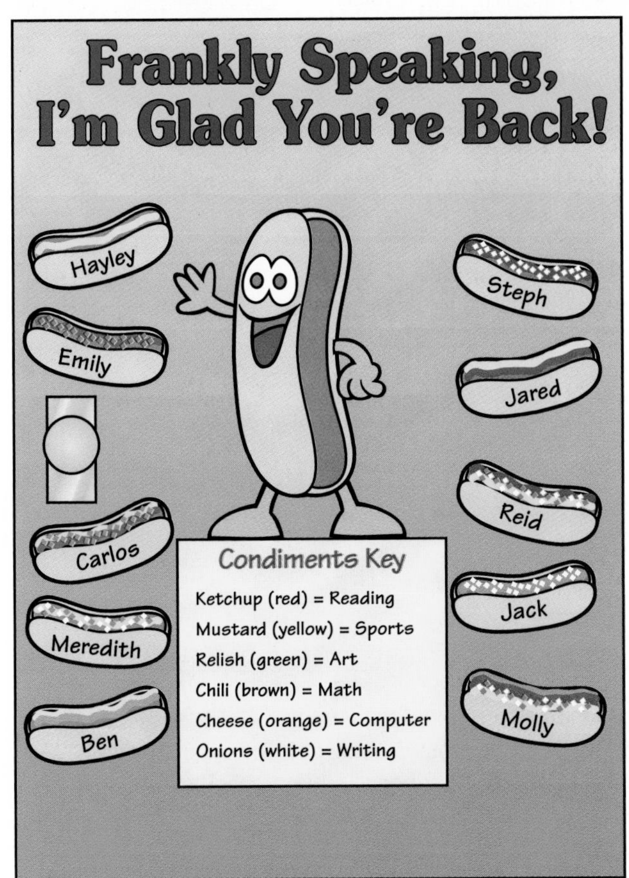

Welcome students back with this "hot-doggity" door display! Post an enlarged copy of the character shown on your classroom door. On the first day of school, have each student label a hot dog pattern (page 22) with his name; then have him decorate it using crayons and the Condiments Key shown to indicate some of his favorite things. Post the hot dogs and a key on your door for a display that's frankly fantastic!

adapted from an idea by Donna DeRosa—Gr. 4
Good Shepherd Academy
Nutley, NJ

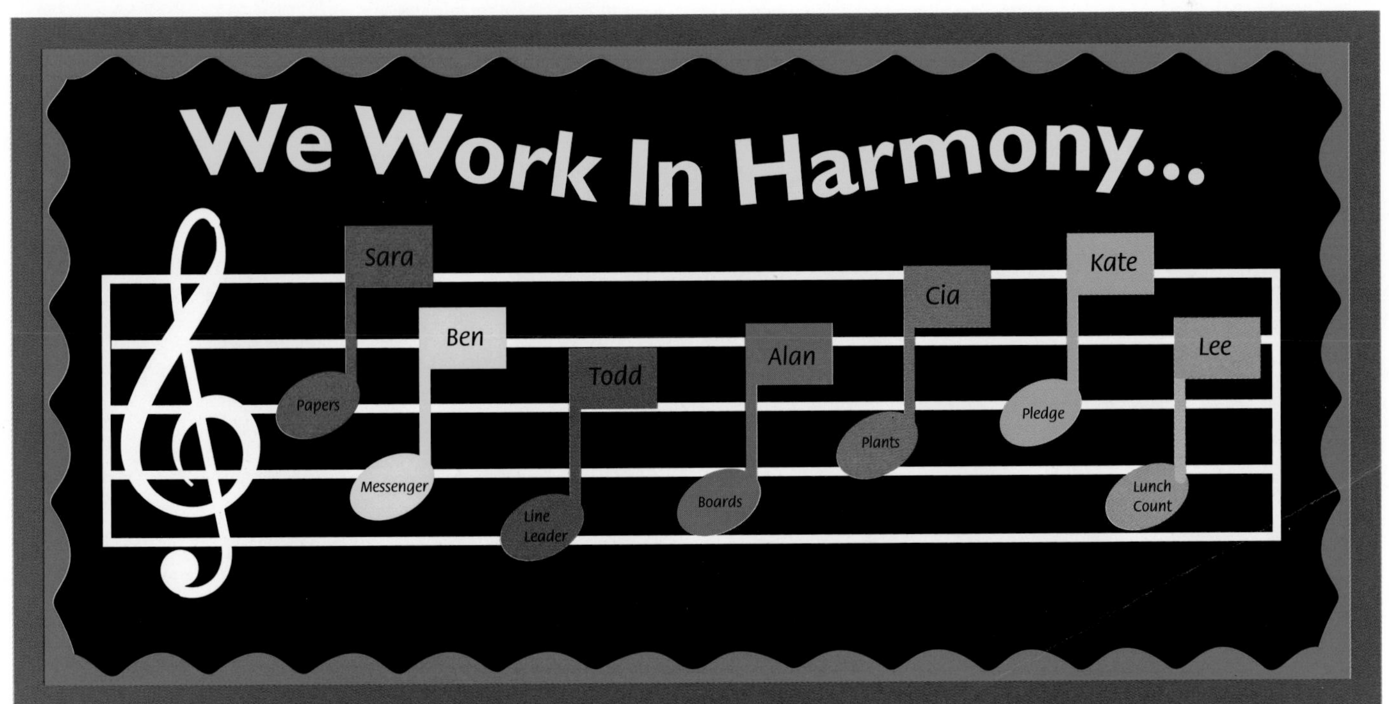

Harmonious helping abounds with this class helpers board! Use chalk to draw a music staff and clef sign on black background paper. Label a note cutout with each job. Laminate the notes; then assign jobs by writing students' names on them with a wipe-off marker. Each week allow new helpers to rearrange the notes' placement. A different melody will always be playing!

Rebecca R. Amsel—Gr. 4, Yeshiva Shaarei Tzion, Piscataway, NJ

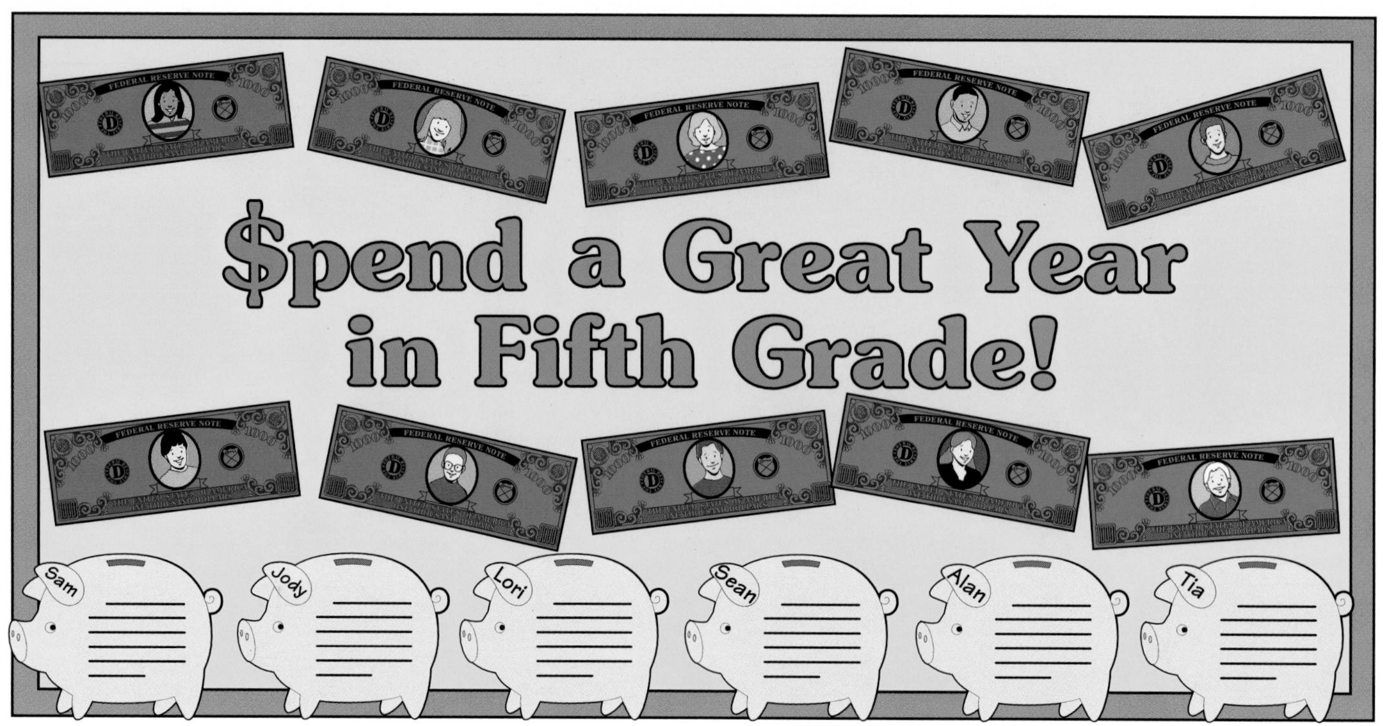

Let your new students know they can bank on a great year! For each child, duplicate the bill pattern on page 23 on green paper. Cut out the center oval; then tape a photo of the new student behind it and post as shown. Add a border of pink paper piggy banks (pattern on page 23) on which students have written paragraphs describing their hopes for the school year or how they'd spend $1,000.

Karen Maresca—Gr. 6, St. Vincent de Paul School, Stirling, NJ

Set aside a spot to share everyone's good news with this idea! Label and display a six-inch paper circle for each student as shown. Encourage students to share their good news—awards, newspaper clippings, birth announcements, photos, etc.—by stapling them onto their spots. Periodically remove old spots and replace them with new ones.

Pat Twohey—Gr. 4, Old County Road School, Smithfield, RI

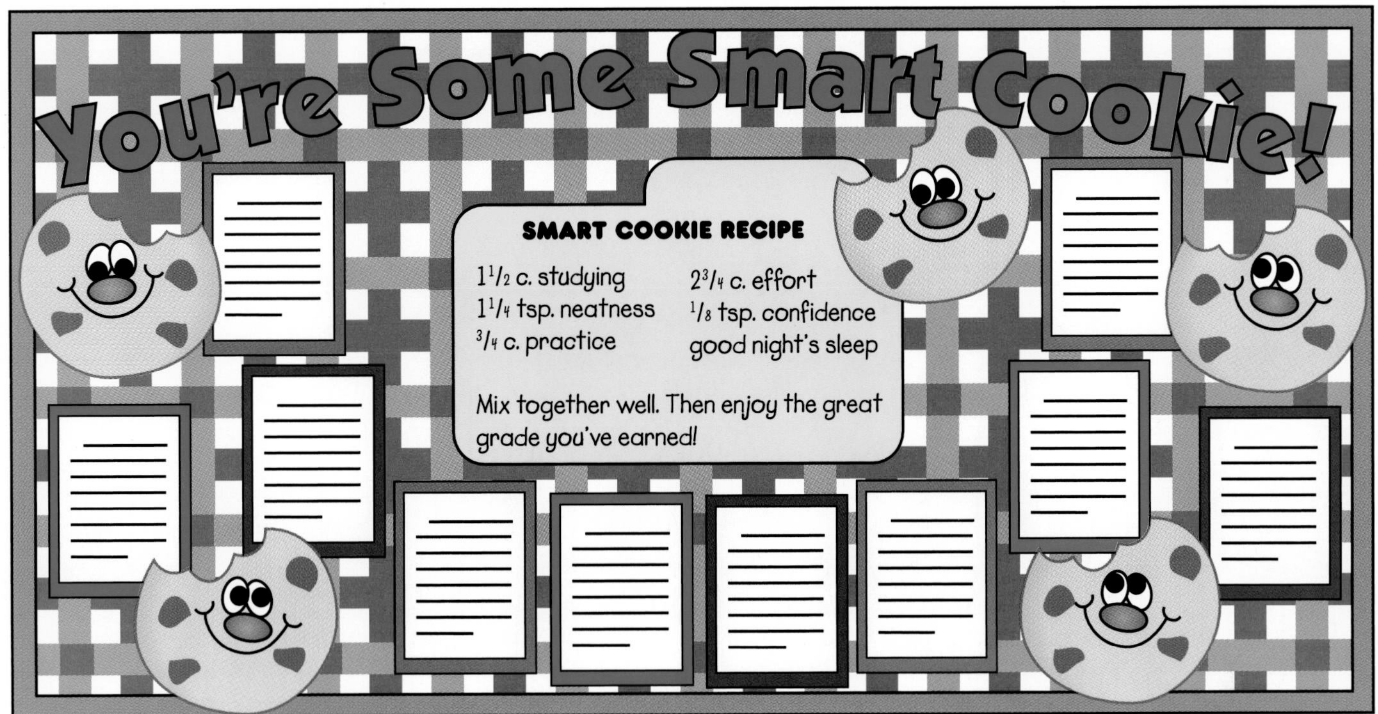

Cook up a batch of better work habits with this yummy display! Decorate a bulletin board with a plastic tablecloth and cutout cookies. Give each of several groups a giant poster board recipe card. On its card, have each group write a recipe that describes the study habits of a "smart cookie." On Monday post one of the group's recipes along with excellent student papers. At the end of the week, replace the card with another group's recipe.

adapted from an idea by Andrea Wohl—Gr. 5, Washington School, Westfield, NJ

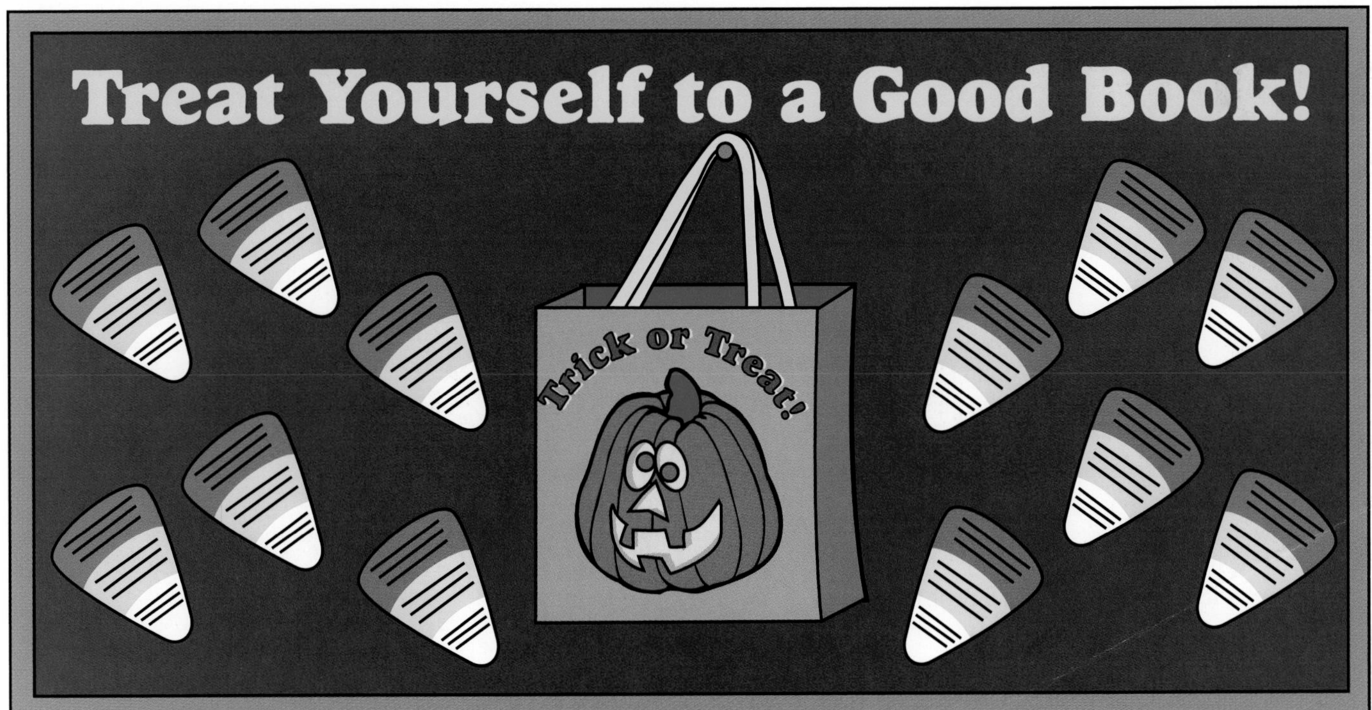

For a book report project that's a treat to complete, duplicate a class supply of the candy corn templates on page 24. Have each student trace his templates onto orange, yellow, and white paper as directed. Then have him cut out the tracings and label them with the information indicated on the templates. Finally, have the student glue his cutouts together on a piece of construction paper and cut out the completed piece of candy. Post the candy corn pieces on a bulletin board along with a trick-or-treat bag.

Brenda A. Keller—Gr. 5, Canadochly Elementary, East Prospect, PA

PUZZLE PATCH

To plant a patch of vocabulary review, have each student cut out a paper pumpkin and add a cutout face that includes a toothy grin. Direct the student to label the teeth with the scrambled letters of a vocabulary word from a current unit. Number and post the pumpkins. Then have students unscramble the words, check their work with an answer key, and use the words in fall writing assignments.

Look Who's Floating
to the Top!

Say cheers to your class's hard work with this frosty display. Make the hand/tray shown and mount it on a bulletin board. Also make and have students color a supply of the float pattern on page 25. Tape a drinking straw behind each float. Each time your class meets a predetermined goal, staple a float to the tray. When the floats reach the top of the board, celebrate with a root beer or ice-cream float party.

Back-to-school variation: Label a float for each of your new students. Change the title of the display to "Look Who's Floating to the Top of [your grade] Grade!"

adapted from an idea by Colleen Dabney
Williamsburg-JCC Public Schools
Williamsburg, VA

Team up with your students' families this Thanksgiving to create a display that shows a lot of heart! Have each student label a red, orange, or yellow paper heart with a sentence describing something for which he's thankful. After posting the hearts flowing out of a giant cornucopia as shown, give each child several smaller heart cutouts to take home. Direct the student to have each family member label a heart with a thankful thought. Add these smaller hearts to the display as a border.

Celebrate class birthdays with the help of a doggie that's long on fun! Duplicate the patterns on page 26 onto brown paper. Connect the head and tail with a long strip of brown paper labeled as shown. Have each student write his name and birthdate on a colorful card; then have students arrange the cards as shown to make a giant bar graph. Add balloons, confetti, and streamers for a display that's hot diggity done!

Perry Stio, M. L. King School, Piscataway, NJ

Deck the halls with this student-made display that sharpens research skills! Give each student an unlined index card. Have the student choose a country's flag to research; then have him illustrate the flag on his card. Arrange the flags in the shape of a holiday tree. Have students add shiny foil stars to the background for a finishing touch.

Julia Alarie—Gr. 6, Essex Middle School, Essex, VT

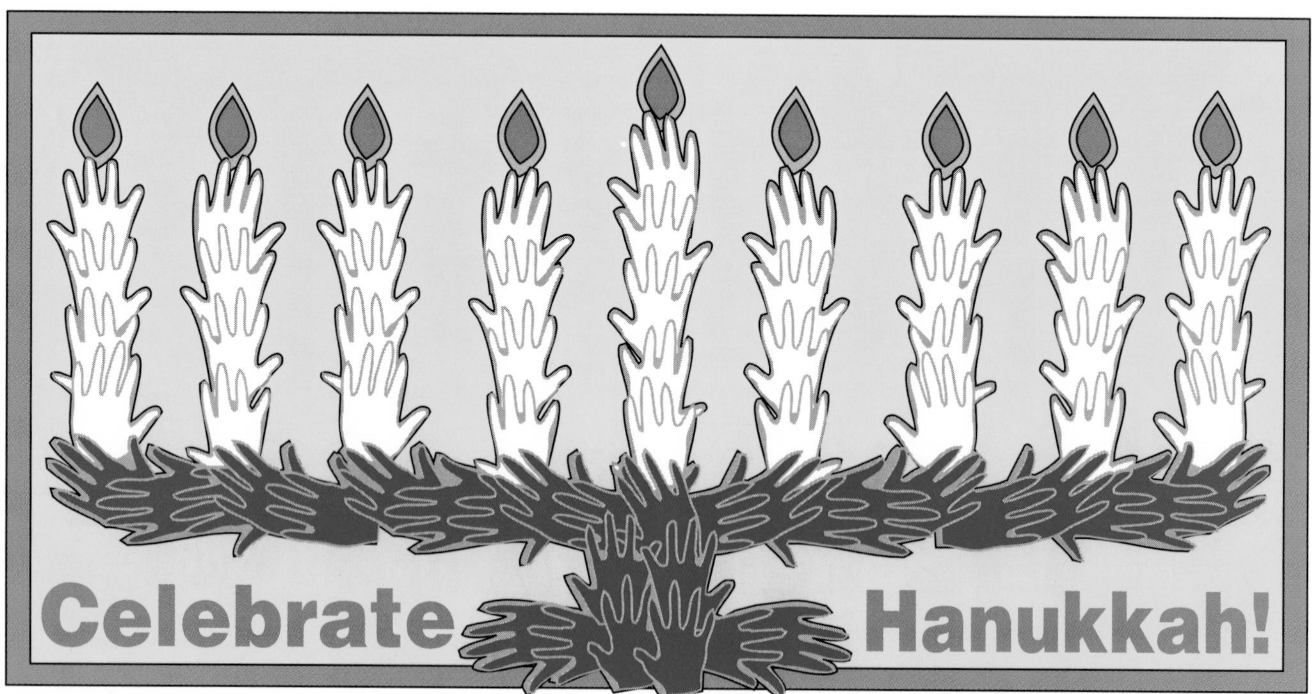

It's the Hanukkah season—a perfect time to promote teamwork with this bright display! Have students trace their hands on bright blue and white paper. After cutting out the tracings, have students outline the cutouts in glitter and arrange them to make a giant menorah as shown. Add cut-out flames; then glow with pride at the shining results of your group effort!

Michelle Kasmiske—Gr. 4, Monroe Elementary, Janesville, WI

No time to make a holiday display? No problem! Mount large, white letters as shown on a background of red foil paper. Ask students, "What is it about the holidays that makes you happy?" Let each child write his answer on a letter using a red or green felt-tipped pen. Have students add shiny gold and green self-sticking stars to the background for a simply dazzling display.

To ring in the New Year, enlarge the phone receiver shown and mount it on a board. Duplicate the pattern on page 27 on light-colored construction paper for each student. Have the student complete the pattern, cut it out, and add it to the board. When you take down the display, keep the patterns. Then return them one morning in February so students can discuss the progress they've made on their goals.

Celebrate the holiday season with a down-home display! Have each student decorate a small paper sack to look like a house (either his own or one that reflects his interests in some way). After stuffing the sack with newspaper and adding a paper roof, have the student pin the house to a board decorated as shown. For a writing extension, have each child write a description of his house. Place the descriptions near the display. Then challenge students to match them to the correct homes.

Karen Riesterer—Gr. 6, Valders Middle School, Valders, WI

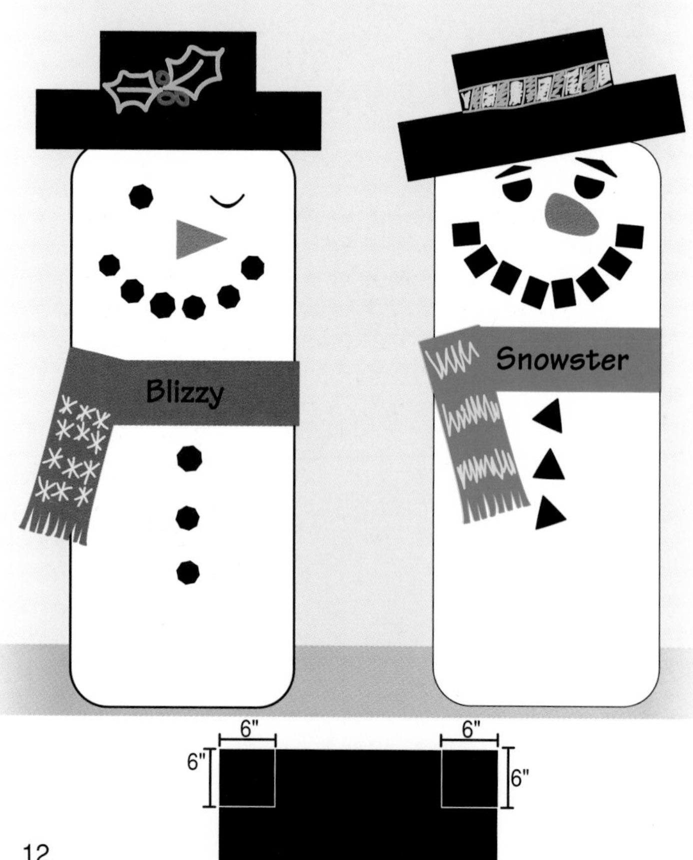

When the weather outside is frightful, have small groups of students create frosty friends that are downright delightful! Display the creations in a hallway. Then have each child write an original story about his group's snowy pal.

Materials per group: 2' x 4' piece of white bulletin board paper with corners rounded, 12" x 30" piece of black bulletin board paper, 4" x 5" sheet of orange construction paper, 12" x 18" sheet of colorful construction paper, ruler, scissors, glue, chalk

Steps:

1. Cut the black paper as shown to create a hat. Glue the hat to the top of the white paper. Save the black scraps for Step 3.
2. Cut a nose out of the orange paper; glue it to the snowman's head.
3. Cut eyes, a mouth, and buttons from the black paper scraps. Glue them to the snowman.
4. Cut the colorful sheet of paper in half lengthwise. Glue the two pieces to the snowman, as shown, to create a scarf. Fringe the end of the scarf.
5. As a group, write a name for your snowman in chalk on the scarf. Add details to the hat and scarf with the chalk.

Patricia A. Wisniewski—Gr. 4
St. Joseph School
Batavia, NY

Piece together an activity on writing personal essays with this colorful display! Have each child write an essay about a personal experience. After editing and proofreading, have the student rewrite her essay on a copy of the puzzle pattern on page 28. Then have her glue the essay onto a larger sheet of construction paper and trim the construction paper to make a $^{1}/_{2}$-inch border. Piece of cake!

Cynthia D. Davis—Gr. 6, Bonaire Middle School, Warner Robins, GA

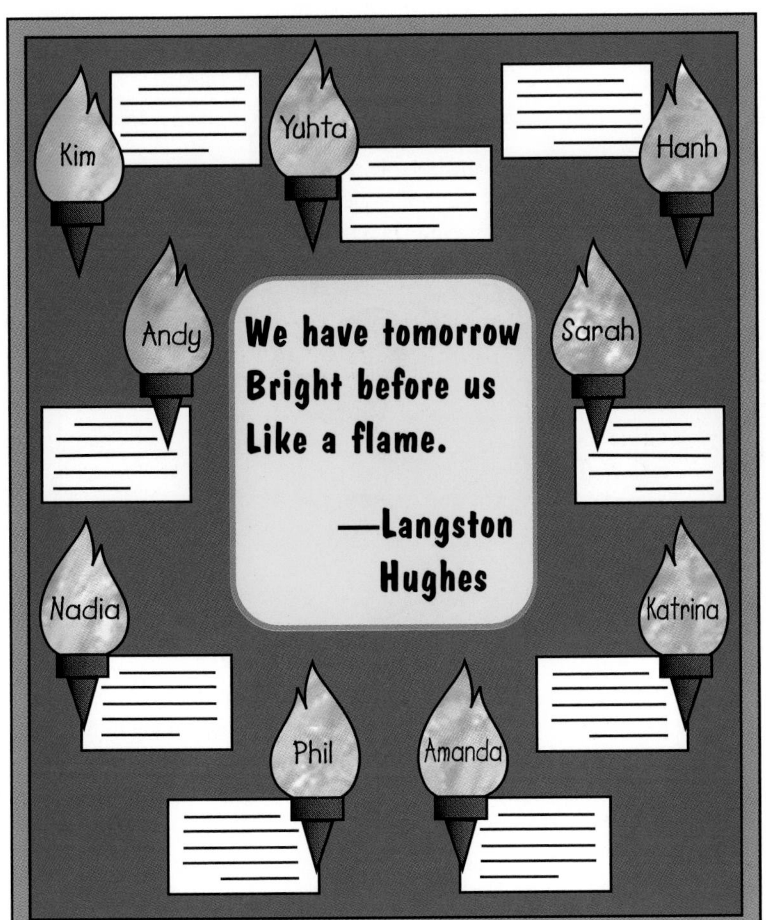

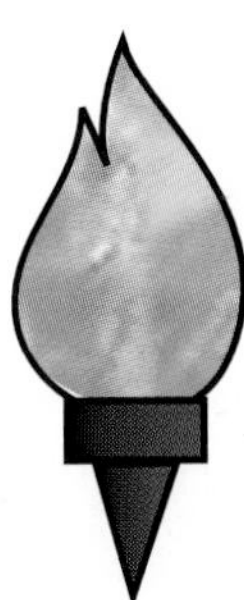

Spotlight Black History Month in February with the help of a famous Black American poet. Have each student cut out a flame shape from white construction paper. After coloring the flame with yellow and orange chalk, the student smudges the colors with a tissue and uses a black marker to label the flame with his name. Then he glues a small black rectangle and triangle to the flame as shown. Post the flames with the lines from Langston Hughes's poem "Youth" as shown. Finally, have each student add to the display a paragraph describing his burning desire for the future or explaining how tomorrow is like a flame.

Andrea Troisi
LaSalle Middle School
Niagara Falls, NY

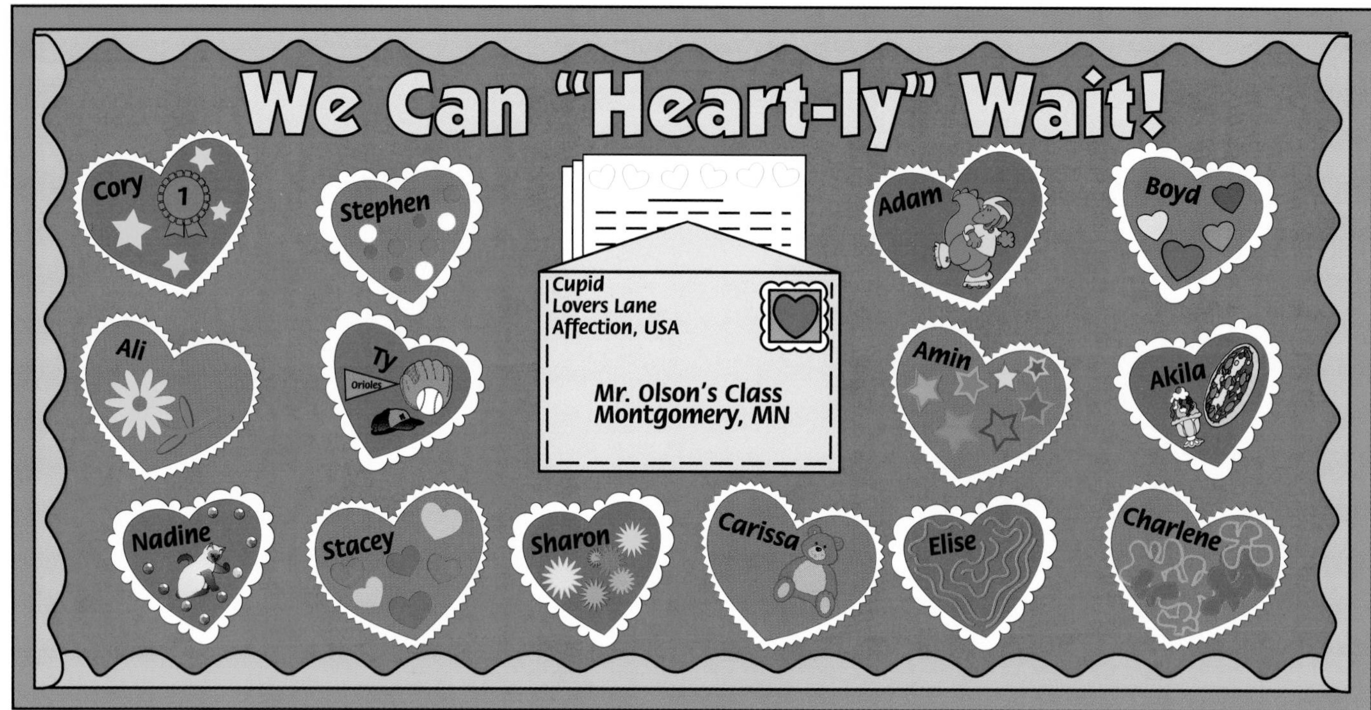

Need a display that "heart-ly" takes any time to make? Staple an envelope cutout to a board as shown to hold seasonal activities. Give each student a heart cutout labeled with his name. Have him decorate his heart at home with family members. Mount finished hearts on doilies. Encourage students to fill their waiting time before Valentine's Day by completing an activity from the board.

David M. Olson—Gr. 5, Montgomery-Lonsdale Middle School, Montgomery, MN

For a heartfelt vocabulary display, have each student label half of a cutout heart with a vocabulary word from the book he's currently reading. Have him use a thesaurus to label the other half with a synonym for the word. Challenge small groups to determine different ways to sort the display's words. Or have students alphabetize the words or use them in sentences that give context clues about their meanings.

Kimberly A. Minafo—Gr. 4, Tooker Avenue School, West Babylon, NY

For a St. Pat's display, duplicate the shamrock on page 29 on green paper for each student. Have each student write about a time when she was lucky—without revealing her identity—on her shamrock. Then have her write her name lightly in pencil on the back of the cutout. Number the cutouts; then pin them to the board. Challenge students to guess the identity of each lucky person. Increase the mystery by adding shamrocks completed by staff members too!

Caroline Chapman, Vineland, NJ

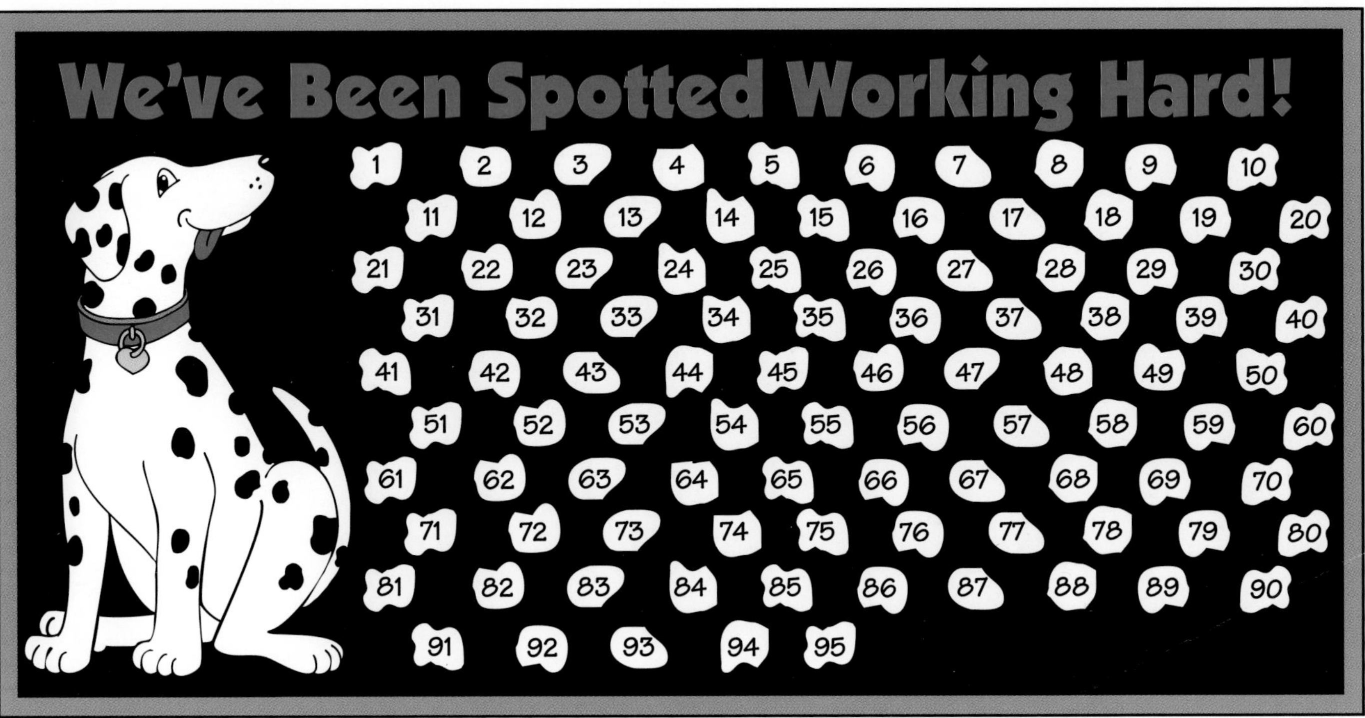

Motivate good work habits with this hot-diggity display! Post an enlarged copy of the pattern on page 30 as shown. Have students help you cut out 101 spots from white paper. Whenever you spot a child working hard, staple a cutout to the board and number it. When the class earns 101 spots, celebrate with cookies-and-cream ice cream or Oreo cookies.

adapted from an idea by Hunter Burrow—Gr. 4, South Salem Elementary, Salem, VA

To grow great grammar skills, have each student draw a large petaled flower on art paper. While students work, label a class supply of paper slips with concepts such as "adjectives," "plurals," and "suffixes." Then have each child select a slip, write its term and definition in his flower's center, and list examples on the petals. After students cut out and lightly color their flowers, post the blooms along with paper stems and leaves on the board.

Patty Smith—Gr. 5 Language Arts, Collins Middle School, Collins, MS

"Orange" you glad this end-of-the-year display is so simple to make? On an orange circle, have each student write a poem telling why one particular event, project, or activity made the year so much fun. Then display the circles with an enlarged orange cutout as shown. Or combine students' poems—each written on a purple grape cutout—into a bunch on a board titled "Fifth Grade Was a Bunch of Fun!"

 Theresa Hickey—Gr. 4, St. Ignatius School, Mobile, AL

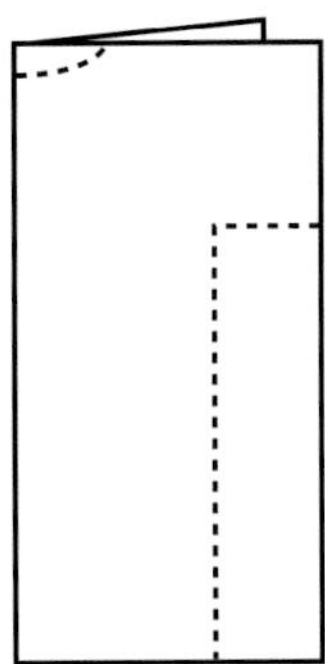

Celebrate a year that suited everyone to a "tee" with this easy-to-make door display! From a large folded sheet of white bulletin board paper, cut a T-shirt shape as shown above. After posting the shirt on the door, place a container of colorful markers nearby so students can autograph the shirt with their favorite memories of the year. Use this idea at other times of the year to celebrate a great book the class has just read, a field trip, or the birthday of a student or staff member.

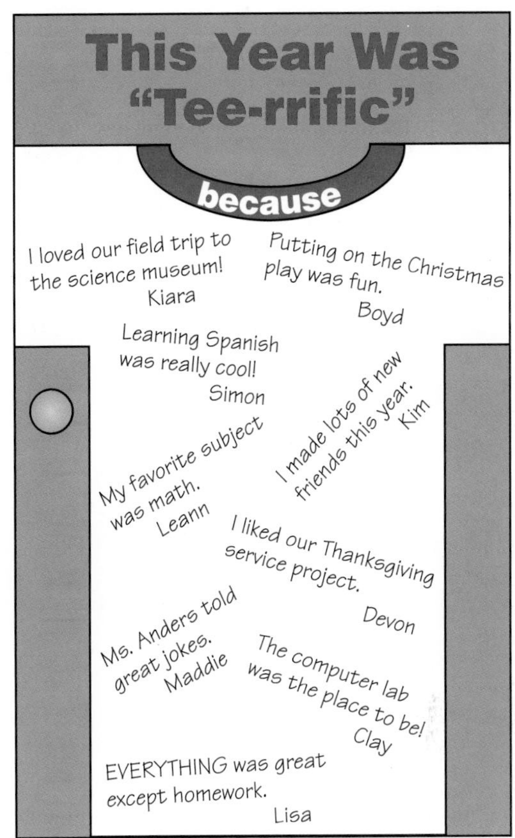

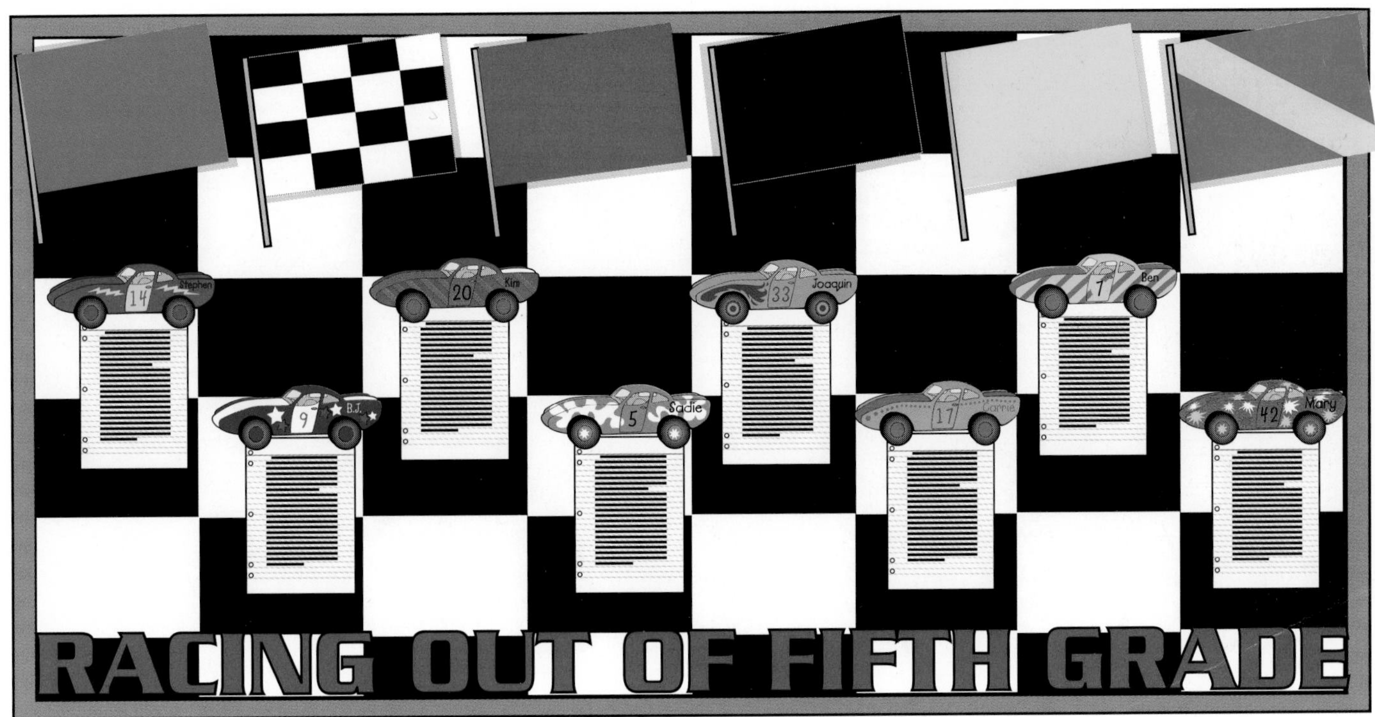

If motivation begins to flag during the final lap of school, rev up everyone's engine with this display! Cover a bulletin board with alternating sheets of black and white paper. Add paper flags as shown to represent those used in real automobile races. Then have each student color, personalize, and cut out a car pattern (page 30) to post on the board with an excellent paper.

Deanna M. Wyrick—Gr. 4, Aboite Elementary, Ft. Wayne, IN

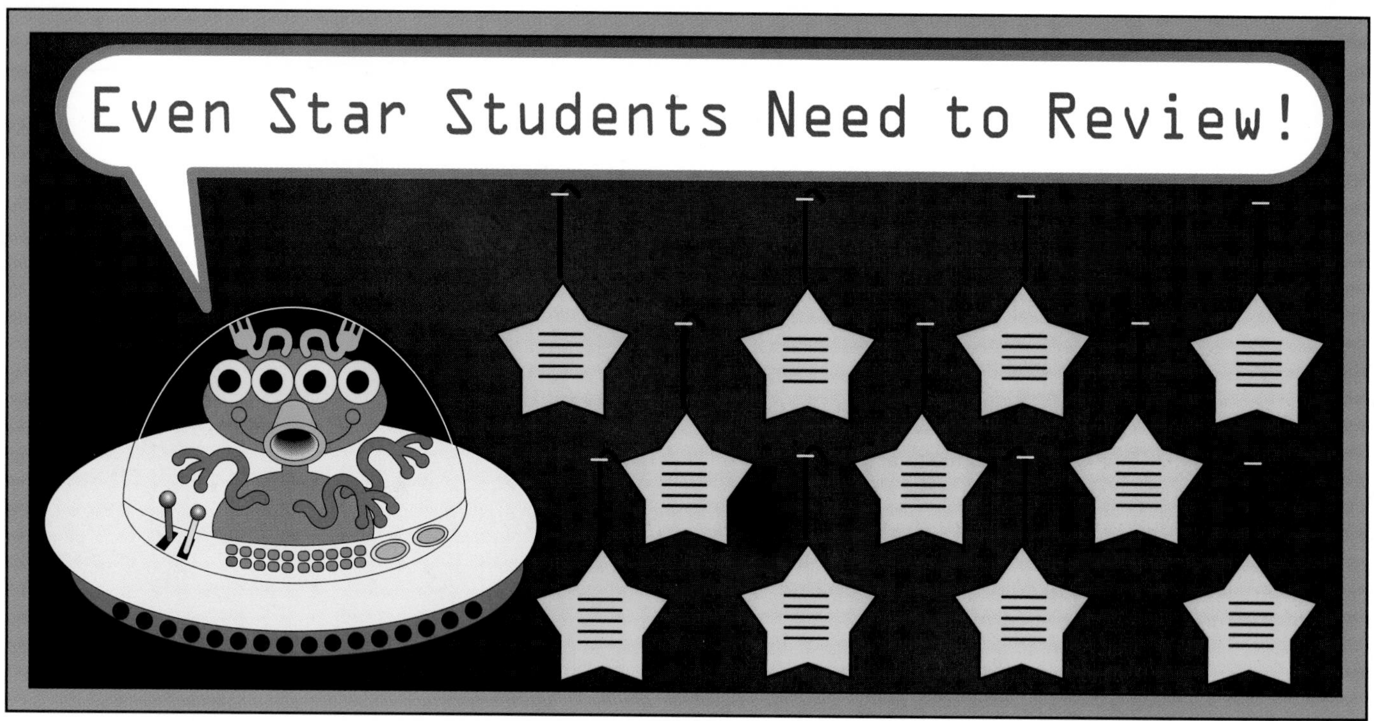

If your students feel alienated from skills taught earlier in the year, help them get ready for testing day with this star-studded display. Enlarge the alien pattern on page 31 to post onto the board. Label cutout stars (pattern on page 31) with review questions; then write the answers on the backs. Hang each star from the board with a length of black yarn. Students check their answers by flipping the cutouts.

Darby Anne Herlong—Gr. 6, Lugoff Elgin Middle School, Lugoff, SC

Help students identify story elements with this homey display! Have each child label a paper roof cutout with his name and post it on a bulletin board. When a student finishes a book, he labels six self-adhesive notes with information about the book, including its title and author, characters, setting, theme, plot, and his favorite part. Finally, he sticks the six notes under his roof. Students will love "remodeling" their houses each time they read a new book!

 Kimberly Minafo—Gr. 4, Tooker Avenue School, West Babylon, NY

Send the message that math rules your roost with this multipurpose display. Each student labels a 2" x 12" strip of yellow paper to resemble a ruler. After adding cutout features, the student posts the ruler on the board. Add to the display students' math papers, puzzles or word problems to solve, current event articles pertaining to math, or other math-related items.

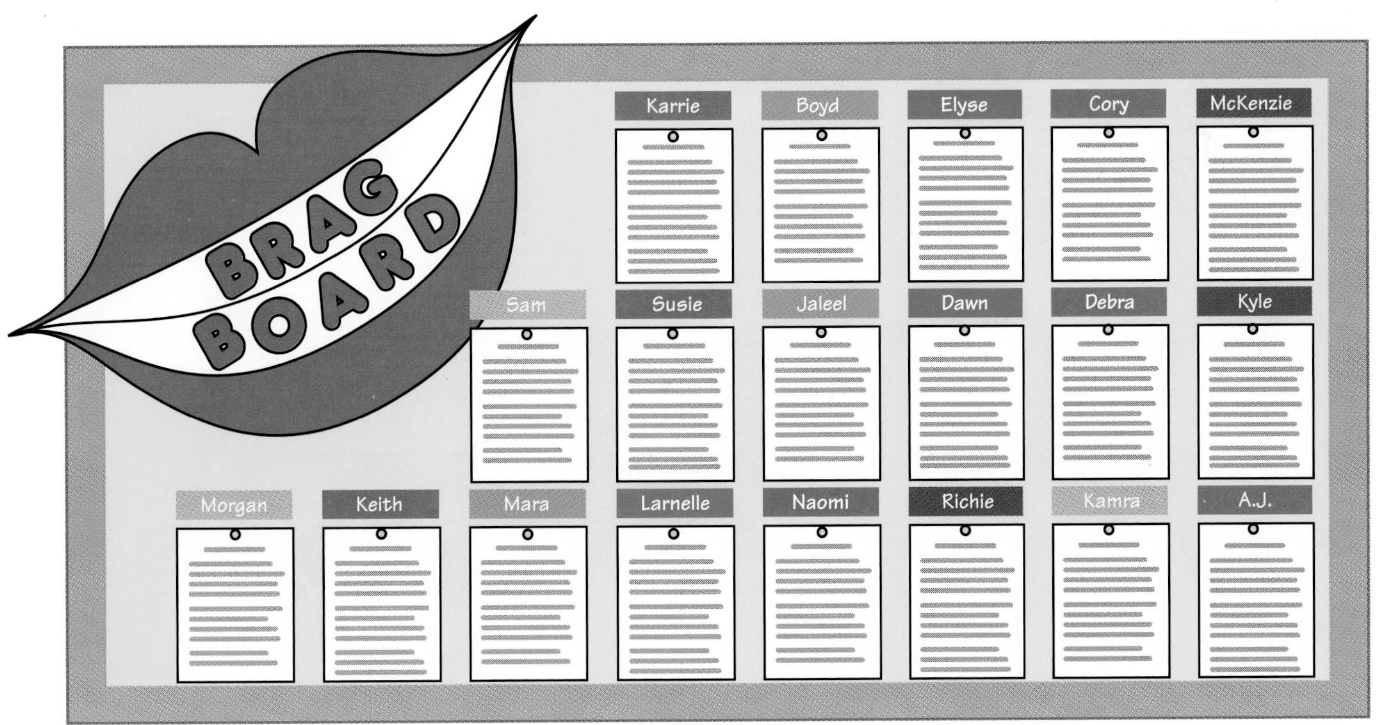

Looking for a display that stays up all year long? Here's one that will put a smile on your face! Post a nameplate for each student on a board decorated with a giant grin. Place a thumbtack under each nameplate. Then let each student post any paper he wants to brag about under his nameplate.

Shannon Hillis—Gr. 5, La Maddalena American School, Italy

Where will *you* be in 2023? Pose this futuristic question on a display that's truly out of this world! Copy page 32 to make a class supply; then have each student complete the page as directed. After each child shares his project, post the astronauts around a cutout globe as shown. Add shiny, self-sticking stars to the display. To extend this activity, have students write narrative stories about their lives in the future.

Julie Alarie—Gr. 6
Essex Middle School
Essex, VT

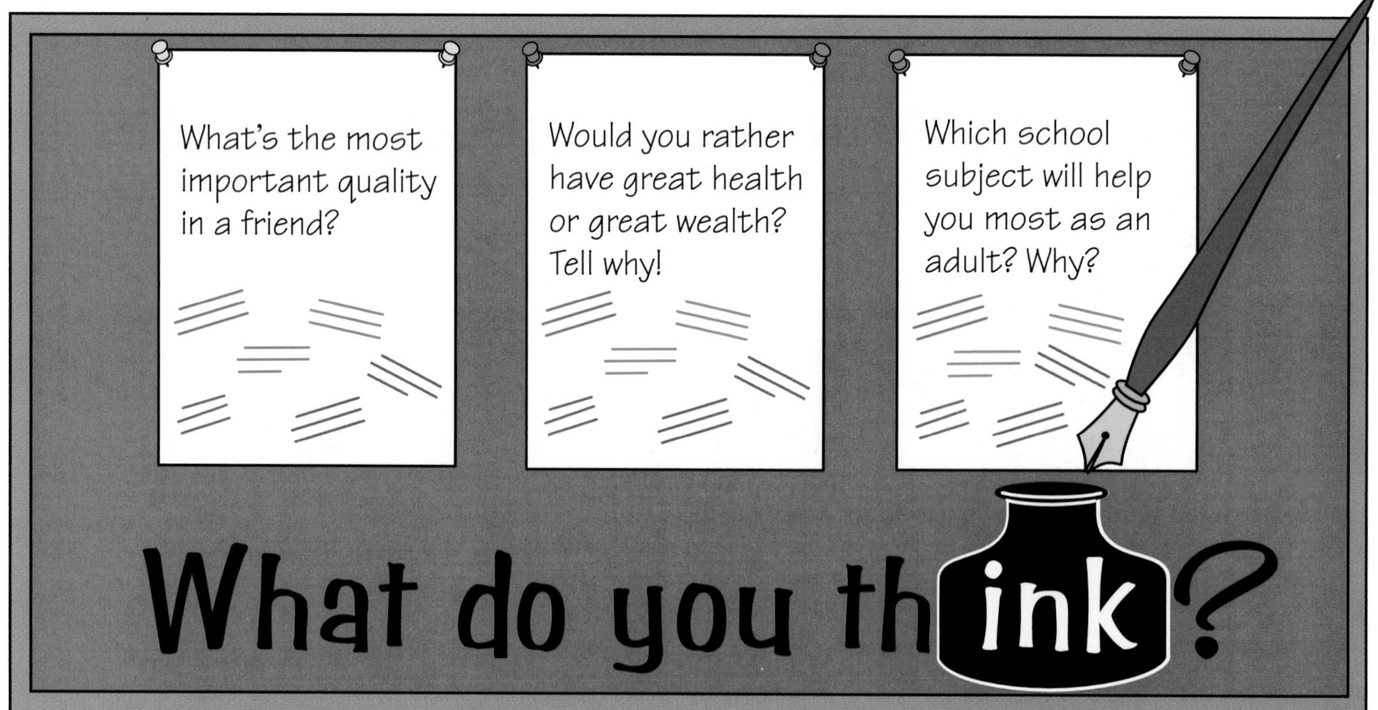

Find out what your students really think with this easy-to-adapt display. Mount a large ink bottle and the title shown. Tack several sheets of poster board—each labeled with a thought-provoking question—to the display (making sure students can easily reach them). Place a supply of fine-tipped markers nearby so students can write their responses on the posters. Change the posters frequently to keep interest high.

Kimberly A. Minafo—Gr. 4, Tooker Avenue School, West Babylon, NY

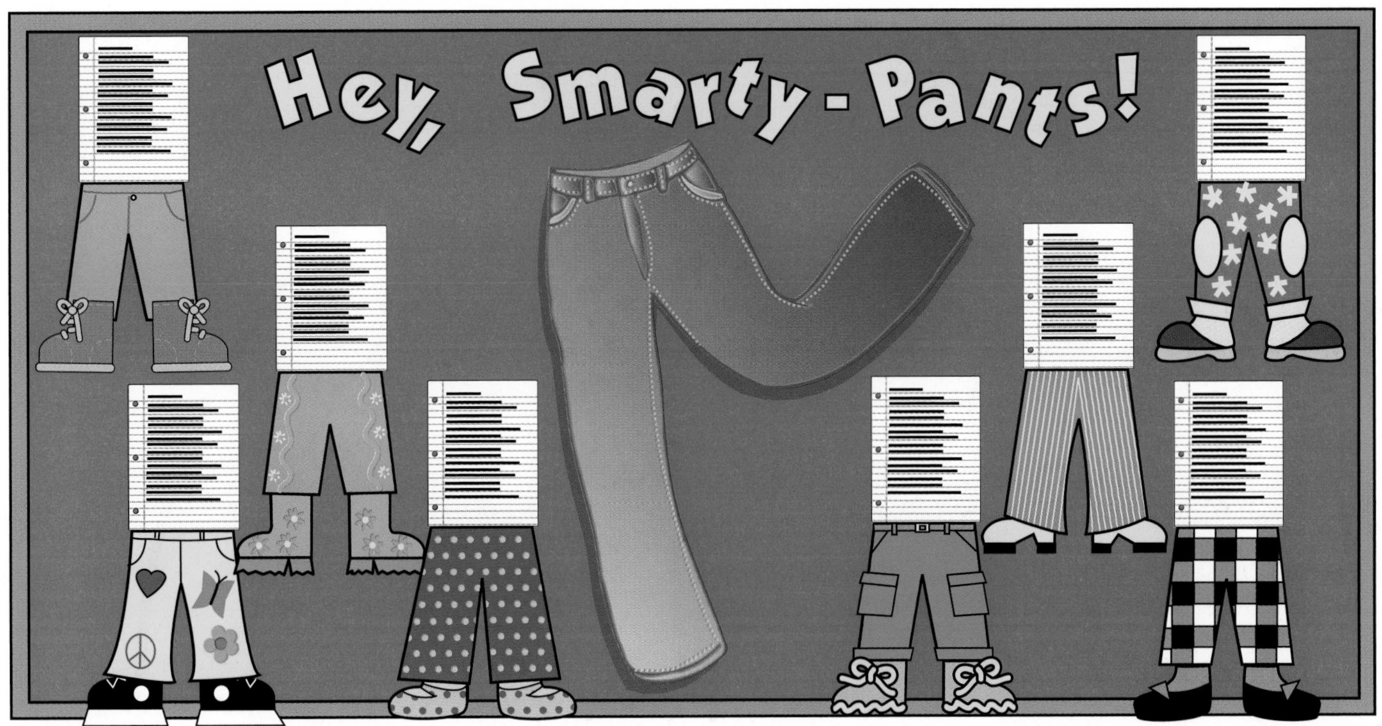

Turn old jeans into a new "denim-ite" display with this idea! Pin a pair of jeans to a board. Have each child use construction paper scraps and glue to fashion a designer pair of pants and shoes as shown. Then have the student attach a favorite paper to the board and pin his cutout just below it. "Pants-tastic!"

Ina Dobkin—Gr. 5, East Elementary, Littleton, CO

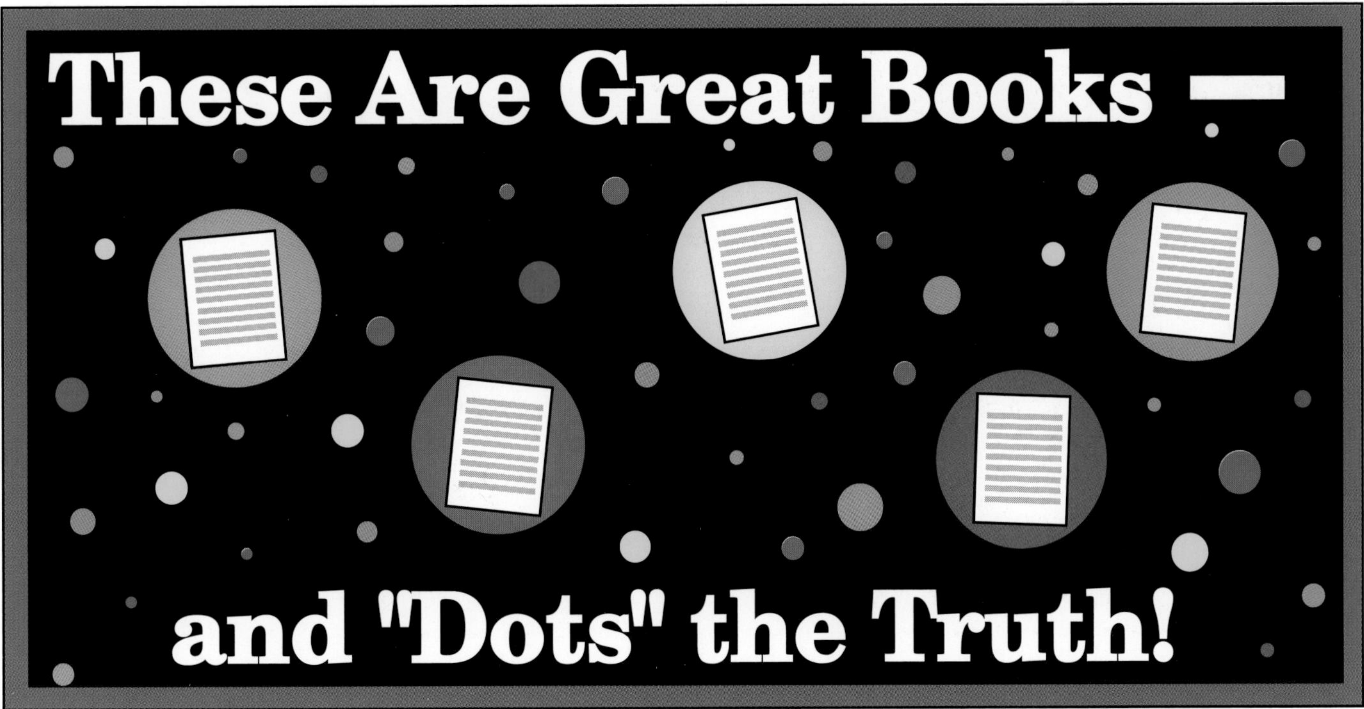

Here's a board that will have your co-workers exclaiming, "Now 'dots' a great idea!" Have each student mount a book report on a large dot cut from neon-colored paper. Decorate the board further with smaller cut-out or self-sticking dots. Change the reports frequently to give students plenty of information about the great books "dot" are in your library!

Marilyn Gill, Noble, OK

Use with the bulletin boards on pages 4 and 5.

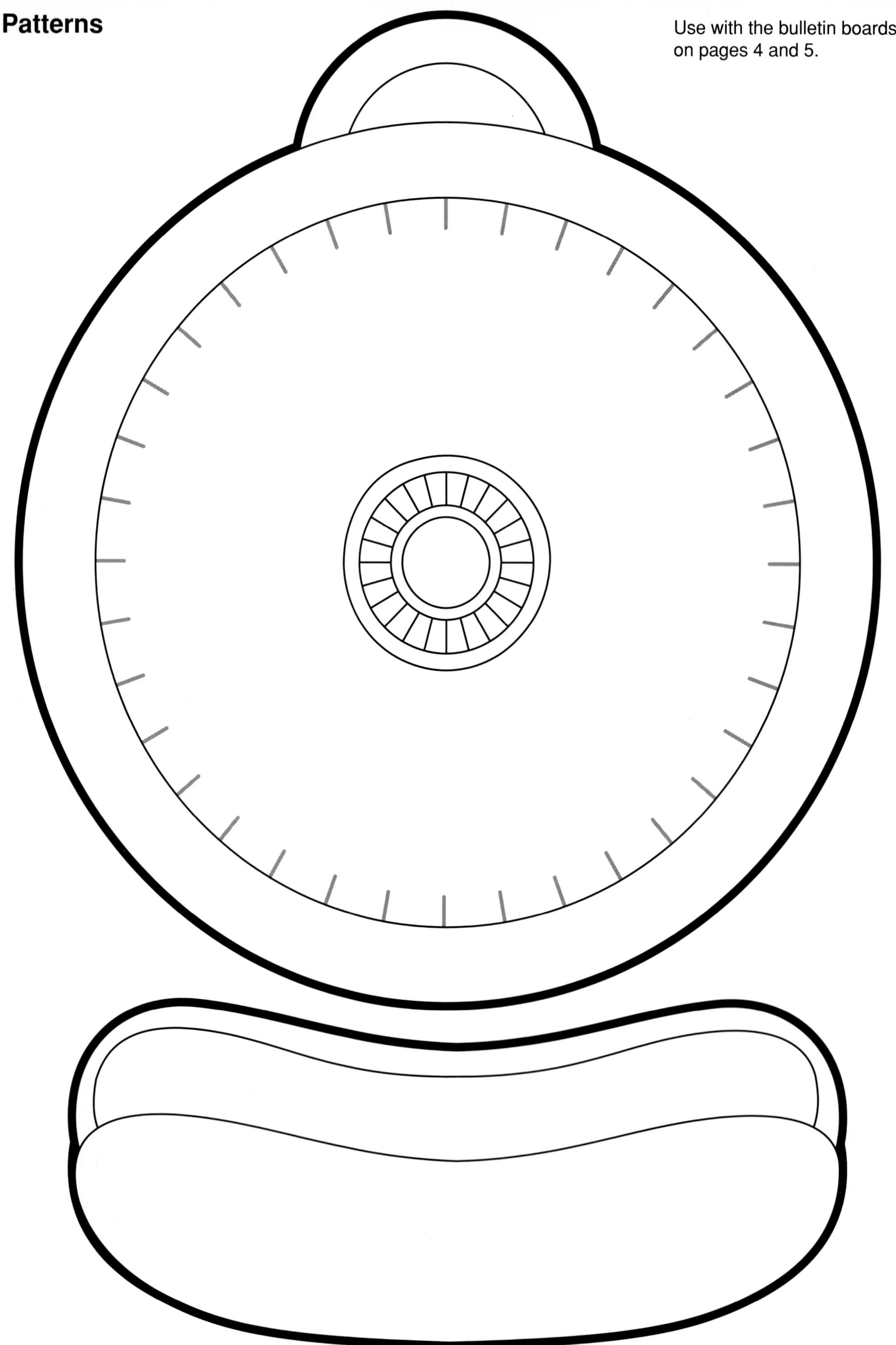

Patterns

Use with the bulletin board on page 6.

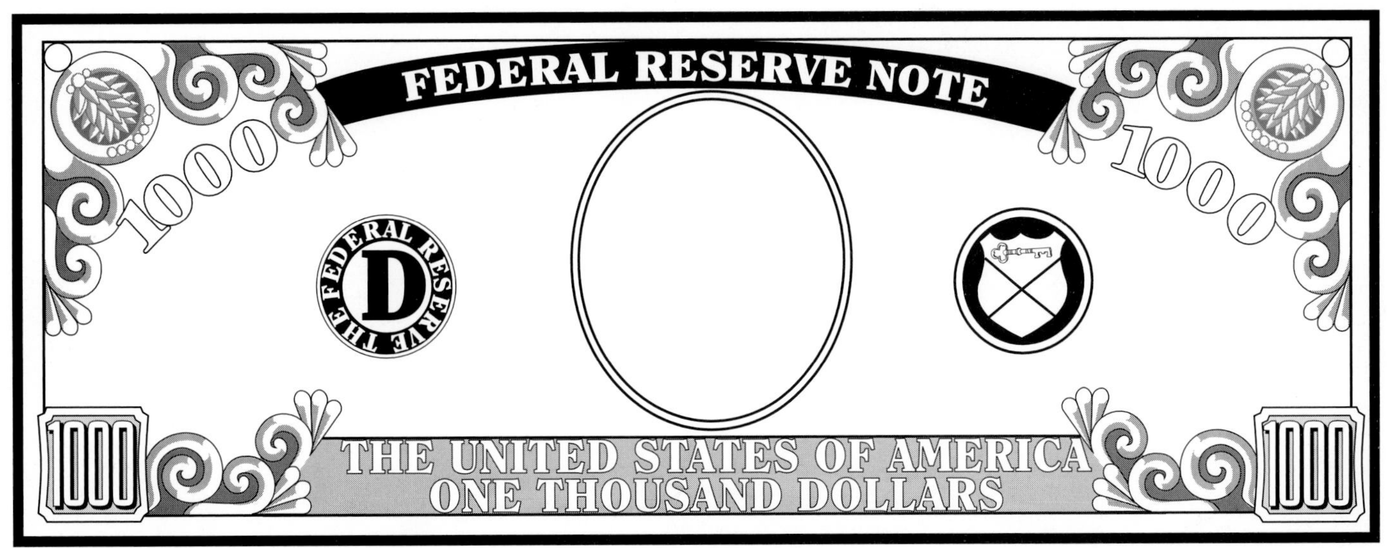

Patterns

Use with the bulletin board on page 7.

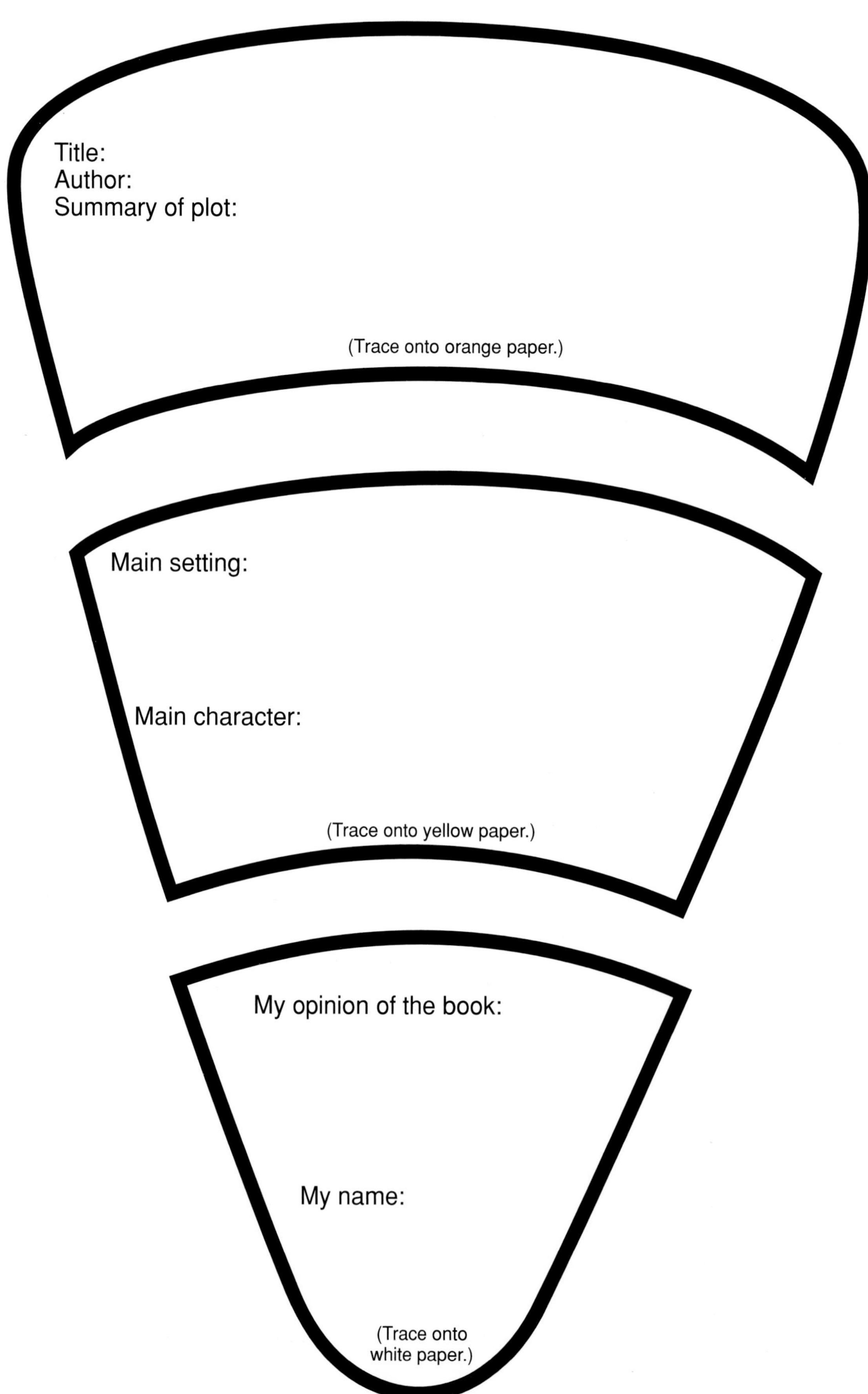

Pattern

Use with the bulletin board on page 8.

Patterns

Use with the bulletin board on page 9.

Pattern

Use with the bulletin board on page 11.

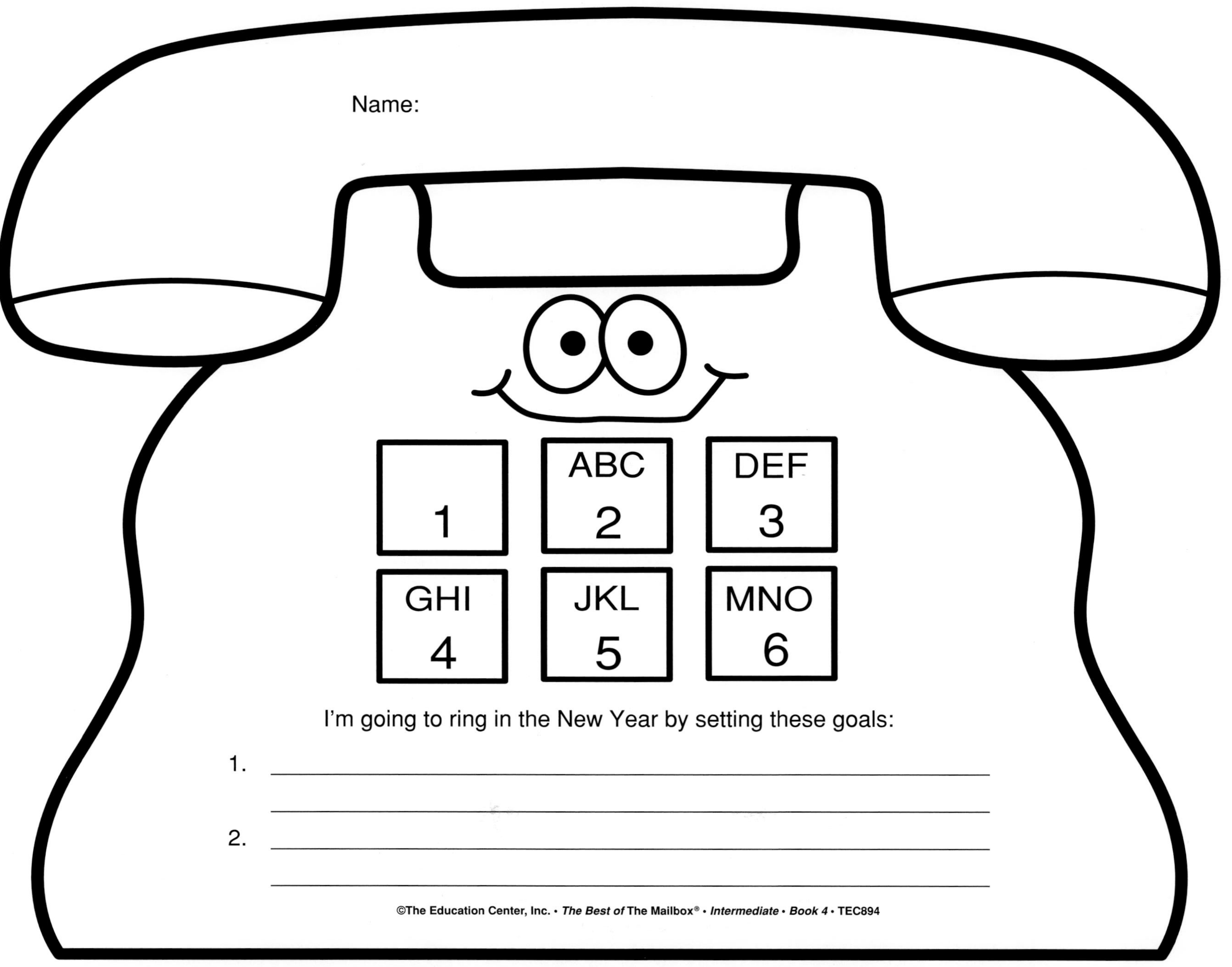

Name:
1
ABC 2
DEF 3
GHI 4
JKL 5
MNO 6
I'm going to ring in the New Year by setting these goals:
1.
2.
©The Education Center, Inc. • The Best of The Mailbox® • Intermediate • Book 4 • TEC894

Pattern

Use with the bulletin board on page 13.

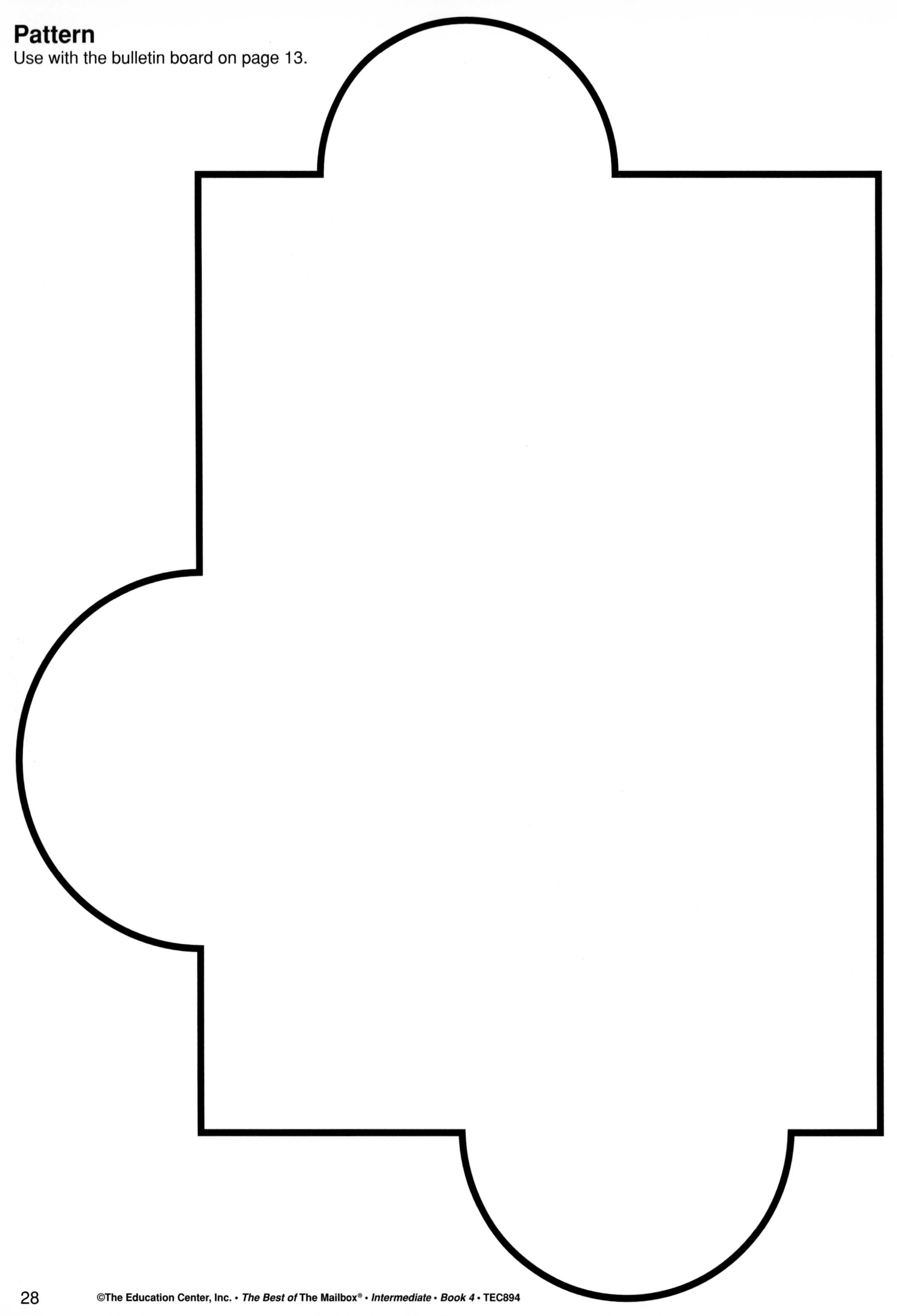

Use with the bulletin board on page 15.

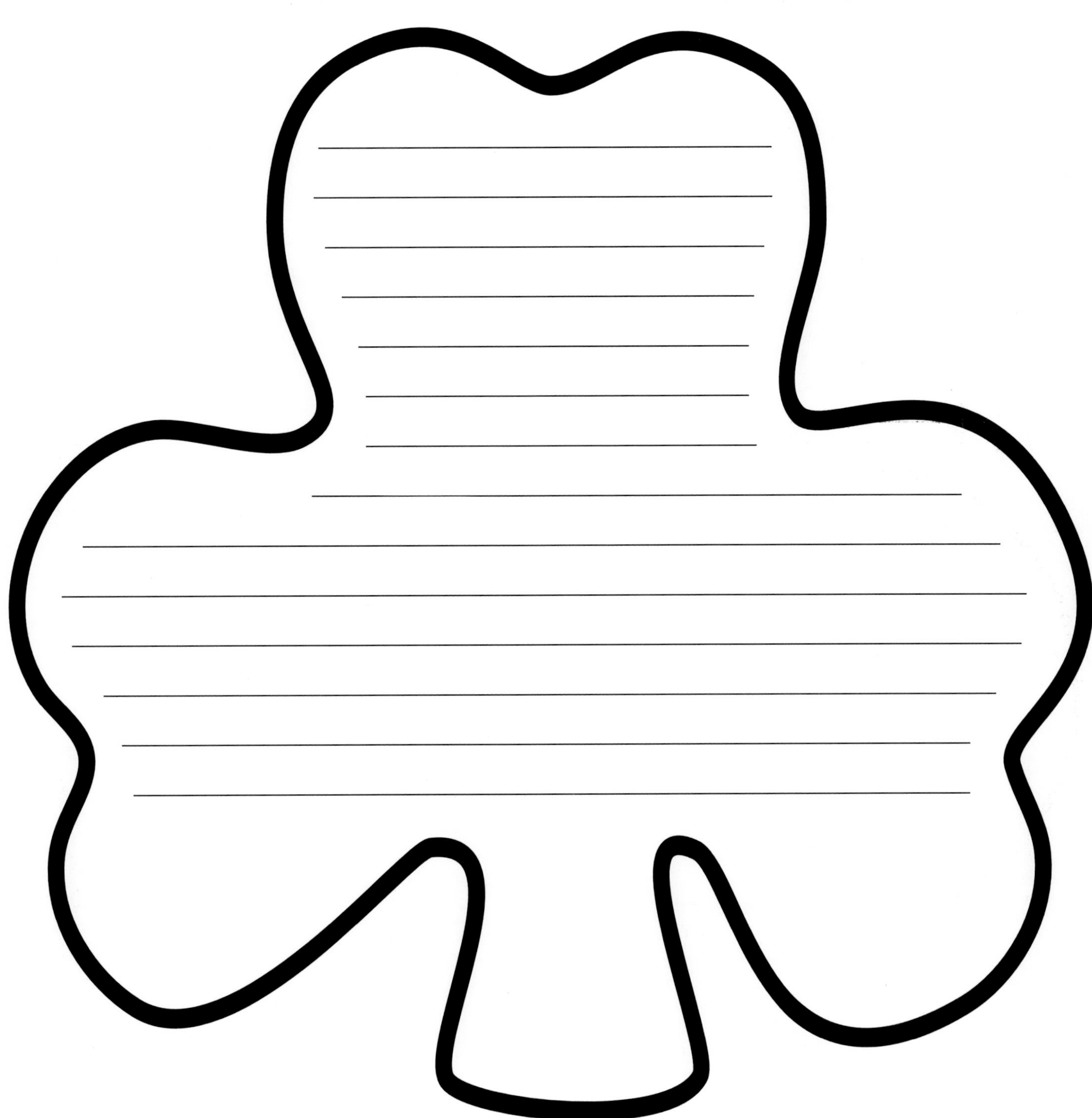

Patterns

Use with the bulletin boards on pages 15 and 17.

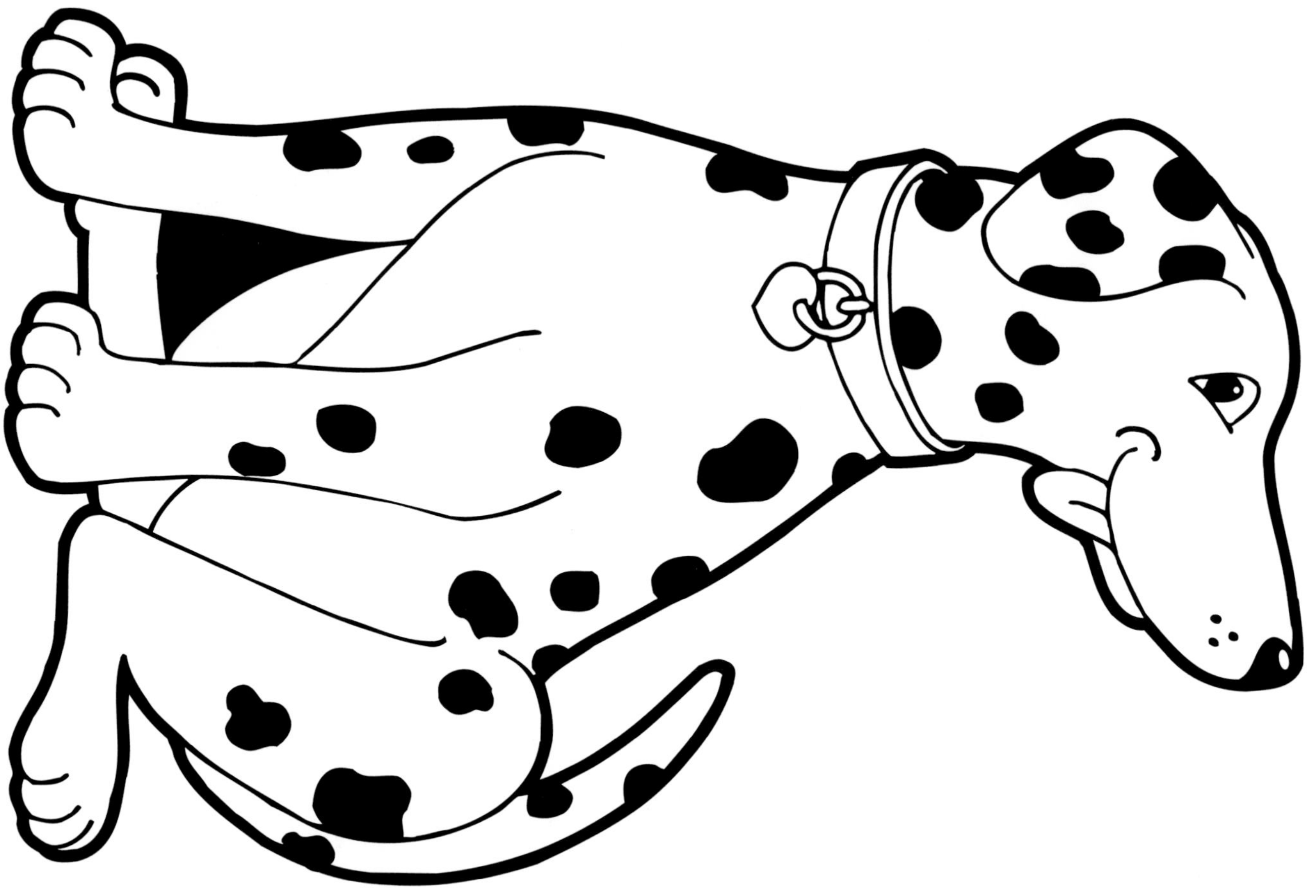

Use with the bulletin board on page 18.

Name____ Following directions, critical thinking

Where Will You Be in 2023?

The future is sure to hold many changes and surprises. What do you think your life will be like in the year 2023? Think about this question; then follow these steps:

1. Cut out the spacesuit and gloves.
2. Draw and color a picture of your face in the visor.
3. Glue the gloves on the spacesuit where indicated.
4. Label an index card with the information shown on the spacesuit.
5. Glue the index card under the gloves as shown.
6. Use colored pencils or markers to add details to your suit.

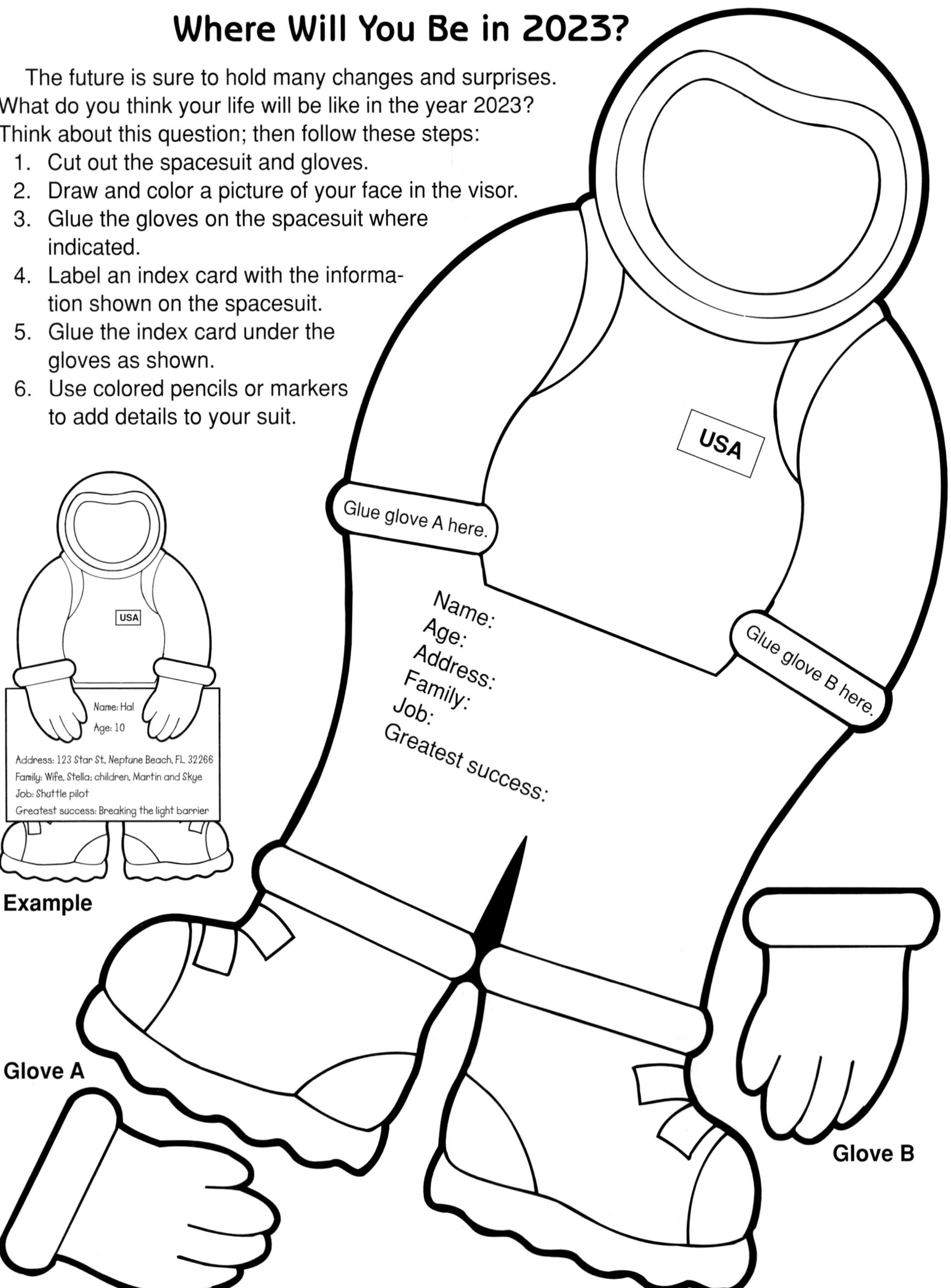

Note to the teacher: Use with the display on page 20. Provide each student with a copy of this page, a 3" x 5" index card, glue, scissors, and colored pencils or markers.

LIFESAVERS...

Smart
Choices
Bucket
June
May
April
March
February
January
Greeting
Cards

LIFESAVERS...

management tips for teachers

Individualized Record Keeping

Looking for a quick and easy method to record observations of your students? At the beginning of each month, I program the dates on a blank calendar page, duplicate a copy for each child, and hole-punch the pages to store in a binder. Then, each day as it's convenient, I record an entry on each student's calendar. At conference time, I share the calendars with parents. Parents always express appreciation for the individual attention that each child receives. In addition, the calendar often reveals a student's behavioral patterns.

January 1998
Jonathan

M	T	W	Th	F
			1 *Holiday! School's out!*	2 *On task all day long!*
5 *Complained of headache most of the day.*	6 *Helped Samantha with her multiplication tables.*	7 *Forgot homework today.*	8 *Art teacher praised behavior.*	9 *Note from Mom: minor crisis at home.*

Beth Pratt—Grs. 5 & 6 Multiage, Eastwood School, Sturgis, MI

Give It Your Best Shot!

Need a simple, inexpensive way to motivate and reward students? How about letting them shoot some hoops! I mount a plastic basketball hoop over a bulletin board in my classroom. Whenever a student answers a question correctly, makes an extra effort to participate in class, or needs recognition in some way, I allow him to take a shot at the hoop with a small soft basketball. The ball and goal are never used for physical education or free time, so students really look forward to the privilege of taking shots. It's a great way to review for tests, reward an individual for a thoughtful deed, or just add some fun to the day.

Pamela C. Broome—Gr. 5, Rockwell Elementary, Rockwell, NC

Hugs, Hugs, and More Hugs!

To encourage good behavior in my class, I arrange my students in six groups of four desks each. Large paper numerals (1–6) hang from the ceiling above the groups so that no matter how often I regroup them, students can easily identify their group numbers. Each group also has a large coffee can covered with bright paper and labeled with the group's numeral. The cans are for storing hugs! My hugs are small strips of colorful paper labeled with the word "hugs." Students earn hugs when any adult compliments their behavior, when they are on task, and when they exhibit good behavior throughout the school. On Monday, the hugs are counted; then students in the group with the most hugs are my helpers for the week. Even though my hugs are paper, students know that this is my way of letting them know how proud I am of their good behavior.

Sandy Carter—Gr. 5, Carpenter Elementary, Deer Park, TX

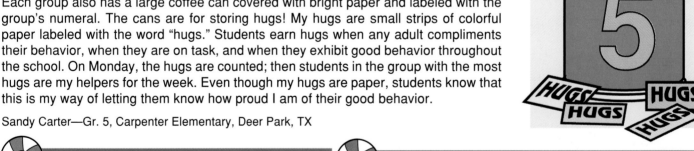

Assignment Board

No more "Do we have any homework?" with this handy assignment board! Each month I draw a calendar grid on a sheet of poster board. I display the calendar on a bulletin board along with a fine-tipped marker. Each week a student helper records all daily work on the calendar. In addition, each student has a notebook in which he records the assignments. Students who are absent can check the board when they return to school. I save each calendar; then, at the end of the year, I show my amazed students all the work they have accomplished.

Julie Kwoka—Gr. 5, George Southard Elementary, Lockport, NY

Reproducibles at My Fingertips

To help me keep up with my favorite reproducibles, I store them in three-ring binders. Each subject-area binder has dividers labeled with skills, such as Context Clues, Synonyms, Homonyms, Creative Writing, etc. When a student needs extra practice with a particular skill, I simply flip to an appropriate reproducible and copy it for her immediate use.

Cynthia T. Reeves—Gr. 4
Albert Harris Elementary
Martinsville, VA

Five In From the End

Eliminate the problem of running out of classroom forms and worksheets with this easy idea. Laminate one copy of each reproducible you use for games, reading, group work, etc.; then place it in the proper file folder five in from the end. When a student goes to get a reproducible from a folder and sees that the next one is the laminated sheet, instruct him to place it on your desk. Not only will the laminated sheet signal you to run off more copies, but there will also still be some reproducibles left in the folder for other students to grab that day.

Barbara Wilkes Delnero—Gr. 4
Tuckerton Elementary, Tuckerton, NJ

Simple Sticker Storage

Solve the sticky problem of sticker storage with this organizational tip! Take advantage of your summer months to transform a greeting card organizer into a handy tool for sorting and storing stickers. Use each month's individual pocket to store stickers for that month or season. Relabel the summer months' pockets for specific themes or curriculum areas, such as "Oceans" or "Math." Place grading or reward stickers in any unlabeled pockets. By getting organized over the summer, your stickers will be ready to use throughout the coming school year.

Patricia A. Faria—Gr. 6
St. Angela School
Mattapan, MA

Pencil Jars

Make sure you're including everyone in class discussions with an idea that makes a point about participating. Write each student's name on a seasonal pencil at the beginning of the month; then place all of the pencils in a jar. When you need a response to a question, pull a pencil out of the jar and read aloud the name written on it. After that student responds, put her pencil in a second, empty jar so you won't call on her again. The next day simply switch jars and repeat the process. At the end of the month, give each student her pencil so she'll really get the point about how important class participation can be!

Missy Jones
Farmington, KY

Stamp Contest

Use reward stamps to reinforce positive behavior with this first-class activity! Divide an $8\frac{1}{2}$" x 11" sheet of paper into two-inch squares. Label each square with a cute slogan, such as "Success Stamp," and a blank for a student's name. Duplicate a class supply of these squares on colored paper and cut them apart. Give a stamp to a student each time you see him use positive behavior in your classroom. Then, each Friday, hold a contest during which students are free to place as many stamps as they wish inside a special container. Remind them that entering is risky, however, since all stamps which have been entered are destroyed after each contest. Choose two stamps from the container and award inexpensive/cost-free prizes, such as books, free homework passes, and snacks to the lucky winners. Then post the winners' names on a bulletin board titled "First-Class Students!"

Helene Singer—Gr. 4
Holbrook Road School
Centereach, NY

Monthly Book Tip

Never miss out on another great monthly idea again with this simple tip! Duplicate the table of contents from each of your monthly idea books; then attach it to the plan book page for a week or more before the new month begins. The copy will remind you to pull your book to find ideas for the upcoming month. You'll have plenty of time to copy worksheets, gather supplies, and make new bulletin boards. Plus, by the end of the month, you'll have a ready-made monthly unit for next year!

Sharon Abell—Gr. 6
Winston-Salem, NC

Smart Choices Bucket

Looking for a way to encourage students to make smart choices? Try this easy-to-implement system. Gather two equal-sized, clear containers and label one "Smart Choices Bucket." Fill the other container with small incentives—such as candy, erasers, stickers, and bookmarks—that have been donated by parents. Each time the class makes a smart choice, such as standing quietly in line or following directions, acknowledge the students' actions by having each child select one incentive and place it in the Smart Choices Bucket. After all incentives have been transferred from one container to the other, equally divide the items into goodie bags for your students. Now that's a smart choice!

Laurel Nascimento and Rebecca Worst—Gr. 4
Saint Joseph School
Marietta, GA

Finished? Check It Off!

Use this handy tip and with one glance you'll identify which students have turned in an assignment. Make a supply of assignment forms similar to the one shown. Store the forms and a few two-pocket folders where students typically turn in their work. The first student to turn in a specific assignment fills out the top portion of a form and clips it to the front of a folder. As each student turns in her assignment, she places her work inside the folder and initials next to her name. Simple!

Subject Math
Date 5-10-01
Assignment pp. 99-100 #s 2-24 even

Name	Initial
Ivan Dominguez	ID
David Gallegos	
Dora Gonzalez	
Jessica Hernandez	JH
Chance Hirschler	
Lucy Kilgore	
Meredith Lee	
Lacey Mann	
Amie Merydith	
Jesus Ramirez	
Douglas Sansen	
Tracey Sheister	
Jody Tweeds	
Sylvie White	
Erin Zender	EZ

Lynsia Sprouse—Gr. 5
Booker Independent School District
Booker, TX

Morning Made Easy

Easily take lunch count and attendance with a little help from your students. Place a laminated name card for each student in a pocket of a pocket chart. Behind the card, place a craft stick (see below). Hang the chart near your classroom door and place two plastic cups—one red and one blue—nearby. When a student arrives each morning, he turns over his name card; then he places his craft stick in the red cup if he is having hot lunch or in the blue cup if he brought his lunch from home. A student volunteer can easily scan the pocket chart to see the names of absent students and then count the number of hot lunch requests. What a timesaver!

Kim Smith, Meyers-Ganoung School
Tucson, AZ

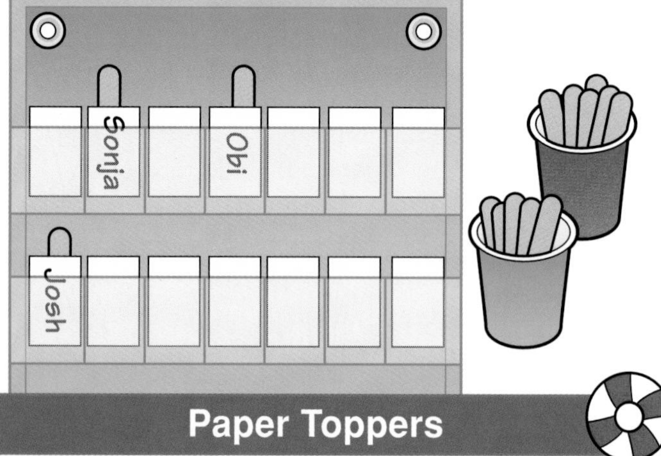

Paper Toppers

Searching for a way to motivate students to turn in neat, legible assignments? Periodically tape a novelty pencil to the top of each neatly done assignment. Students will be thrilled to receive this reward even though their work may contain mistakes. Top that!

Patricia E. Dancho—Gr. 6
Apollo-Ridge Middle School
Spring Church, PA

Student Book Recommendations

Try this class library tip to help students select books to read. Glue a library card pocket to the inside back cover of each class library book. Then place an index card in each pocket. After a student has finished reading a book, he writes his comments about it on the card and places the card back in the pocket. Students will love sharing their opinions and reading those written by their classmates.

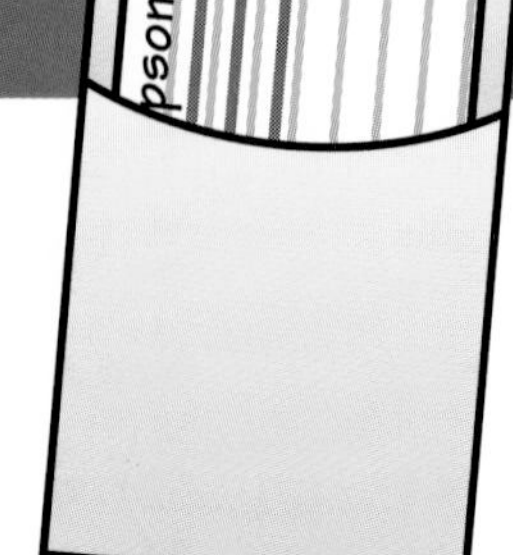

Susan Richardson, Snow Hill Elementary
Salisbury, MD

Classroom Specials

TUCK EVERLASTING
Is there really a fountain of youth?

Blockbuster Book Projects Go to the Movies!

Find an intermediate kid and you're likely to find an avid moviegoer. So grab a bucket of popcorn, a soda, and the following book-report projects to turn your students' movie mania into an exciting reading adventure!

by Rusty Fischer

Casting Call

Make each student in your classroom a casting director with the following letter-writing activity. Tell each student that he has been hired to cast the lead actor in the movie production of the book he's just read. As the casting director, he needs to write a letter to persuade the male or female actor that he feels will best portray the main character to take the job. Direct each student to follow business-letter format and to include information about the main character, the setting of the story, and the basic plot. Encourage each student to also express to the actor why he or she is just perfect for the role. Have each student post his persuasive letter on a bulletin board with a magazine picture or original drawing of his star. (Now *there's* a way to get Brad Pitt into your classroom!)

123 Glendale Avenue
Wilmore, Kentucky 40390

Jonathan Taylor Thomas
ABC Studios
Burbank, California

Dear Jonathan:

I'm offering you the role of a lifetime portraying Brian in the movie version of Gary Paulsen's book, Hatchet.

Sincerely,
Penny Evans

Soundtrack Selections

It's often the music that makes a movie so special. Play a recording of "The Circle of Life" from the movie *The Lion King.* Have students explain why this song works so well as the movie's theme song. Then direct each student to think of a song that would work well as the theme song for his novel. Instruct the student to write the song's lyrics and explain in a brief paragraph how they fit the theme of the novel.

Movie-Poster Projects

Movie posters are just one way films are advertised to the public. Obtain a few appropriate movie posters from your local theater to display in the classroom. Then ask your students to describe what they see. Point out that a movie poster's job is to let the public know the title of the movie and the major actors in it, and to hint at the movie's plot to spark the moviegoers' curiosity. Distribute one sheet of white poster board and markers or crayons to each student. Instruct each student to create a movie poster for her novel, including the book's title and illustrations of its basic plot. Also direct the student to select one actor for each major character and illustrate them on the poster. Culminate the activity by having each student share her poster with the rest of the class while everyone munches on a moviegoer's meal of popcorn and soda. Have each student explain her illustration and why she feels the actors she selected are the best ones for the parts.

Movie Scripts

A movie script gives the actors their lines, but it also gives them information on the setting and directions. Have each student select a scene in his novel in which the characters are engaged in dialogue, then write a script for this scene. Tell the student to begin the script with a basic description of the scene, the characters, and the setting. Then have him write the dialogue between at least two characters using the text in the novel as a guide. Tell the student to also include directions to the actors in parentheses informing them to express certain emotions or move in a specific direction. Extend the activity by having groups of students perform some of the student-written scripts. Quiet on the set!

Screamers!

A classroom full of screamers? You bet! A *screamer* is a tag line that moviemakers use to entice viewers to see a movie. Distribute several copies of your newspaper's movie section. Have students identify the screamer used to describe each movie. Then have students predict what each movie might be about. If a student has already seen a movie, have him tell whether the screamer was accurate or not and why. Next, give each student a long strip of paper and markers or crayons. Direct him to write on the strip the title of a novel he's read and a one-line screamer that summarizes its plot. Have each student present his screamer to the class; then post the screamers on a bulletin board to entice students to read each book.

TUCK EVERLASTING
Fountain of Youth or Curse of a Lifetime?

JUMANJI
Roll the Dice—I Dare You!

Critic's Corner

Turn your students into budding movie critics with the following activity. First, have the class create a movie-rating scale such as the "thumbs-up/thumbs-down" system or the four-star rating scale. Then show your class the movie version of a novel or picture book you've recently read with the class (see the list below). Instruct students to watch the movie carefully to evaluate how well the producers stick to the book's original story line, the casting selections, and whether the movie is as good as the book. After viewing the movie, have each student use the class rating scale to critique it. Compile the results on the board for all to see; then have students explain why they gave the movie a positive or a negative review. As a follow-up, have each student write a paragraph telling why she thinks the novel she's read independently either has or has not been made into a movie.

NOW PLAYING:
A FEW BOOKS WITH MOVIE ADAPTATIONS

- Hatchet (A Cry in the Wild)
- My Side of the Mountain
- Jumanji
- Sarah, Plain and Tall
- Old Yeller
- The Wonderful Wizard of Oz (The Wizard of Oz)
- Shiloh
- Caddie Woodlawn
- The Incredible Journey (Homeward Bound: The Incredible Journey)
- Mrs. Frisby and the Rats of NIMH (The Secret of NIMH)
- Charlie and the Chocolate Factory (Willy Wonka and the Chocolate Factory)
- James and the Giant Peach
- Charlotte's Web
- From the Mixed-Up Files of Mrs. Basil E. Frankweiler (Hideaways)
- The Phantom Tollbooth
- Island of the Blue Dolphins
- Roll of Thunder, Hear My Cry
- The House of Dies Drear
- The Secret Garden
- The Indian in the Cupboard

Name ______________________________ Project checklist

Designing a "Geobread" House

Get set to design a geometric house that would make any gingerbread man proud! For your design to be approved, it must include all of the details below. As you complete each step, check (√) it off the list.

____ 1. **Graph sheet 1:** Use colored pencils to draw two pentagons side by side, each having the dimensions shown. Label one pentagon "Front" and the other "Back." Find the perimeter and the area of each pentagon. Record the measurements on the graph paper. *Hint: To find the area, think of the pentagon as two shapes: a square and a triangle. Then use the formulas* $A = s^2$ *and* $A = \frac{1}{2}bh$.

7.5 cm, 7.5 cm, 12 cm, 12 cm, 12 cm

____ 2. **Graph sheet 2:** Draw two 12 cm squares side by side. Label one square "Left Side" and the other "Right Side." Find and label the perimeter and area of each square.

12 cm, 12 cm, 12 cm, 12 cm

____ 3. **Graph sheet 3:** Draw two 12 cm x 15 cm rectangles side by side. Label one "Left Roof" and the other "Right Roof." Find and label the perimeter and area of each rectangle.

15 cm, 12 cm, 12 cm, 15 cm

____ 4. Classify each item below as a different space figure.

caramel: ______________________

Bugles corn snack: ______________________

a piece of Toblerone chocolate: ______________________

peppermint stick: ______________________

gumball: ______________________

Jolly Rancher: ______________________

____ 5. Add drawings to your graph-paper designs that show how you'll use the candies and snacks as decorations. Make sure your design has a labeled example of each geometric part listed below.

Lines and angles:
- ___ 2 sets of parallel lines
- ___ 1 set of perpendicular lines
- ___ 2 or more sets of intersecting lines
- ___ 4 right angles
- ___ 1 obtuse angle
- ___ 1 acute angle

Plane figures:
- ___ 1 circle
- ___ 1 rectangle
- ___ 1 square
- ___ 1 parallelogram
- ___ 1 rhombus
- ___ 1 triangle
- ___ 1 trapezoid
- ___ 1 hexagon

Space figures:
- ___ 1 cube
- ___ 1 cone
- ___ 1 triangular pyramid
- ___ 1 sphere
- ___ 1 rectangular prism

____ 6. Show your design to your teacher for approval. Once it's approved, you're ready to construct your "geobread" house!

 Note to the teacher: Use with "Home, Sweet 'Geobread' Home" on page 41.

WHO KIDNAPPED TED E. BEAR?

SOLVING A SCIENTIFIC MYSTERY USING CHROMATOGRAPHY

A young bear has been kidnapped, and students will need to observe and experiment in order to nab the nefarious kidnapper! Try this ready-to-use lesson plan about the science of chromatography to help students solve this puzzling case.

by Terry Healy

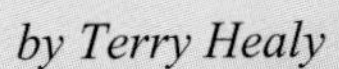

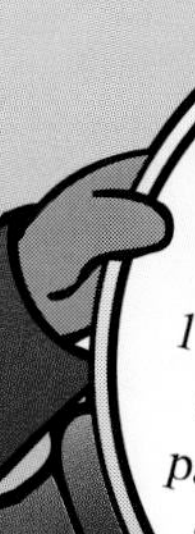

Materials:
4 coffee filters
3 black, water-based markers, each one manufactured by a different company
1 clear plastic cup of water for each group of four students
paper towels
scissors
rulers

STEP 1: TEACHER PREPARATION

1. Gather the materials on the list.
2. Label the markers "A," "B," and "C."
3. Use one of the markers (A, B, or C) to write the following ransom note on the first filter:

Dear Students,

I have taken Ted E. Bear. If you are sly enough to discover who I am, you'll get your bear back.

The Kidnapper

4. Label the three remaining filters "A," "B," and "C."
5. Use marker A to color a dot in each section of filter A, leaving about $1/2$ inch between each dot and the edge of the filter. (See the illustration.)
6. Repeat Step 5 with markers B and C and the corresponding filters.
7. Make one copy of page 44 for each group of four students.

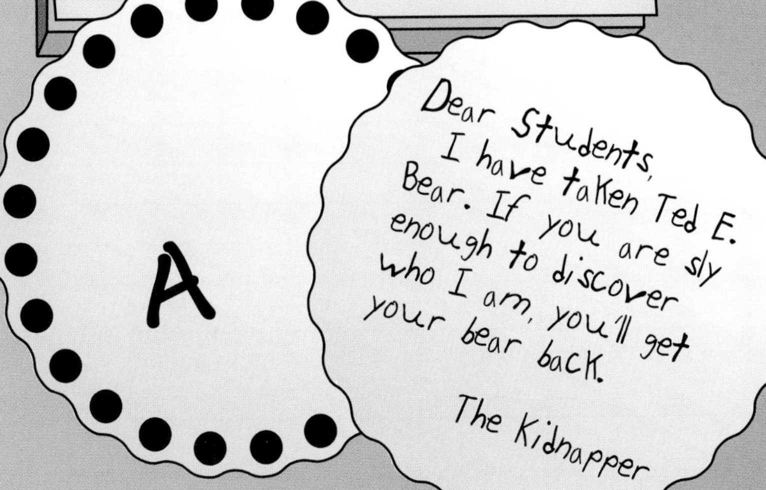
A
Dear Students,
I have taken Ted E. Bear. If you are sly enough to discover who I am, you'll get your bear back.
The Kidnapper

STEP 2: DEFINING CHROMATOGRAPHY

Share the definition of *chromatography* from the reproducible on page 44 with students. Explain that chromatography will help them identify which marker matches the ransom note's ink.

STEP 3: SHARING THE SCENARIO

Read the following to your class: *A terrible thing has happened! Mr. Ted E. Bear has been kidnapped. The three suspects are Mr. Squirre Ell, Miss P. Q. Pine, and Master Kyle Otey. We've received a ransom note from the kidnapper.* (Read the ransom note to the class.) *By comparing the dyes used in each of the suspect's markers against the ink of the ransom note, we should be able to discover the kidnapper's identity.*

STEP 4: PERFORMING THE EXPERIMENT

Divide your class into groups of four. Direct each group to cut a 2" x 1" ink sample from filters A, B, and C, labeling each sample appropriately. Provide each group with a same-size sample cut from the ransom note and a small cup of water. Direct each group to carefully dip the lower edge of filter A's sample into the water for 10 seconds, making sure that the ink dot stays above the water level. Then have the group lay the sample in its correct place on page 44's chart to dry. Students should observe the water spreading through the sample. Have them repeat this process for each of the other samples.

STEP 5: DRAWING A CONCLUSION

Guide the groups in recording their observations on their reproducibles. Have the group members write down the colors seen on each filter sample. Then have them identify the kidnapper by comparing the ransom-note ink to each sample.

Name ____ Experiment: color chromatography

WHO KIDNAPPED TED E. BEAR?

Chromatography is the process that lets scientists separate a mixture into its different parts by their colors. The color record that results is called a *chromatogram.* This experiment will help you see what colors are mixed together to make each marker's ink.

Directions: Carefully dip just the lower edge of one sample into the water, **making sure that the ink dot stays above the water level**. Then lay the sample in its correct place on the chart to dry. Repeat this process for each of the other samples, including the ransom note.

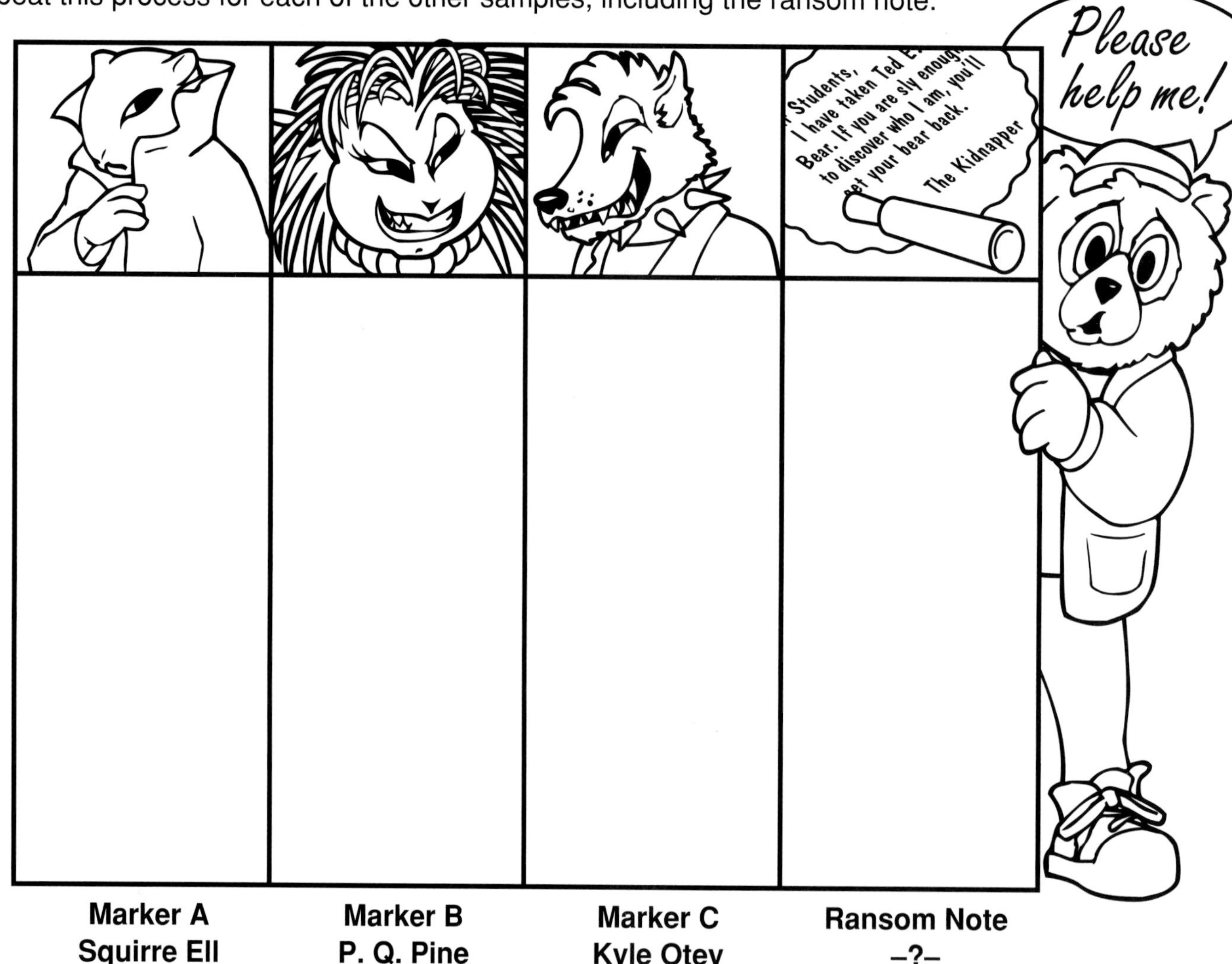

Please help me!
Students,
I have taken Ted E.
Bear. If you are sly enoug
to discover who I am, you'll
get your bear back.
The Kidnapper
Marker A
Squirre Ell
Marker B
P. Q. Pine
Marker C
Kyle Otey
Ransom Note
–?–

Conclusions: What colors were added together to make each ink mixture?

Marker A: ____

Marker B: ____

Marker C: ____

Which one best matches the ransom note: A, B, or C? ____________________

Who kidnapped Ted E. Bear? ______________________________

Bonus Box: Pretend you are Ted E. Bear. On another sheet of paper, write a story describing how you were kidnapped and the feelings you experienced.

 Note to the teacher: Use with the activity on page 43.

GAME PLANS
Dictionary

Name ______________________________

Investigate Reading

A good detective asks questions and looks for answers while investigating a mystery. A good reader does the same thing, whether he or she is reading a story, a novel, or a chapter from a textbook.

Below are some questions that you will need to stop and investigate while you're reading. As a reminder, place a piece of scrap paper at each page where you should stop. Listen to your teacher's directions for what you are to do once you have completed this activity.

Investigative File

Stop on page __________, *paragraph* __________.

Investigate this: ______________________________

Findings: ______________________________

Investigative File

Stop on page __________, *paragraph* __________.

Investigate this: ______________________________

Findings: ______________________________

Investigative File

Stop on page __________, *paragraph* __________.

Investigate this: ______________________________

Findings: ______________________________

Investigative File

Stop on page __________, *paragraph* __________.

Investigate this: ______________________________

Findings: ______________________________

 Note to the teacher: See "Exhibit B…" on page 56 for information on using this activity.

Name ______________________________

Be a Reading Detective!

Reading is a lot like detective work! Detectives face a lot of questions when they begin a case. By using what they already know—plus what they learn while investigating—detectives can solve a mystery! Become a reading detective with your next reading assignment. Before you begin to read, fill in the information on the clipboards. When you finish reading, see how many of the things that you thought you knew were correct. How many of your questions can you answer now that you've finished reading?

Reading Detective Notes
What I already know:
Reading Detective Notes
Questions I want to answer:

Bonus Box: Begin your own investigation of a famous person whom you would like to know more about. On a sheet of paper, list everything you already know about the person. Then list what you would like to find out. Now investigate, write your findings, and close the case on this mystery!

Note to the teacher: See "At the Scene of the Crime" on page 56. Use this reproducible with any reading assignment: a textbook selection, a novel chapter, a basal story, etc.

High-Flyin' Homework Hints

Make homework a breeze for everyone with these high-flyin', practical ideas from our readers!

HOT Tickets

When spring fever hits—or a big holiday is approaching—minds turn anywhere but to homework! Increase the motivation to complete homework with this simple solution. Make copies of the "HOT Ticket" (Homework on Time) pattern on page 62 on neon orange paper. Each time a student completes his homework and turns it in on time, let him fill out a ticket and place it in a special container. At the end of the week, draw one or more tickets; then award a special prize to each lucky winner. Want to work a little math practice into this incentive? On Friday morning, announce the number of tickets in the container; then have each student determine the probability of his name being drawn, based on the number of tickets he earned during the week.

Joy Allen & Marcia Crouch—Gr. 4, Sam Houston Elementary, Bryan, TX

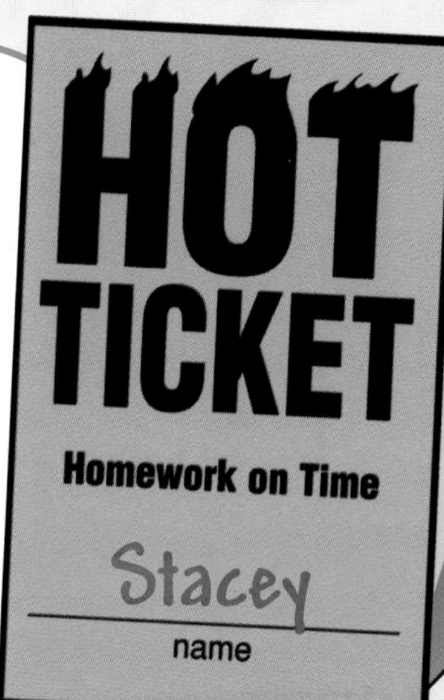

Homework Club Card

Want to increase students' motivation for doing homework? Then join the club—the Homework Club, that is! Make a class supply of the Homework Club Card pattern on page 62. Explain to the class that you understand that circumstances occasionally make it difficult to complete homework. Then distribute the homework cards, each of which entitles its owner to one free homework pass per month, plus one additional "FREE" space to use any month. When a student wants to use a pass, he brings the card to you; then you punch a hole in the appropriate month's space (or the "FREE" space). In the beginning, students will probably rush to use the cards right away. But gradually they'll learn the advantages of saving the pass for emergencies, such as when an assignment is accidentally left at home or forgotten.

Joy Allen & Marcia Crouch

When Parents Help

Just because a student makes 100 percent on a homework assignment doesn't necessarily mean that she understood a concept. At the beginning of the year, ask parents to sign the top of any homework assignment they needed to help their children with. If a parent's signature is across the top of an assignment, it will signal to you that the student needs extra help on that skill.

Joan Cuba—Gr. 5, Pleviak School, Lake Villa, IL

Hooray for Homework!

Students who shout "Hooray for homework"? It could happen with this monthly motivator. At the end of each month, hold an awards ceremony to honor students who turned in all of their homework assignments. Present each deserving student with a special certificate that entitles her to skip homework one night during the upcoming month. Did someone just say "Hooray"?

Kirsten Sasaki—Gr. 6, Copiague Middle School, Copiague, NY

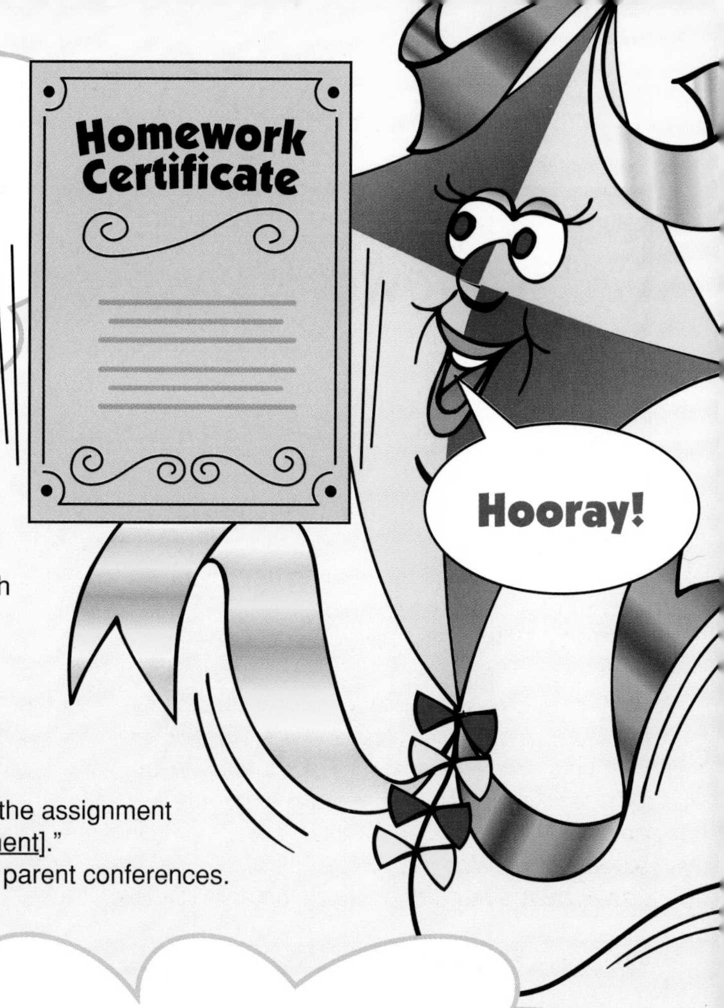

Homework Certificate

Hooray!

"Gimme" One of Three, Please!

If you've got lots of kids and lots of papers to grade, it's often easy to be in the dark about whether a student was absent or just didn't do an assignment. Solve this challenge by asking each student to hand in one of the following each time you collect a homework assignment:

- the homework assignment
- a sheet of paper labeled with the student's name, the date, the assignment name, and the phrase "I was absent on [the date the student missed school]."
- a sheet of paper labeled with the student's name, the date, the assignment name, and the phrase "I did not complete [name of assignment]."

File any "I did not complete…" papers to use during student and parent conferences.

Patricia E. Dancho—Gr. 6, Apollo-Ridge Middle School
Spring Church, PA

Handy Homework Helper

Turn a bulletin board into a tool that keeps track of missing assignments and rewards students for responsible homework habits. For each student, cut the front from a manila file folder as shown. Staple the folder to a bulletin board along the sides to form a pocket; then label the folder with the student's name. Also make a supply of forms similar to the two shown on yellow and blue paper.

If a student is absent, place copies of the assignments he missed in his pocket. If a student owes you an assignment, fill out a yellow form and place it in his pocket to remind both him and you that he owes work. Slip a completed blue form into the pocket of any student who turned in all assignments for the week. How handy!

Carol Jorgensen, Lena Elementary, Lena, WI

I OWE MY TEACHER THESE ASSIGNMENTS:

Spelling: ________
Reading: ________
Math: ________
Science: ________
Social Studies: ________
Writing: ________
Other: ________

Please do the above homework as soon as possible.

Date:

I've Got to Hand It to You!

You've done a great job this week with your assignments. Thanks for keeping up with your homework.

You deserve a hand!

Homework Organizer

Avoid the paper chase that homework can sometimes create with this tip. Type a class list and make copies. Each time you collect homework, place a copy of the list atop the papers. Then follow these steps:

1. Cross out the names of students who turned in the assignment.
2. Highlight the names of students who didn't turn in the assignment.
3. Paper-clip the list to the top of the papers.
4. Label the list with grades as you assess the work.
5. Transfer the grades to your gradebook.

Keep the list until Friday so you can refer to it when informing students about who owes work for the week.

Jennifer Peterman—Gr. 6, Eli Whitney Elementary, Stratford, CT

Patterns

Use with "HOT Tickets" and "Homework Club Card" on page 60.

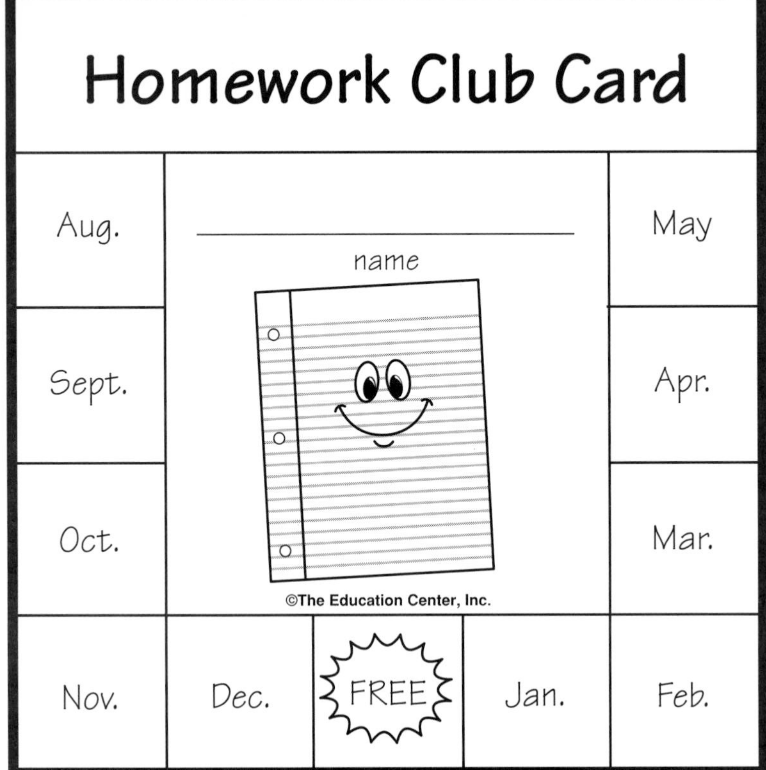

Homework Club Card
Aug.
Sept.
Oct.
Nov.
Dec.
FREE
Jan.
Feb.
Mar.
Apr.
May
name
©The Education Center, Inc.

HOT
TICKET
Homework on Time
name
©The Education Center, Inc.

Homework Club Card
Aug.
Sept.
Oct.
Nov.
Dec.
FREE
Jan.
Feb.
Mar.
Apr.
May
name
©The Education Center, Inc.

HOT
TICKET
Homework on Time
name
©The Education Center, Inc.

This Must Be the Place!

Creative Map Activities That Really Hit the Spot

On the lookout for mapping activities that will keep intermediate kids tuned in? Just point your compass in the direction of the following fun-filled, hands-on learning ideas!

by Julia Alarie

More Information, Please!

Skill: Comparing information on different kinds of maps

Extend the activity on the left below by giving each group a different kind of map of the same area. For example, provide one group with a population density map, another with a climate regions map, a third with a products or natural resources map, a fourth with a physical features map, and a fifth with a political map. Have the students in each group brainstorm all the information they can gather from studying their map. Check each group's observations for accuracy. Then compare the kinds of information acquired from the different maps. Lead the students to draw conclusions about the relationships among the facts gathered. For example: How does elevation affect population density? How is climate related to kinds of products? What natural features form boundaries? Now that's a booty of solid-gold learning!

Information, Please!

Skill: Reading a map

How much knowledge do your students already have about maps? Find out by presenting them with this challenge! Divide your class into groups of three or four students each, and have each group choose a recorder. Provide each group with a copy of the same map (political, physical, products/natural resources, or population density) of an area you're about to study. Also give each group a large sheet of paper. Instruct the students in each group to brainstorm everything they learn by studying the map. Have the recorder jot down each observation. After about ten minutes, compare all the information generated and check it for accuracy. Discuss how students discovered each fact. Proclaim the group with the most accurate information the "Official Class Cartographers"!

Welcome to Rectanguland!

Skills: Using map symbols, following directions

Provide students with plenty of practice using map symbols and following directions with the reproducible on page 65. First, go over the directions with students. Stress that they should complete steps 1 and 2 before beginning their maps. When all the maps are finished, compare and discuss the results; then have students color their finished products. Display the marvelous maps on a bulletin board titled "Rectanguland: You *Can* Get There From Here!"

Maps in the News

Skills: Current events, geography

What's often buried between the pages of today's news? Maps, mateys! Reserve a section of a wall or bulletin board on which to create a "Maps in the News" collage. Encourage students to be on the lookout for maps that accompany articles in newspapers and newsmagazines. Post the maps—along with their captions and the articles—as an ongoing reminder that maps are a big part of our everyday lives. In addition, post the following questions on the board to spark classroom discussions:

- What type of map is shown? (political, physical, population, products, etc.)
- What is the purpose of the map?
- On what continent does the news story take place? In what country? In which state?
- What type of story does the map accompany? (politics, culture, climate, disaster, etc.)
- List three facts you can learn from the map.

Can Someone Give Me Directions?

Skill: Cardinal directions

Using wall-mounted maps ("north is up, south is down") to teach cardinal directions is often confusing for students. To help them better understand the true cardinal directions, use colored masking tape or paint to make a compass rose right on your classroom floor. First, get students' input to help you determine the actual directions; then make the compass rose accordingly. Since the compass is a permanent part of your classroom, refer to it whenever you're discussing directions.

Puzzled About Maps

Skill: Geography

Even intermediate kids think a good puzzle is worth its weight in gold! Turn any map—like those included in *National Geographic* magazine—into a floor map by gluing it onto a large piece of poster board. Use a different color of poster board for each map to make it easy to keep puzzles separate. After the map has dried, cut it into interesting shapes and store it in a labeled shoebox. Make map puzzles of any region you cover in social studies or of the settings of books the class is reading. Recruit parent volunteers to help you make these puzzles, which are perfect do-at-home projects!

Location, Location, Location!

Skills: Cardinal and intermediate directions

Give students practice in giving directions by playing Location. Choose a small but distinctive object in the classroom, such as a special eraser or figurine. Have your students close their eyes while one student places the object in a secret, but visible, location. Have students take turns asking directional questions to try to determine the object's location. For example:

- Is the object located in the northern part of the classroom?
- Is it southeast of the teacher's desk?
- Is the object located west of the aquarium?
- Is it near the northwestern corner of the classroom?

Let the first student to locate the object hide it for the next round.

Name ______________________________

Welcome to Rectanguland!

Welcome to Rectanguland! It's a nice place to visit...if you can find it! And that's where your help is needed. Follow the directions below to make an accurate map of Rectanguland. Tourists all over the world are counting on you!

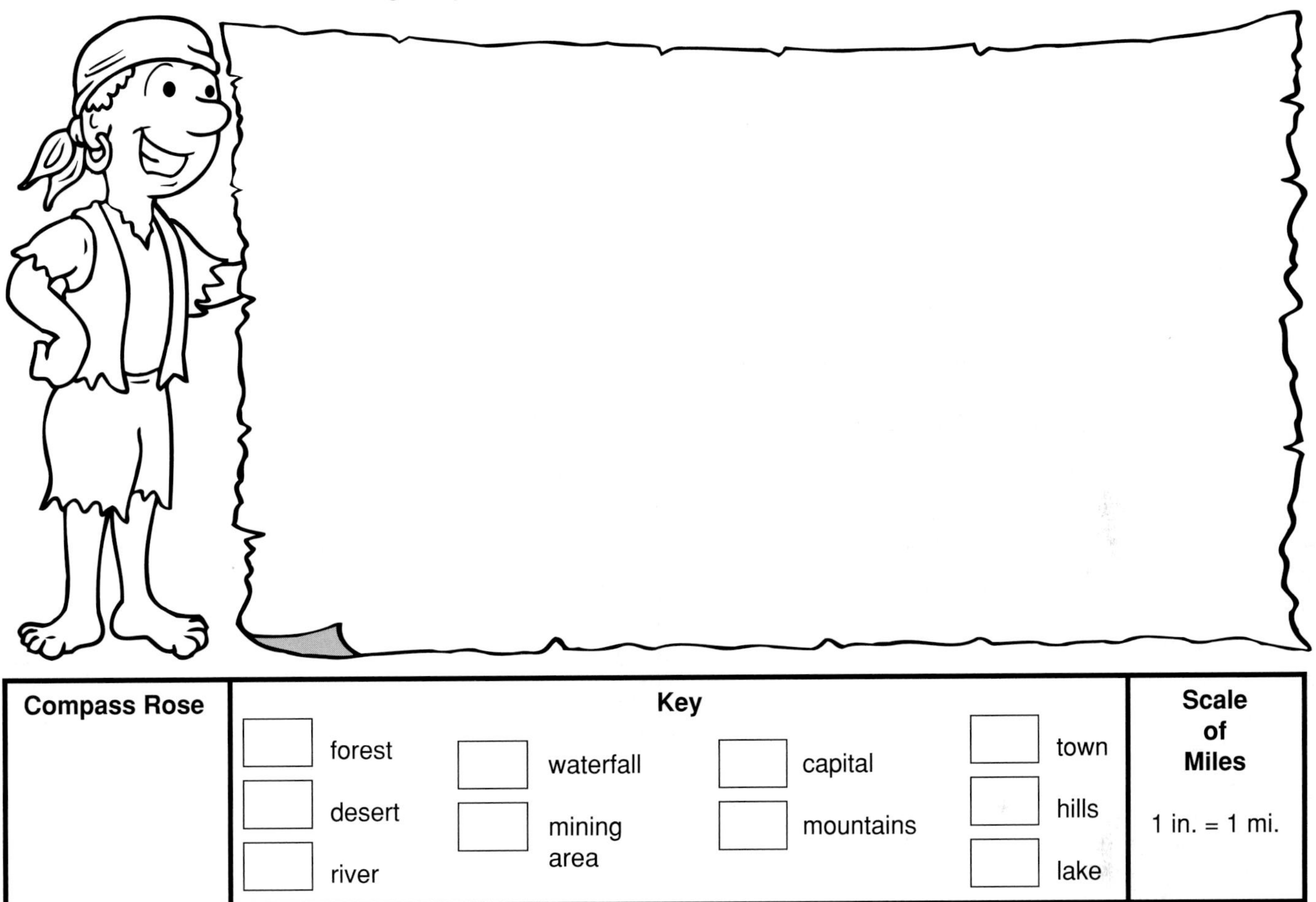

Compass Rose	Key								Scale of Miles
	☐	forest	☐	waterfall	☐	capital	☐	town	
	☐	desert	☐	mining area	☐	mountains	☐	hills	1 in. = 1 mi.
	☐	river					☐	lake	

Directions:

1. Look at each feature listed in the key. Draw and color a symbol for each feature in the box beside it.
2. Draw the compass rose. Include both cardinal and intermediate directions.
3. Now follow the steps below to make your map in the space above. Include each feature and its name.
   a. Rectanguland is a country shaped like a rectangle. (Surprised?) Its northern and southern borders are longer than its eastern and western borders.
   b. The Angular Mountains are located along the northern border.
   c. Winsome River flows down from the mountains in a southeasterly direction. Then it flows through Hiccup Hills.
   d. Winsome River forms Cascade Falls as it empties into Lake Linger. Lake Linger is near the eastern border.
   e. The capital city, Rightanglia, is located on the central western border of Rectanguland.
   f. The Great Piney Forest is also along the western border.
   g. The town of Needling is located at the northeast edge of the forest.
   h. Two miles south of Needling is its twin town of Noodling.
   i. In the south central area of the country is the DooWaka Desert.
   j. The mining center, with the town of Nugget at its center, is north of the desert.

Bonus Box: Find the area of Rectanguland. Round the length of each border to the nearest half-inch.

Note to the teacher: Use with "Welcome to Rectanguland!" on page 63.

Dishin' Up Good Nutrition!

Healthy eating habits and kids don't tend to go together, do they? But they can when you serve students these fun-to-do activities and reproducibles on nutrition!

by Lisa Waller Rogers

Split Pea Soup? Yuck!

Ask kids if they've ever had to eat a yucky food, and you'll hear a horror story from everybody! Introduce your nutrition unit with a picture book that features this dietary dilemma, *George and Martha* by James Marshall (Houghton Mifflin Company, 1974). Read aloud the first story in the book and invite students to share about times when they ate a yucky food. Then have them brainstorm two lists—"Foods Most Yummy" and "Foods Most Yucky"—while you list their responses on the board. Ask each child to vote on his favorite yummy food and least favorite yucky food; then have him graph the results of both polls. Finally, have students compare the lists and graphs. Ask, "How are the foods in the yummy list different from those in the yucky list?" Help students understand that making healthful food choices keeps our bodies healthy.

Good for You!

Is good food food that tastes good or food that's good for you? Parents and kids usually disagree! That's the case in *Gregory, the Terrible Eater* by Mitchell Sharmat (Scholastic Inc., 1989). But in this tale, Gregory the goat exasperates his parents by eating healthful foods rather than the "junk" they prefer. After reading and discussing the story, display a picture of the Food Guide Pyramid. Point out that the foods at the pyramid's bottom should be eaten in the largest amounts, while those at the top should be eaten only sparingly. Then give each student a white paper plate. On the plate, have the student draw a meal for Gregory that illustrates the compromise at the book's end (healthful foods plus only one "junk food"). Post the plates on a bulletin board titled "Good for You, Gregory!" Point out to students that it's okay to eat some junk food, like Gregory, as long as most of their choices are healthful ones.

Give Grains a Go!

Why is the bread, cereal, rice, and pasta group so important? Because its foods are our body's main source of energy. To motivate students to give grains a go, collect an empty pasta box for each child. Read aloud the poem "Pasta Parade" from *Food Fight: Poets Join the Fight Against Hunger With Poems to Favorite Foods* edited by Michael J. Rosen (Harcourt Brace & Company, 1996). With students, list kinds of pasta on the board. Next, have each child use the words to write a poem about pasta on an index card. Direct him to glue the card to a pasta box. Place the boxes in a basket at your reading center. If desired, hold a pasta-tasting party using recipes from *Pretend Soup and Other Real Recipes: A Cookbook for Preschoolers & Up* by Mollie Katzen and Ann Henderson (Tricycle Press, 1994). Have small groups of students whip up batches of Noodle Pudding, Green Spaghetti, and Noodle Soup. Seconds, anyone?

Veggie Bingo

Familiarize students with the variety of vegetables available—and their nutritional benefits—with this "veggie-rific" game! Give each student a copy of page 69. Discuss how to read the chart. Then ask students which veggies they have eaten, might try, or have never heard of. Next, have each child draw a 5 x 5 bingo grid on her paper and label the middle "free space." Have her write the name of a veggie from the list in each square.

To play, describe a vegetable from the chart. For example, "It's white, has about 60 calories, and contains 20 percent of the U.S. RDA of vitamin C." *(onion)* Each student uses her chart to identify the veggie and then covers it on her card with a marker. Continue describing various vegetables. When a student has bingo, have her read the names of the covered veggies and give a nutrition fact about each one. If successful, let the student take your place as caller.

Fruit and Veggie Vendors

Sell students on neglected fruits and vegetables with this fun activity! Label a set of index cards with vegetables from page 69 (ones seldom eaten by kids) and the fruits listed below. Display the cards at a center with a variety of cookbooks. Challenge each child to select a card and complete the following tasks:

- Research your fruit or vegetable to find out its nutritional benefits.
- Draw a picture of your fruit or vegetable. If desired, personify the drawing.
- Find a recipe featuring your food. Prepare the recipe (with an adult's help) and sample it.
- Write a paragraph describing the recipe, your taste test, and the food's benefits.
- In a presentation, try to sell your fruit or veggie to the class.

Fruits: apricot, avocado, blackberry, blueberry, cherry, cranberry, currant, fig, kiwifruit, lime, mandarin, mango, nectarine, olive, papaya, persimmon, plum, pomegranate, raspberry, tangelo

I'm really quite tasty!

kale lime mango

Life in the Fast (Food) Lane

Two food groups—the milk, yogurt, and cheese group and the meat, poultry, fish, dry bean, eggs, and nuts group—are essential in providing our bodies with protein. So why do they reside near the top of the pyramid instead of the bottom? Because many protein-rich foods are also high in fat. One example is the fast-food hamburger meal, which packs lots of protein but also a day's worth of fat, sodium, and calories.

To help students get the lowdown on fast-food nutrition, write the following on the board: calories = 2,000; sodium = less than 2,400 mg; fat = less than 65 g. Explain that each figure gives the approximate recommended daily value for children their age. Next, divide the class into groups. Give each group a nutrition guide from a local fast-food restaurant and a copy of the half-page reproducible on page 70. Have the group complete the reproducible as directed and share its work with the class. Discuss how this nutritional information might alter students' dining habits.

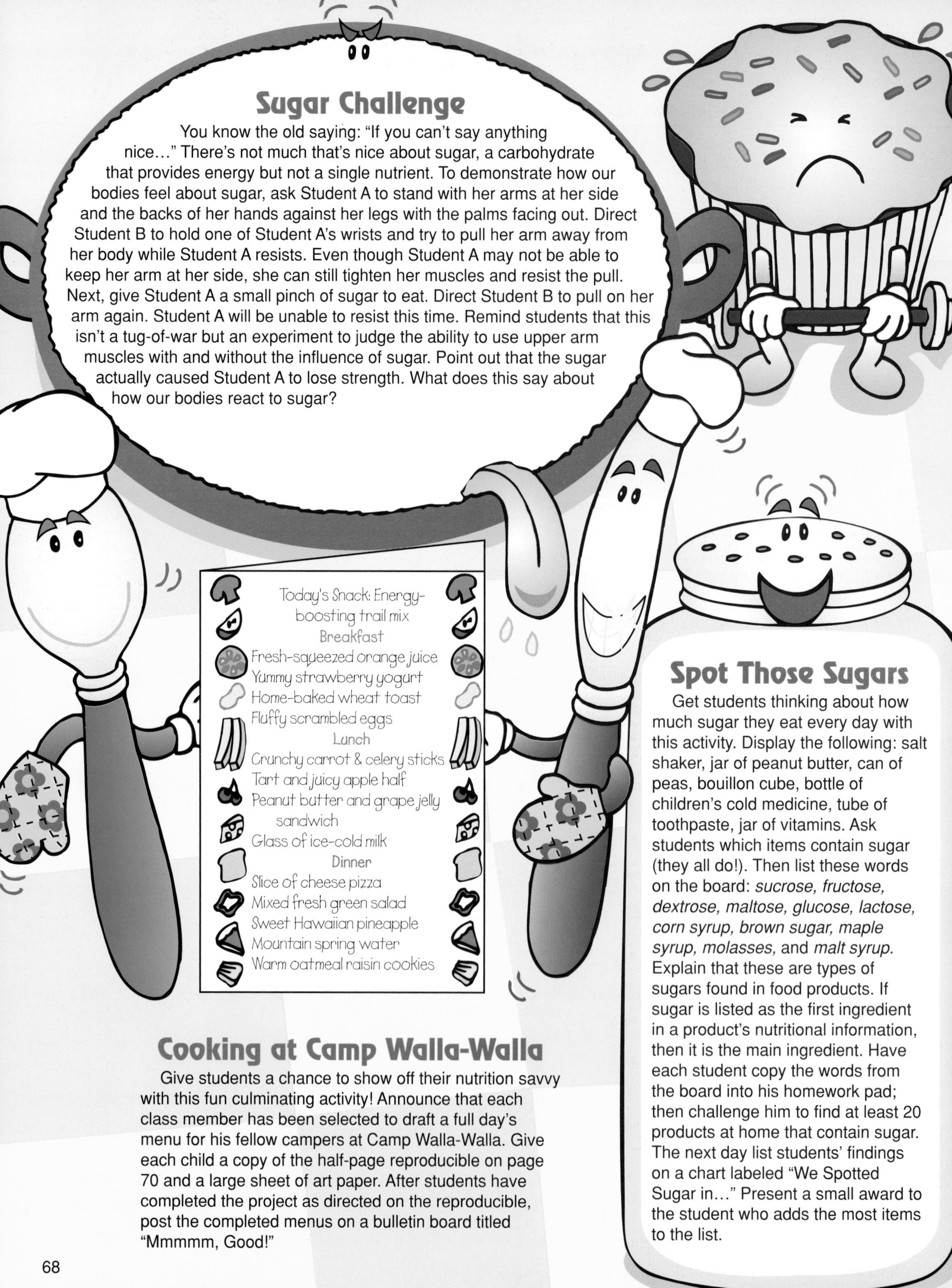

Today's Snack: Energy-boosting trail mix
Breakfast
Fresh-squeezed orange juice
Yummy strawberry yogurt
Home-baked wheat toast
Fluffy scrambled eggs
Lunch
Crunchy carrot & celery sticks
Tart and juicy apple half
Peanut butter and grape jelly sandwich
Glass of ice-cold milk
Dinner
Slice of cheese pizza
Mixed fresh green salad
Sweet Hawaiian pineapple
Mountain spring water
Warm oatmeal raisin cookies

Sugar Challenge

You know the old saying: "If you can't say anything nice…" There's not much that's nice about sugar, a carbohydrate that provides energy but not a single nutrient. To demonstrate how our bodies feel about sugar, ask Student A to stand with her arms at her side and the backs of her hands against her legs with the palms facing out. Direct Student B to hold one of Student A's wrists and try to pull her arm away from her body while Student A resists. Even though Student A may not be able to keep her arm at her side, she can still tighten her muscles and resist the pull. Next, give Student A a small pinch of sugar to eat. Direct Student B to pull on her arm again. Student A will be unable to resist this time. Remind students that this isn't a tug-of-war but an experiment to judge the ability to use upper arm muscles with and without the influence of sugar. Point out that the sugar actually caused Student A to lose strength. What does this say about how our bodies react to sugar?

Cooking at Camp Walla-Walla

Give students a chance to show off their nutrition savvy with this fun culminating activity! Announce that each class member has been selected to draft a full day's menu for his fellow campers at Camp Walla-Walla. Give each child a copy of the half-page reproducible on page 70 and a large sheet of art paper. After students have completed the project as directed on the reproducible, post the completed menus on a bulletin board titled "Mmmmm, Good!"

Spot Those Sugars

Get students thinking about how much sugar they eat every day with this activity. Display the following: salt shaker, jar of peanut butter, can of peas, bouillon cube, bottle of children's cold medicine, tube of toothpaste, jar of vitamins. Ask students which items contain sugar (they all do!). Then list these words on the board: *sucrose, fructose, dextrose, maltose, glucose, lactose, corn syrup, brown sugar, maple syrup, molasses,* and *malt syrup.* Explain that these are types of sugars found in food products. If sugar is listed as the first ingredient in a product's nutritional information, then it is the main ingredient. Have each student copy the words from the board into his homework pad; then challenge him to find at least 20 products at home that contain sugar. The next day list students' findings on a chart labeled "We Spotted Sugar in…" Present a small award to the student who adds the most items to the list.

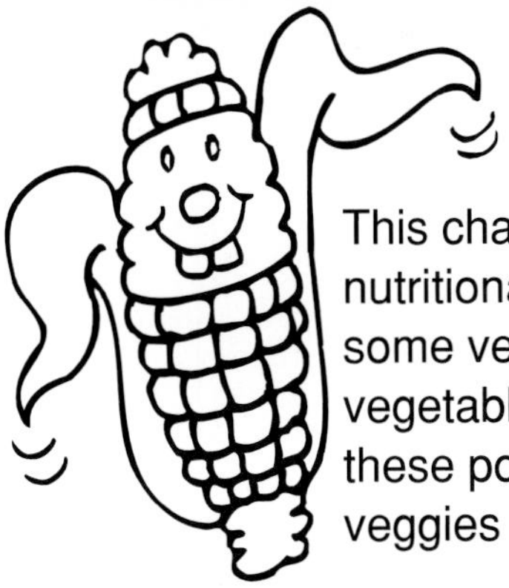

Very "Veggie-rific"!

This chart shows the nutritional values for some very "veggie-rific" vegetables. Pile plenty of these positively palatable veggies on your plate!

	Total calories	Protein (g)	Carbohydrates (g)	Total Fat (g)	Dietary Fiber (g)	Sodium (mg)	Vitamin A (% of U.S. RDA)	Vitamin C (% of U.S. RDA)	Calcium (% of U.S. RDA)	Iron (% of U.S. RDA)
Artichoke, 1 medium, cooked	75	5	17	0	12	140	3	25	7	11
Asparagus, 5 spears, raw	18	2	2	0	2	0	10	10	★	★
Beets, 2, cooked	31	1	7	0	2	49	★	9	★	3
Bell Pepper, 1 medium, raw	20	1	5	0	1	2	5	112	★	2
Broccoli, 1 cup chopped, raw	25	3	5	0	3	24	14	137	4	4
Brussels Sprouts, 1 cup, cooked	38	3	8	0	4	22	8	125	4	7
Cabbage, 1 cup shredded, raw	17	1	4	0	2	12	★	55	3	2
Carrot, 1 medium, raw	40	1	8	1	1	40	330	8	2	★
Cauliflower, 1 cup pieces, raw	18	2	3	0	2	45	★	110	2	2
Celery, 1 stalk, raw	6	0	2	0	1	35	★	5	★	★
Collard Greens, 1 cup, raw	11	1	3	0	1	7	12	14	★	★
Corn, Sweet, 1 ear, raw	75	3	17	1	1	15	5	10	★	3
Cucumber, 1/3 medium, raw	18	1	3	0	0	0	4	6	2	2
Eggplant, 1 cup cubed, raw	21	1	5	0	3	3	6	★	3	3
Green Beans, Snap, 3/4 cup cut, raw	14	1	2	0	3	0	2	8	4	★
Green Onions, 1/4 cup chopped, raw	7	0	1	0	0	0	3	20	★	5
Kale, 1 cup, raw	33	2	7	0	4	29	60	134	9	6
Leeks, 1 cup, raw	64	2	15	0	3	20	★	21	6	12
Lettuce, Iceberg, 1 cup shredded, raw	7	0	2	0	0	5	★	4	★	★
Lettuce, Leaf, 1 cup shredded, raw	10	1	2	0	1	5	11	17	4	4
Mushrooms, 5 medium, raw	25	3	3	0	0	0	★	2	★	★
Mustard Greens, 1 cup, raw	14	2	3	0	1	14	30	65	6	5
Okra, 8 pods, raw	27	2	6	0	2	4	5	23	5	2
Onion, 1 medium, raw	60	1	14	0	3	10	★	20	4	★
Parsley, 1/4 cup chopped, raw	10	1	2	0	1	12	16	45	4	10
Peas, Snow, 1 cup, raw	60	0	11	0	4	6	2	145	6	17
Potato, 1 medium baked in skin	220	5	51	0	5	16	★	44	2	25
Radishes, 7, raw	20	0	3	0	0	35	★	30	★	★
Sprouts, Alfalfa, 1 cup, raw	10	1	1	0	1	0	★	4.5	★	★
Spinach, 1 cup, raw	12	2	2	0	2	44	38	26	6	8
Squash, Yellow, 1 cup sliced, raw	25	1	5	0	2	3	4	18	3	3
Squash, Winter, 1 cup cubed, baked	18	2	4	0	1	4	4	20	2	3
Squash, Zucchini, 1 cup sliced, raw	136	3	36	0	7	10	11	44	11	13
Sweet Potato, 1 medium, baked	154	3	36	0	5	15	327	61	4	4
Tomato, 2 1/2" diameter, raw	26	1	6	0	2	11	8	39	★	3
Turnips, 1 medium, raw	23	0	5	0	2	57	★	30	3	★

★ less than 2%

Note to the teacher: Use with "Veggie Bingo" and "Fruit and Veggie Vendors" on page 67.

Name ____________ Nutrition, creative writing, and thinking

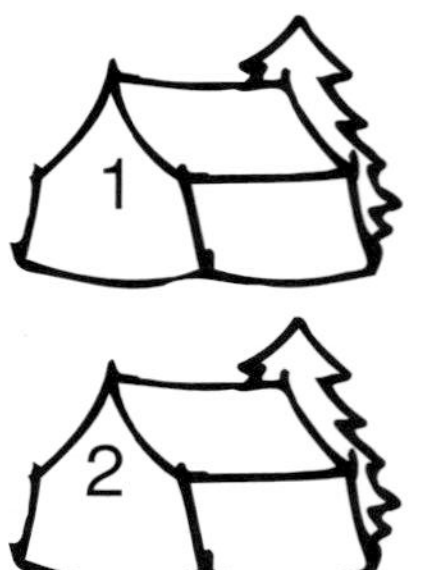

Things Are Cookin' at Camp Walla-Walla!

When you think of summer camp, do you think of fantastic food? Probably not. Well now's the time to change that! The director of Camp Walla-Walla has just asked you to plan a day's menu for your campmates. Follow these steps:

1. On a sheet of paper, brainstorm menu items for each of these meals: breakfast, lunch, dinner, campsite snack. These four meals must be delicious or the kids won't eat them; they must also be nutritious or the parents won't approve!
2. Look through your brainstormed list of menu items. Select the items you plan to include in each meal. Double-check to make sure your choices are nutritious.
3. On another sheet of paper, write each meal's menu. Use lots of colorful adjectives so that your campmates will be eager to dig in to your delicious cuisine! After you've written about your meals, have a classmate help you proofread your work.
4. Fold a sheet of art paper in half to make a menu. Open the menu. Use colorful markers and crayons to copy your meals in the menu. Add pictures too!
5. Illustrate the front of your Camp Walla-Walla menu. Include your name somewhere on the cover.

6. Share your menu with the class. Any mouths watering?

Note to the teacher: Use with "Cooking at Camp Walla-Walla" on page 68. Provide each student with a large sheet of art paper and markers or crayons.

Name ____________ Reading for information

Life in the Fast (Food) Lane

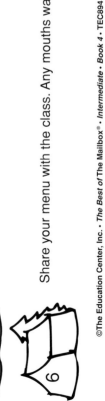

Name of restaurant: ____________

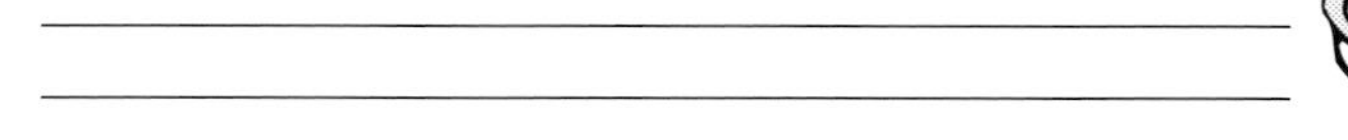

For your restaurant, list the following in order:

The top four high-sodium foods:
1. ____________
2. ____________
3. ____________
4. ____________

The top four low-sodium foods:
1. ____________
2. ____________
3. ____________
4. ____________

The top four fatty foods:
1. ____________
2. ____________
3. ____________
4. ____________

The top four lowfat foods:
1. ____________
2. ____________
3. ____________
4. ____________

Answer these questions on the back or on another sheet of paper.
1. In terms of sodium and fat, what would be the worst meal to order at your restaurant?
2. What would be the healthiest meal to order?
3. If you could add something to the menu that was nutritious and tasty, what would it be?

Note to the teacher: Use with "Life in the Fast (Food) Lane" on page 67. Provide each student group with a nutrition guide available from a local fast-food restaurant.

Looks Like Stormy Weather!

Hands-On Activities for Studying Storms

Your students may not be able to chase a tornado or fly an airplane inside a hurricane. But they *can* learn to track clues that will help them predict that a storm's on the way! Complement your studies of weather with the following creative activities, teacher demonstrations, and reproducibles on severe storms. *by Gail Peckumn, Jefferson, IA*

A Close-Up Look at How a Storm Develops

1—Hot Air's on the Rise

How exactly does a hurricane develop? Three ingredients must be present.

- Warm water: During the summer and fall months, the sun continually warms tropical ocean waters.
- Moist air: Warm, moist air rises above the water and drifts up into the sky.
- Converging winds: Cooler air moves in to take the place of the rising warm air. As warm air continues to rise, the air pressure drops, making stronger winds.

Help students understand that warm air rises with the following demonstration:

1. Tape the bottom of one paper lunch bag to each end of a meterstick.
2. Balance the meterstick on your index finger. Hold it so that the opening of one bag is directly over a heat source (a lamp without its shade), but not touching it.
3. Ask students to observe what happens.

The air inside the bag will heat up, so the air expands and some of it escapes. This reduces the weight of the air inside the bag. The heavier, cooler air around the bag will exert a force on the lighter, warm air, causing the bag to rise. Remind students that they see warm, moist air rise when steam rises above boiling water. The same thing happens over warm ocean waters. The more heated water in the atmosphere, the more likely that a storm will occur.

2—A Cold Front's Moving In

Cold air forces warm air upward, creating an area of low pressure. As warm, moist air rises, it can produce towering storm clouds. Show your students how this movement of cold air happens with the following demonstration. Remind students that since both air and water are considered fluids, water represents air in the demonstration.

1. Punch two holes in the bottom of a paper cup.
2. Secure the cup to the corner of a large, clear container (a plastic storage box or an empty aquarium) with duct tape. The bottom of the cup should be about two centimeters from the bottom of the container.
3. Fill another cup with ice-cold water and add a few drops of blue food coloring.
4. Fill the large container with hot water to about one centimeter from the top of the cup.
5. Quickly pour all of the cold, blue water into the cup. Have students view the bottom of the container to see what happens.
6. Have students touch the water in the paper cup that's inside the large container.

The cold, blue water will sink to the bottom of the container as it pushes up the hot water. The water in the cup will be warm because all of the cold water sank to the bottom of the container.

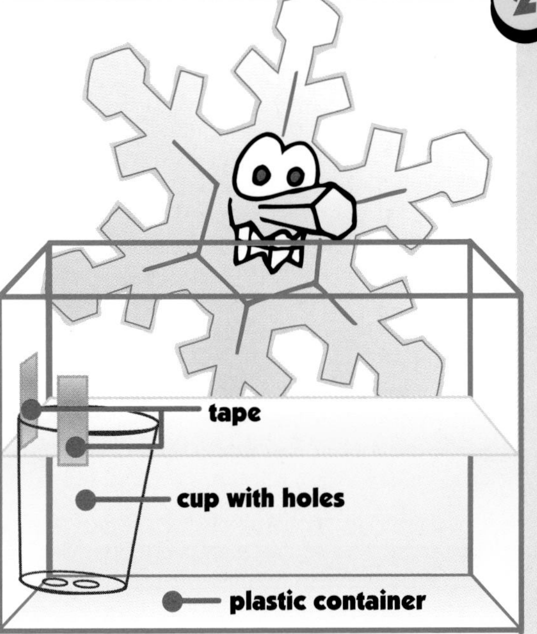

3—Moisture's Building

Hot air can hold a lot of moisture. This moisture, in vapor form, rises in the atmosphere. Air temperatures become cooler with increased elevation, so all the moisture in the hot air starts to condense into clouds. The more moisture, the bigger the clouds. Demonstrate how hot air holds more moisture than cold air with the following activity:

1. Fill two glasses—one with hot water and the other with cold water and ice.
2. Let them sit for several minutes as students observe what happens.

Moisture will form on the outside of the cold water glass. Why? Because the cold water has cooled the air around the glass, and since cooler air cannot hold as much moisture as warmer air, the moisture in the air begins to condense into droplets on the glass.

Extend this demonstration by showing how clouds form.

1. Fill a small cake pan with ice.
2. Fill a large, widemouthed glass jar about 1/4 full of hot water.
3. Light a match and hold it down inside the jar for a few seconds; then drop it in. (This forms dust particles around which water vapor can condense.)
4. Place the pan of ice over the top of the jar.
5. Have students observe what happens.

Warm air will rise off the water in the jar, then cool and condense when it hits the pan of ice. The result will be the formation of a cloud near the top of the jar. Whenever there is a large amount of heated, moist air, it can cool and condense into huge cumulonimbus storm clouds, producing thunder, lightning, and rain.

A tornado in Broken Bow, Oklahoma, carried a motel sign 30 miles and dropped it in Arkansas!

In early times, people thought that lightning and thunder were signs of the gods' anger.

Pam Crane

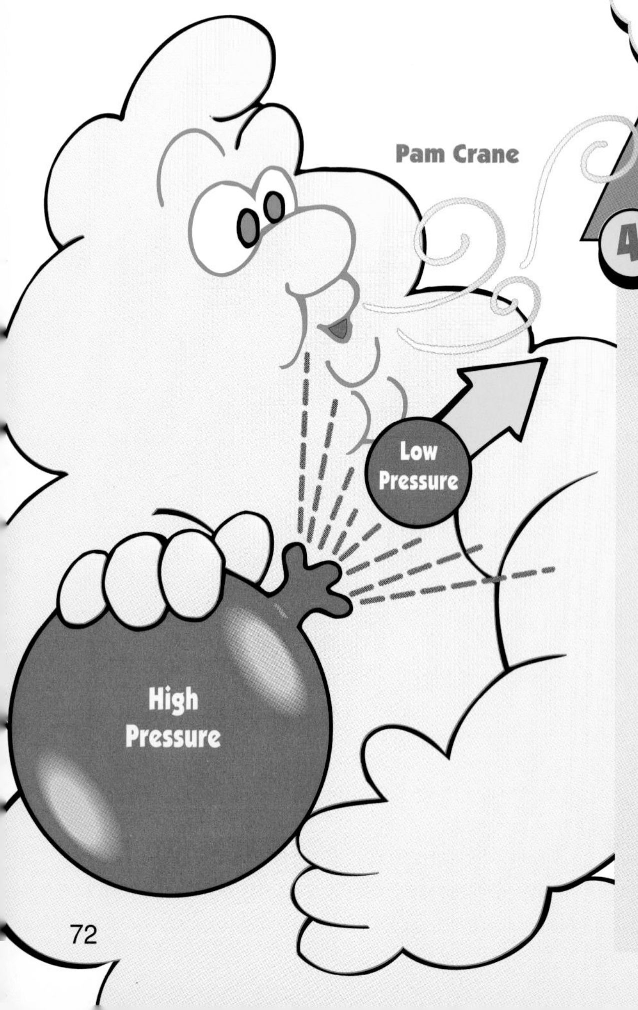

Low Pressure

High Pressure

4—Pressure's Dropping

When stormy weather hits, high winds follow! Differences in air pressure cause winds. Demonstrate this concept with the following activity:

1. Blow a little bit of air into a balloon and hold the end so the air stays inside.
2. Ask your students where the air has greater pressure—inside or outside the balloon. *(inside)* Ask what will happen if you loosen your grip on the opening of the balloon. *(The air will come sputtering out.)*
3. Have a volunteer hold his hand in front of the balloon opening as you let the air out. Ask the class why the air left the balloon instead of staying inside it. *(Air moves from an area of high pressure to an area of low pressure.)*
4. Next fully inflate the balloon and hold its end. Ask students if the balloon has more air pressure inside than when you first blew it up. *(yes)*
5. Let out the air, as the same volunteer feels it escape. Ask the volunteer which time there was a stronger flow of air. *(the second time)*

Share with your students that this is what makes the wind in a storm blow—but on a much larger scale! Like the air that rushed out of the fully inflated balloon, surface air is always on the move between high- and low-pressure areas, trying to even them out. The bigger the difference in pressure between the two areas, the harder the wind will blow.

5—Lightning's Flashing

What exactly is lightning? Demonstrate for your students how lightning is formed on a smaller—and safer!—scale.

1. Blow up two large balloons and tie off the end of each one.
2. Tie a one-meter length of thread to each balloon.
3. Suspend the balloons from the top of a door frame so that they are about ten inches apart.
4. Label two sticky notes—one A and the other B—and attach a note to each balloon.
5. Have a student rub balloon A against her hair about a dozen times, then gently release the balloon.

The balloons will move toward each other and stay together. Why? Electrons are rubbed off the hair and collected on balloon A, giving it a negative electrical charge. Since like charges *repel* (push away) each other, the negative charges on balloon A repel the negatively charged electrons of balloon B. This causes the surface of balloon B to become more positively charged. Since the balloons now have opposite charges, they are attracted to each other.

Explain to your students that most scientists think this is what happens in a thundercloud. Light, rising water droplets and tiny pieces of ice collide with hail and other heavier, falling particles, creating electric charges. The heavier particles gain a negative charge; the lighter ones, a positive charge. The negatively charged particles fall to the bottom of the cloud and most of the positively charged particles rise to the top. Lightning occurs when these separated charges flow toward each other (or toward opposite charges on earth), creating an electric spark.

Hurricane comes from a Carib Indian word for "big wind."

When a snowstorm's winds reach 39 mph, it's called a *blizzard*.

Check out the following Web site (current as of October 1998) to learn more facts about lightning; plus read firsthand accounts from people who have actually been struck by lightning:
www.azstarnet.com/~anubis/zaphome.htm

6—Thunder's Rumbling

Is that thunder rumbling in the distance? The bright light that we see in a flash of lightning is called a *return stroke*. Return strokes heat the air in their paths, causing it to expand very quickly. It then cools and contracts. This rapid expansion and contraction causes air molecules to move, which produces the sound waves that we hear as thunder. To help students "experience" thunder, provide each small group with a 1" x 8" plastic strip (cut from a transparency), a small lump of modeling clay, a large paper clip, a ruler, and a piece of wool (any item made of 100% wool). Then direct each group to follow these steps:

1. Use the clay to stand the paper clip upright.
2. Wrap the wool around the plastic strip.
3. Quickly pull the strip through the cloth at least three times.
4. Immediately hold the plastic near the top of the paper clip. What happens? Each group should hear a snapping sound. Why?

Electrons are rubbed off the wool and onto the plastic. The electrons cluster together until their energy is great enough to move them across the air between the plastic and the metal clip. The movement of the electrons through air produces sound waves, resulting in a snapping sound.

number of letters in name	number of students
2	
3	|||
4	卌
5	||
6	卌 |||
7	||
8	||||

Tally Sheet

Tally Up!

Using a *tally sheet* is a simple way to collect data. Ask students, "Who in our class has the longest first name? How many other students have names with that many letters?" Call on several volunteers to suggest how they would organize the data you're asking for. Their responses will likely include:

- List students' names. Then count the letters in each one. Write that number beside the name.
- Make columns with number headings (2 letters, 3 letters, etc.). Write each name in the matching column.
- List numbers (2 letters, 3 letters, etc.) in a column. Write each name beside the matching number.

Next, make a tally sheet, like the one shown, on a transparency or the chalkboard, adding more numbers if necessary. In turn, have each child state his name and the number of letters it has. As each number is given, make a tally mark beside the corresponding number on the transparency. When finished, ask students if your original questions have now been answered. Also ask if this method was an efficient way to answer the questions. Then continue with the next activity to show a simple way to display this information.

Using a Frequency Table

Beside the tally sheet (from the preceding activity), make a *frequency table* like the one shown. Then ask, "Which number of letters on the tally sheet has the most matching names? How many names?" Write this information in the first line of the table. Continue with the number of letters that has the second-most matching names. Add this information in the second line of the table. Continue filling the table until every student is represented. Then ask, "Which display is easier to read: the tally sheet or the frequency table?" *(The frequency table is easier to read because the information is listed in an orderly fashion. Also there are no tally marks to count, and facts can be found more readily.)*

Frequency Table

number of letters in name	number of students
3	8
4	5
5	4
6	3
7	2
8	2

1. Let A be the *year* in which you were born.
   A = 1988
2. Let B be the *day of the year* on which you were born.
   January: 31 days
   February: 29 days (1988 was a leap year.)
   March: 31 days
   April: 12 days
   B =103rd day of the year (31+ 29 + 31+12 = 103)
   B = 103
3. Find C: C= (A – 1) ÷ 4. Ignore the remainder.
   C = (1988 – 1) ÷ 4 = 1987 ÷ 4 = 496 r. 3
   C = 496
4. Find D: D = A + B + C
   D = 1988 + 103 + 496
   D = 2,587
5. Divide D by 7.
   2,587 ÷ 7= 369 r. 4. Note the remainder: **4**

Use the table below to see which day of the week matches the remainder of the division problem in Step 5. *(The student born on April 12, 1988, was born on a Tuesday.)*

Remainder:	Birthday:
0	Friday
1	Saturday
2	Sunday
3	Monday
4	Tuesday
5	Wednesday
6	Thursday

Bar Graphs and Pictographs

Ask students what kinds of graphs they see most often in magazines and textbooks, and they'll likely say *bar graphs* and *pictographs*. Share with students that these graphs show comparisons of data. And although a pictograph is usually colorful and eye-catching, it doesn't show specific data as well as a bar graph does. Have students collect data to display in a bar graph or pictograph by asking, "On which day of the week were you born?" Share the steps for determining one's day of birth shown in the chart at the left. Then, as you guide students, have them complete each step. (The chart includes a completed sample birthdate: April 12, 1988.) When everyone has finished, draw a tally chart and frequency table on the chalkboard. Ask each student to state his day of birth as you complete the tally sheet. Then organize the tally sheet results in the frequency table, beginning with the day of the week with the most tally marks.

To complete the activity, give each student a copy of page 80. Direct half of the class to make bar graphs—and the other half pictographs—of the information listed in the frequency table. Suggest that students review the information on their miniposters to help them.

Introducing the Histogram

A *histogram* is a special bar graph that shows the number of times data occurs within a certain range. While the bars in a bar graph and in a histogram are of the same width, the bars in a histogram are connected with no space between them. Another difference between the two is that a bar graph shows specific information and a histogram's information is much more general.

To collect data for students to use in a histogram, tape two yardsticks end-to-end on a wall so that each student can measure her height. Then divide students into pairs. Have the students in each pair measure each other's height to the nearest inch. When all heights are determined, have each student write her initials and her height on the chalkboard. Ask students to study the data and think about what intervals (ranges) should be included in a histogram to display the data (examples: 50–54 in., 55–59 in., 60–64 in., etc.). Stress that the intervals must all be equal. Next, provide each student with a copy of page 80 on which to make a histogram of the class data.

hour	number of visitors
8:00 – 9:00	
9:00 – 10:00	
10:00 – 11:00	
11:00 – 12:00	
12:00 – 1:00	
1:00 – 2:00	
2:00 – 3:00	

On the Line

A *line graph* shows changes and variations over a period of time. To make a line graph, students follow the same guidelines as those for making a bar graph—except that lines are drawn instead of bars.

Early one morning before your instructional day begins, direct each student to label a sheet of paper as shown. Then tell students that they are going to keep a record of the number of visitors to your class during the day—both adults and children. Beginning with the 8:00 to 9:00 interval, have each student make a tally mark for each individual who comes to the classroom door during that hour. Even if the visitor does not enter the classroom, have students make a tally mark for him or her. Then, near the end of the day, instruct each student to make a line graph displaying the collected data for homework. Have each student draw his graph on a copy of the reproducible on page 80. Have student groups compare their graphs the next day.

A Piece of the Pie

A *circle graph* (also called a pie chart) shows the parts of a whole and the relationships among those parts. Model a circle graph by sharing with students a typical Saturday in your life! Since a day has 24 hours, such a graph should be divided into 24 equal parts. Approximate the time you spend on each activity to the nearest hour; then list the data on the board. To get—and keep—your students' attention, embellish your day somewhat. For example, list the following data on the board: 7 hours—sleeping, 1 hour—schoolwork, 2 hours—meals, 3 hours—skateboarding, 4 hours—skydiving lessons, 5 hours—mountain climbing, and 2 hours—training your pet boa constrictor.

Next, draw the 24-section circle graph shown on the chalkboard (or make a transparency of the one on page 79). Have students assist you as you complete your graph. As a follow-up, give each student a copy of page 79. Instruct each student to complete the 24-section circle graph to show a typical Saturday in his life—or perhaps one he would like to experience!

____
(architect's name)

Tally Sheet

Best Building Materials*	
straw	III
sticks	~~IIII~~ II
bricks	~~IIII~~ ~~IIII~~ II

*according to P.B.A. (Pig Builders Assoc.)

Frequency Table

Material	Number of Votes
bricks	12
sticks	7
straw	3

TIPS FOR BUILDING A GREAT GRAPH

1. Give your graph a title.
2. Label the *vertical axis*—from the base to the top.
3. Label the *horizontal axis*—from left to right at the bottom.
4. If you're making a *pictograph,* show the symbol and its value in a key.
5. If you're making a *bar graph,* make sure the bars are the same width. Also use equal space between the bars.
6. If you're making a *histogram,* all of the bars should be side by side.
7. Use the correct number scale. Make sure the intervals are equal (for example: 1–5, 6–10, 11–15, 16–20, etc.).

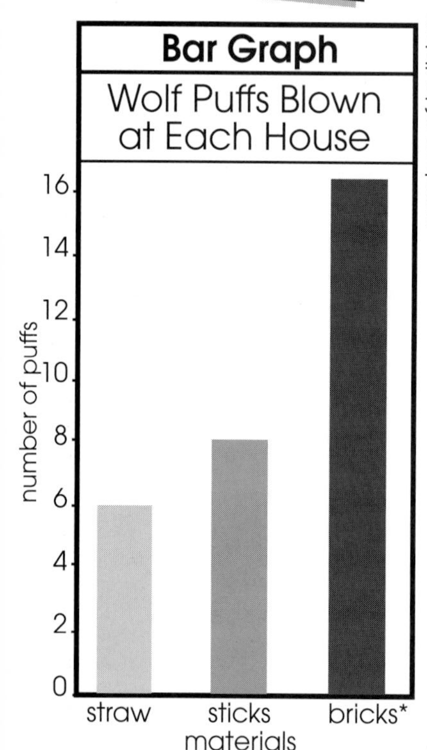

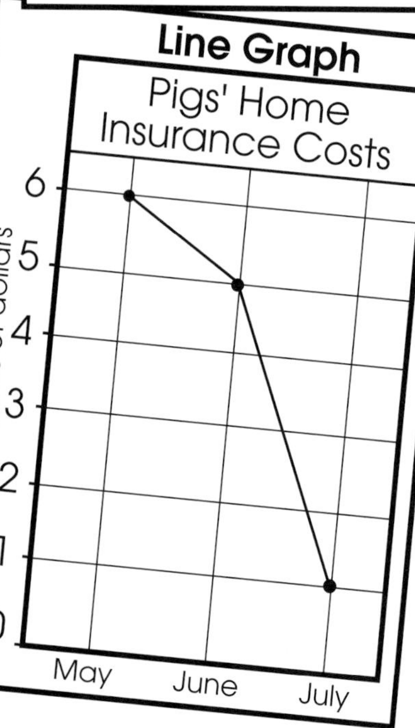

 Note to the teacher: Use with "Keeping It All Together" on page 75.

Name________________________

BUILDING CIRCLE GRAPHS

A circle graph divided into 24 equal sections can be used to show a variety of data:

- Use the graph to display data about a 24-hour day.
- Divide the graph into 3, 4, 6, 8, or 12 (all factors of 24) equal sections to display other data. For example: 1 of 12 equal sections equals 5 minutes of an hour.

A circle graph divided into 100 equal sections can be used to show a variety of data:

- Use the graph to display percentages, which are based on 100.
- Use the graph to show parts of a dollar. For example: 10 of 100 equal sections equals 10¢.
- Divide the graph into 5, 10, 20, 25, or 50 (all factors of 100) equal sections to display other data. For example: 8 of 50 equal sections equals 8 U.S. states.

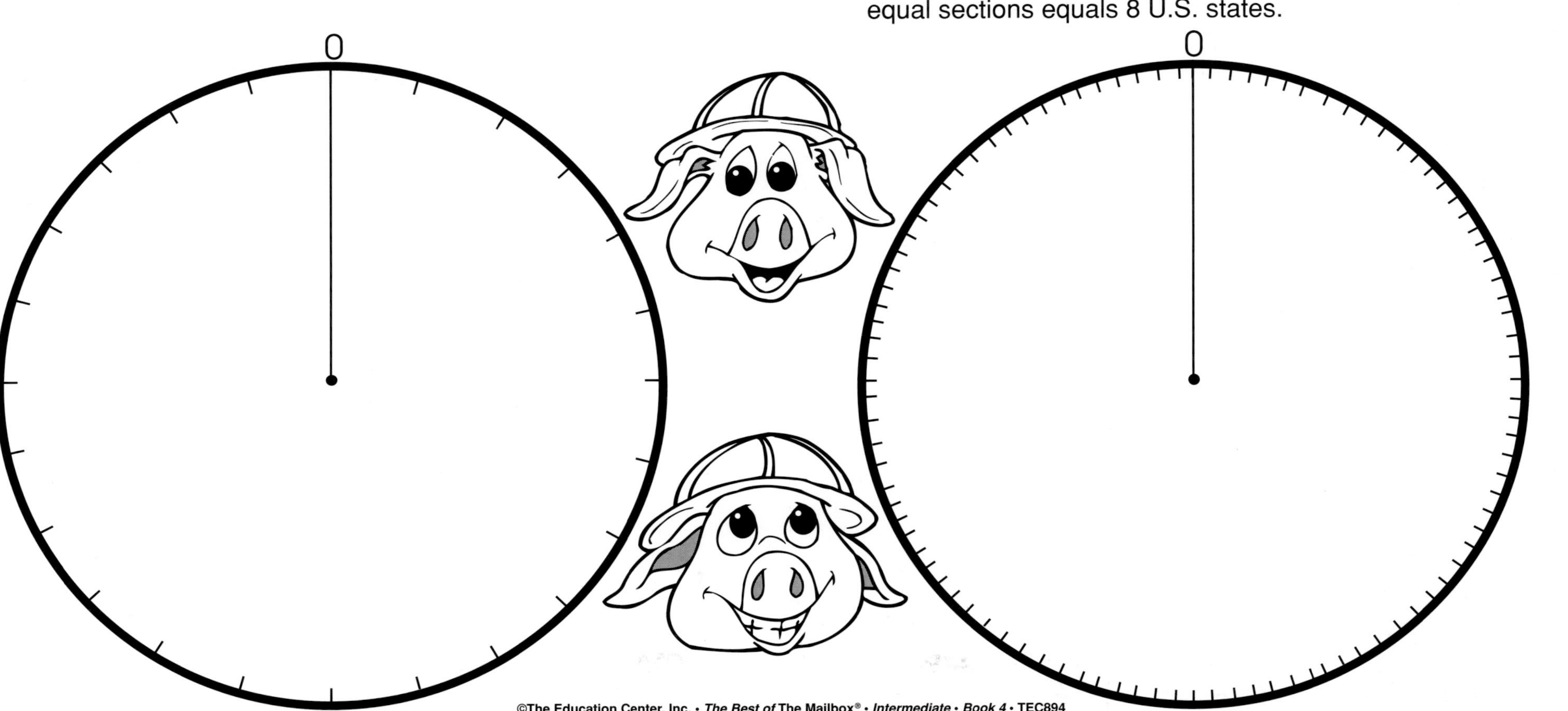

Note to the teacher: Use with "A Piece of the Pie" on page 77.

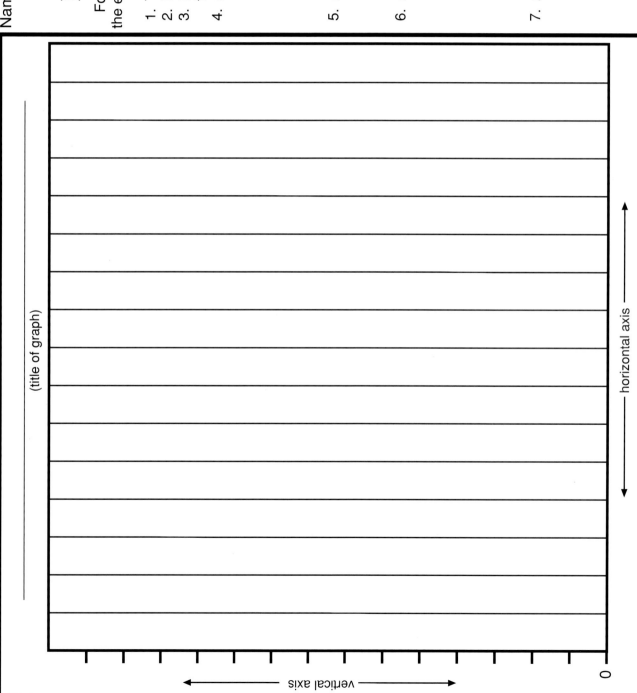

(title of graph)

vertical axis

0

horizontal axis

Name ____________

A BLUEPRINT FOR BUILDING GRAPHS

Follow this plan to create graphs that are the envy of the neighborhood!

1. Title the graph.
2. Label the vertical axis: base to top.
3. Label the horizontal axis: left to right at the bottom.
4. *Bar Graph:*
   a. Bars should be of equal width.
   b. Use equal space between bars.
   c. Use a number scale with equal intervals (ranges).
   d. Use a ruler to make sure the bars are the right heights.
5. *Pictograph:*
   a. Use a key to show the symbol and its value.
   b. Label only one axis.
6. *Histogram:*
   a. Bars should be of equal width.
   b. Bars are connected. There is no space between them.
   c. A histogram gives general information. For example: the number of runners who finish a race between 50 and 60 minutes.
7. *Line Graph:*
   a. Make a bar graph, but leave off the bars!
   b. Mark points on a line graph.
   c. Connect the points with straight lines.

Note to the teacher: Use with "Bar Graphs and Pictographs" on page 76 and "Introducing the Histogram" and "On the Line" on page 77.

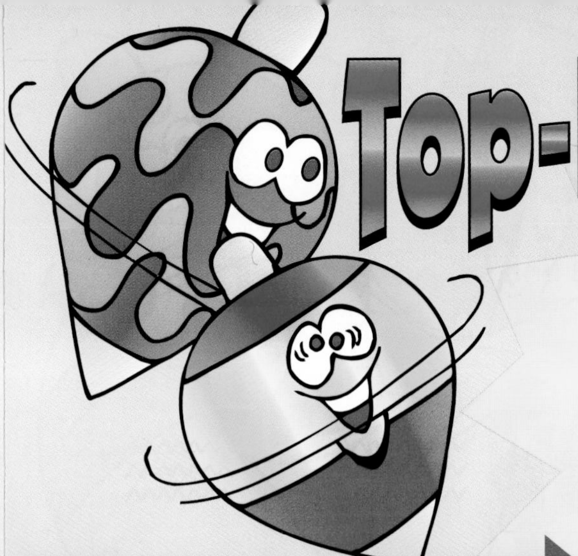

Top-Notch Narratives

Creative Ideas for Teaching Narrative Writing

Spinning a story off the top of one's head is a pretty tall order for even the most eager young writer. Help your students learn how to write a personal or imaginative narrative from top to toe with the following ready-to-use activities and reproducibles!

with ideas by Pat Twohey and Becky Andrews

Writing a Personal Narrative

A *personal narrative* is a story about a personal memory. The main character in the story is the author.

It Starts With a Great Idea

Skill: Gathering ideas for personal narratives

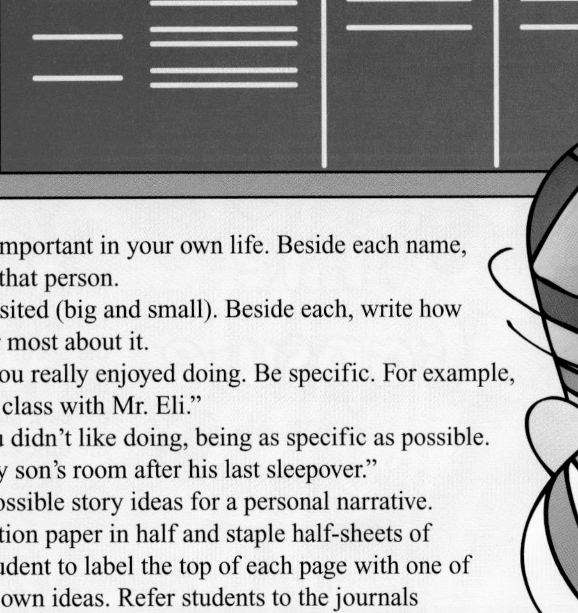

Help students gather ideas for personal narratives with this easy-to-do activity. First, explain to the class that the best experiences to write about are memorable ones that caused the author to feel a strong emotion, such as happiness, fear, or surprise. Then divide the chalkboard into four columns labeled as shown. Write the following in each column.

- **"Important People":** List five people who are important in your own life. Beside each name, list a memorable experience you've shared with that person.
- **"Places I've Visited":** List five places you've visited (big and small). Beside each, write how the place made you feel and what you remember most about it.
- **"Things I Liked Doing":** List five things that you really enjoyed doing. Be specific. For example, instead of "pottery," list "taking my first pottery class with Mr. Eli."
- **"Things I Disliked Doing":** List five things you didn't like doing, being as specific as possible.

For example, instead of "housework," list "cleaning my son's room after his last sleepover." Point out that the result of this activity is a list of 20 possible story ideas for a personal narrative. Then have each child fold a 9" x 12" sheet of construction paper in half and staple half-sheets of notebook paper inside to make a journal. Direct the student to label the top of each page with one of the categories above, and then fill the journal with his own ideas. Refer students to the journals whenever you want them to write personal narratives. Also make your own journal to share with reluctant writers who need a little extra modeling or motivation.

Tip-Top Dialogue

Skill: Writing dialogue

A story without dialogue is like soup without a sandwich—something's definitely missing! Give your young writers practice writing dialogue with this lots-of-fun lesson! Review with students the basic rules for punctuating dialogue (see the list on page 85). Then divide the class into pairs. Have each twosome sit together with one sheet of paper between them. Then challenge the pair to hold a silent conversation by writing in dialogue format what they wish to say. After the first student in the pair writes his first line of dialogue, have his partner check it for correct punctuation. Then have Partner #2 write her response. Continue until each pair has written at least four lines of dialogue. Follow up this activity by having each student complete a copy of the reproducible on page 85. Use this same activity to help students write dialogue for imaginative narratives, too.

Name ________________________________ Writing checklist

Spinning a Top-Notch Imaginative Narrative

Follow these steps to write an imaginative narrative that can't be topped!

An *imaginative narrative* is a story with imaginary characters and events.

____ 1. **Invent your characters:** Think of a main character and one or two other characters. They can be real people, creatures you invent yourself, talking animals, etc. Give each character a name. Write a description of each character's appearance and interests.

____ 2. **Choose a problem to solve:** Think of a problem for the main character to solve. (The way that your main character solves the problem will be the *plot* of your story.)

____ 3. **Choose a setting:** Decide where and when your story will take place. Write a description with so many details that readers can see the setting for themselves.

____ 4. **Start your first draft:** Begin your story by introducing the main character and setting. Or start with an event that leads up to the story's main problem.

____ 5. **Continue writing your draft:** As you write, make the main character's life more and more difficult because of the problem. Don't forget to include dialogue and lots of details. Finish your story when the problem is solved.

____ 6. **Put it down:** Leave your story alone for a while. Then pick it up and reread it.

____ 7. **Ask someone to read your draft:** Have a classmate review your draft. Listen to any questions your friend has. Make any needed changes.

____ 8. **Edit and proofread your draft:** Check for errors in spelling, capitalization, and punctuation. Make any needed changes.

____ 9. **Write a neat, error-free copy:** After you rewrite your story, proofread it one last time.

Note to the teacher: Use with "I'm Glad You Asked!" on page 83 and the activities on page 84.

Name ________________________________ Writing checklist

Spinning a Top-Notch Personal Narrative

Follow these steps to write a personal narrative from top to toe!

A *personal narrative* is a story about a personal memory that is so important you never want to forget it.

____ 1. **Choose a subject:** Think of an unforgettable experience that happened to you over a short period of time.

____ 2. **Think:** If the experience is very clear in your mind, go ahead to Step 3. If it's not really clear, list the details you can remember. Try to answer the five *W*s: *Who? What? When? Where?* and *Why?*

____ 3. **Write the first draft:** Remember to write the events of this experience in order. Add details to each event as you think of them.

____ 4. **Revise the first draft:** Look over the draft. Did you leave anything out? Is anything in the wrong order? Are there any confusing parts? Did you include dialogue? Make any needed changes.

____ 5. **Ask someone to review your draft:** Have a classmate review your draft and ask the same questions you did in Step 4. Make any needed changes.

____ 6. **Edit and proofread your draft:** Check for errors in spelling, capitalization, and punctuation. Make any needed changes.

____ 7. **Write a neat, error-free copy:** After you rewrite your story, proofread it one last time.

Note to the teacher: Use with the activities on page 82.

Name ______________________________

Top Secret!

Color in the top after you complete each step.

Your mission: to write a description that is so clear that anyone who reads it will be able to picture what you're describing exactly as you did!

1. On a sheet of drawing paper, draw and color a picture of a one-of-a-kind character in a unique setting. *Don't let anyone see your picture!*

2. Look at your picture. On the lines below, list details that describe your character's appearance. Be very specific. List information about color, size, and shape, along with adjectives that clearly tell what the character looks like. Also tell what the character is doing and where he/she is located in the scene. Use the back of this sheet if you need more room.

______________________ ______________________

______________________ ______________________

______________________ ______________________

______________________ ______________________

______________________ ______________________

3. Review your list. Then number the items on your list to show the order in which you will include them in your paragraph.

4. On another sheet of paper, write a paragraph that clearly describes the character in your picture. Use the numbered items in your list above.

5. Reread your paragraph. Does it match your picture? Is it in a logical order? Are the details clear enough? Revise and proofread your paragraph.

6. Look at your picture and study the setting. On the lines below, list specific details that describe the setting. Use the back of this sheet if you need more room.

______________________ ______________________

______________________ ______________________

______________________ ______________________

______________________ ______________________

7. Review this second list. Then number the items to show the order in which you will include them in a second paragraph about the setting.

8. On the back of your character paragraph, write another paragraph that clearly describes your picture's setting. Use the numbered items listed above.

9. Reread your setting paragraph. Ask yourself the questions in Step 5. Then revise and proofread the paragraph.

Note to the teacher: Use with "What You Write Is What They See" on page 83. Provide each student with a sheet of drawing paper and crayons or markers.

Name ______________________ Writing a personal narrative: sequence, details

Go With the Flow!

Did you know that you have some top-notch stories to tell? Think about things you've done or that have happened to you that you'll never forget. Every one of these events is a story that's just waiting to be told!

To write a personal narrative about one of your adventures, you must first list the events in order. Then you need to add enough details so that your reader can feel like he or she is on the adventure with you. Follow these directions to plan and write a top-notch tale!

Step 1: Select an adventure that you've had. (Choose one that happened over a short period of time.) Summarize the main idea of this event. ______________________

Step 2: Close your eyes. Picture the events that happened in your adventure. In the flowchart boxes below, list the events in the order in which they happened (one event per box). Draw more boxes and arrows on the back of this page if you need more space.

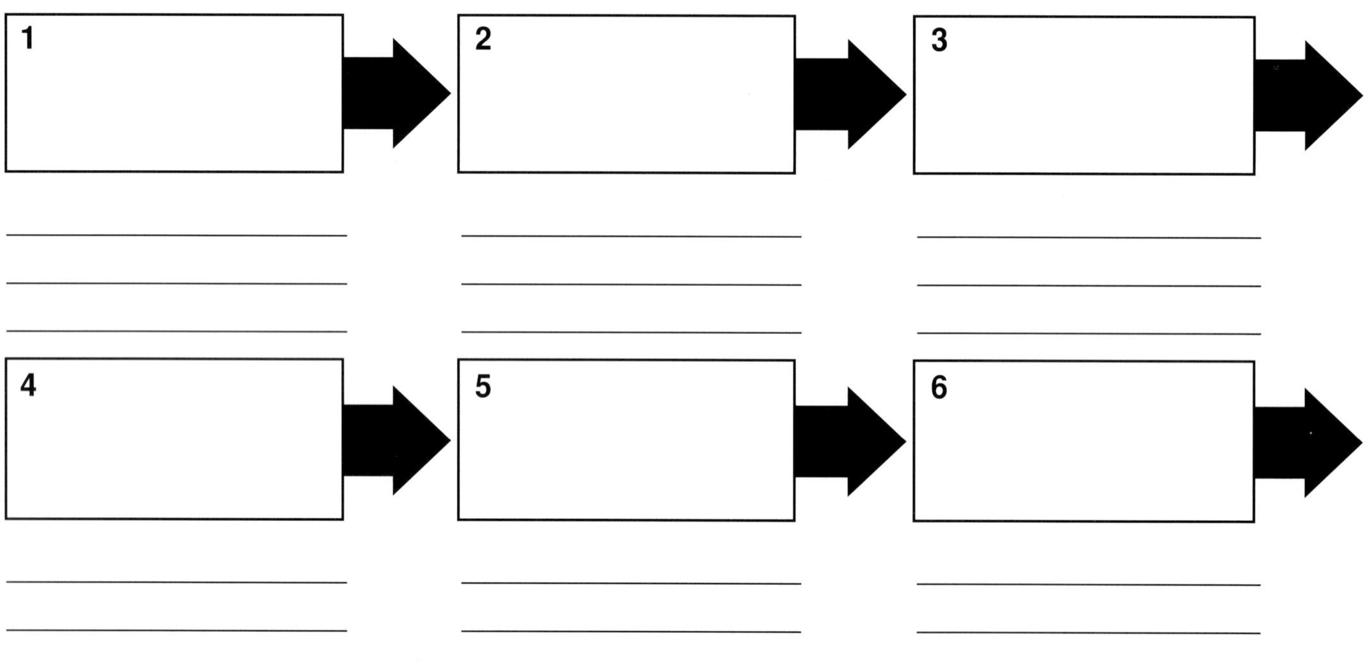

Step 3: Picture the part of the adventure described in box #1. What do you see? Hear? Smell? Touch? Taste? Also, what were you thinking and feeling during this part of the adventure? On the lines under the box, list important details that will help your reader see the details that matter and understand your thoughts and feelings. Repeat this step for the other boxes.

Step 4: Now use your flowchart to write a personal narrative about your adventure on another sheet of paper. Follow the steps described on the writing checklist provided by your teacher.

 Note to the teacher: Use with "Go With the Flow!" on page 82 and "Spinning a Top-Notch Personal Narrative" on page 86.

Globe-trottin' It!

Creative Ideas for Studying Other Countries

From one hemisphere to another, a curious globe-trotter will find hundreds of countries filled with intriguing people, exotic places, and amazing cultures. Make the study of another land an unforgettable adventure with the following creative ideas and reproducibles—all designed to be used with any country on the globe.

ideas by Hellen Harvey

"Geogra-Tree" Bulletin Board

Skill: Research skills

Bring a paper tree—and your students' research skills—to life with this colorful display! Draw, color, and label a large tree cutout; then mount it on a bulletin board. Have each child cut a leaf shape from light green paper and program it like the one illustrated. Next, direct the student to research the country of her ancestors and fill in the information on her leaf. (If a student is unable to identify the country of her ancestors, allow her to research any nation that interests her. Have her change the top two lines on the leaf to read "[student] would love to visit [country].") After she fills in her leaf, have the student decorate an unlined index card to represent her country's flag. Tape the completed flag to its leaf; then staple the project to the tree. Use the information on the leaves to spark many interesting discussions or as informative five-minute fillers!

Help Wanted!

Skills: Drawing conclusions, narrative writing

Have students investigate the relationships between a country's economy and the jobs available to its people with this thought-provoking activity. First, review with students what they've learned about the natural resources, climate, agriculture, and manufacturing of the country you're studying. Based on this information, what jobs might be most abundant in this land? For example, forestry and forest products provide 40% of Finland's exports, so jobs in forestry, woodworking, and paper-manufacturing industries would probably be plentiful there. Next, have each student pretend that she has found herself without money in the country you're studying. Instruct her to write a narrative in which she explains her situation, lists five jobs she applies for and her qualifications for them, and tells about the job she finally gets. After the student shares her story with the class, challenge her to explain why the job she wound up getting is likely to be available in that country.

"Geo-Bingo"

Skills: Research skills, categorizing

Whether you're studying one country or several countries at a time, this version of bingo is guaranteed to generate lots of learning! A few days before the game, list the categories shown on a sheet of chart paper. Give each student three index cards. Assign a category to each child; then have him find three facts about the country being studied that relate to his category. Direct him to write his category and one fact on each index card. Collect and shuffle the cards; then number them sequentially. When you're ready to play, follow these steps:

1. Give each student one sheet of unlined paper and a supply of paper squares to use as markers.
2. Instruct the student to fold his paper in half four times to create his game card. (When opened, the paper's folds should create a grid of 16 spaces.)
3. Have the student randomly copy one category from the chart in each space on his paper, repeating a category if he desires.
4. Read the fact from the first card. Have each student determine the fact's category.
5. If the student has the matching category on his sheet, have him cover it with a marker. Announce the number on that fact card so students who covered that category can write the number on that marker.
6. Repeat Steps 4 and 5 until a student has four markers in a row horizontally, vertically, or diagonally.
7. Check the winner's matches for correctness by having him read aloud the numbers written on his four markers. If they correctly match the numbers on the facts you've read, declare him the winner. If not, continue play.

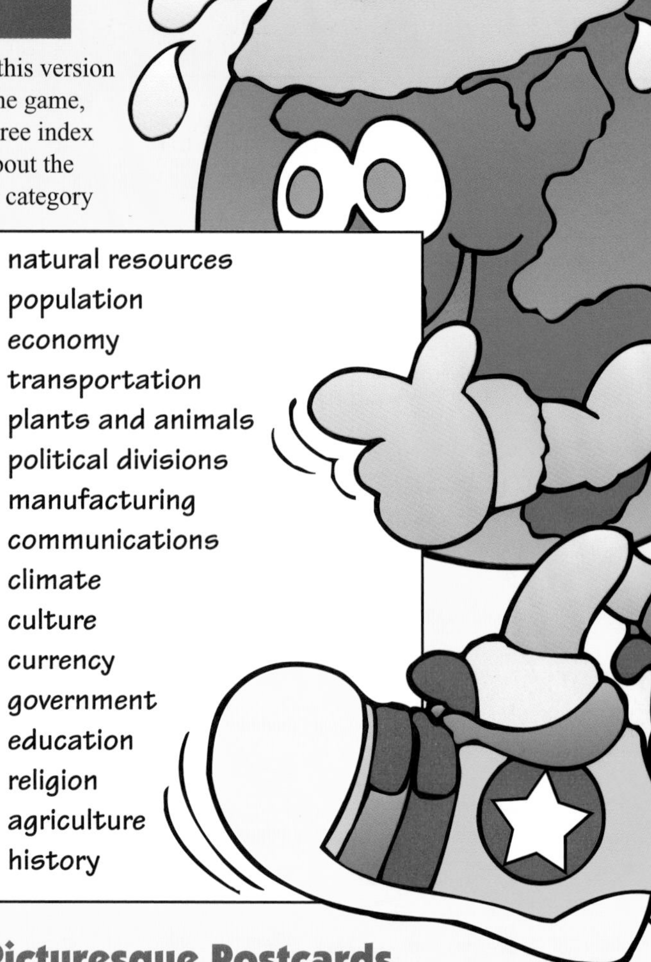

natural resources
population
economy
transportation
plants and animals
political divisions
manufacturing
communications
climate
culture
currency
government
education
religion
agriculture
history

Welcome to the Lake District
Dear Jacob,
Wow! Wish you were here to fish with me in Finland's Lake District. The hiking has been great, too!
The Lake District is in central Finland. It has thousands of lakes. Many boats travel on the lakes and rivers in the Lake District.
Jackson
Jacob Harvey
123 Curtis Drive
Anytown, U.S.A.
12345

Picturesque Postcards

Skill: Writing a description

Treat your students to this geography project worth writing home about! Give each student a 4" x 6" unlined index card, colored markers, and a 1" x 3/4" piece cut from a self-sticking nametag. Assign each student a landmark from a country currently being studied. Direct the student to draw a picture of the landmark on one side of his card and address the other side like a postcard, leaving space for a note. Next, have him write the note, including a description of the landmark, its location, and its historic or geographic significance. Then, on the nametag piece, have the child design a postage stamp that's representative of that country and affix it to his postcard as a stamp. Pin these postcards on a bulletin board. With such picturesque postcards to admire, you might have to stop yourself from mailing them!

Unlikely Sports

Skills: Research skills, critical thinking

Bobsledding in Jamaica? Sounds nuts, but it's true. Share with students that despite an average temperature of 80°F, Jamaica sent a bobsled team to the Winter Games. Then divide students into groups. Have each group list the sports played in a country you're studying; then have it think about how that country's climate, topography, and culture might affect the playing of those sports. If the group thinks a sport is "unlikely" based upon one or more of the three factors, ask its members to determine what adaptations were made to make playing that sport possible. For example, even though the average temperature in Iceland is about 41°F, people there can swim year-round in heated indoor pools. Finally, challenge each student to list three sports she would not expect to be played in that country and why. Provide time for students to share their lists.

Name ______________________________ Note-taking guide

Fact-Finding Sheet on ____________________
country

★ Location in World ★	★ Capital ★	★ Money ★
★ Type of Government ★	★ Agriculture ★	★ Population and People ★
★ Head of Government ★	★Most Important Industry★	★ Early History ★
★ Special Foods ★	★ Recreation ★	★ Education ★
★ Famous Citizen ★	★ Flag ★	★Official Language ★

Note to the teacher: Give each student a copy of this page to guide his note taking when researching a country. After the student fills in the sheet's boxes with notes, have him use those notes to write a paragraph for each box.

All Set to Travel!

Finding out as much as you can about a place before you visit it can make the trip more pleasant and memorable. Complete the activities below to make sure your trip is nothing but fun!

PASSPORT

Destination:

________, ________
capital city, country

Departure:

________, ________
city, state/province

________ ________, ________
month date, year

Find out which unit of money is used in the country you'll visit.

Hint: *Look for "Money" in the encyclopedia article about the country you're studying.*

____

Find the average temperature for the month you'll be traveling.
Hint: *Use an atlas.*

____

List the clothing you'll pack.

____
____
____
____

Locate the latitude and longitude of the capital city you'll visit.

________ ________
latitude longitude

Measure the distance from your home to your destination.

Hint: *Use a piece of string and a globe. Then use the globe's key to change inches to miles.*

____

List three things a native from the country you're visiting could share with you about his or her country. Use the back if you need more space.

1. ________________
____
2. ________________
____
3. ________________
____

Find out what time it is at your destination if your flight leaves at 1 P.M.

Hint: *Use the world time zones chart in an encyclopedia.*

____

Bonus Box: What souvenir could you bring back from your trip? On the back of this sheet, write a paragraph describing it and explaining why you bought it.

Note to the teacher: Provide an atlas, a globe, string, scissors, a ruler, and a set of encyclopedias for students' use.

MISSION: Possible!

Math Projects to Improve Problem-Solving Skills

Your mission—should you choose to accept it—is to use one or more problem-solving strategies to complete a variety of investigative math projects. Will your students accept this mission? You bet! Challenge your young problem solvers with this collection of fun hands-on math projects.

by Irving P. Crump

It's in the Files

MISSION: MAKE A PLAN

What's the problem? That's the first question problem solvers ask themselves when they set out to solve a problem. Next, they choose one or more strategies. If a strategy doesn't work, they try a different one. The last step is checking the results. Help your students organize for problem solving by providing each of them with a copy of the outline on page 96. Have each student cut out the file folder art and then attach it to the inside cover of his math folder, composition book, or journal. Remind students to refer to this plan when solving any kind of problem.

Student resource page

Name Janet

TOP SECRET

MISSION:

Make a Plan!

Step 1: Examine the problem.
1. Do you understand the problem?
2. What facts are given?
3. What conditions are given?
4. What's the goal of solving the problem?

Step 2: Choose one or more strategies.
1. Act out the problem or use objects.
2. Draw a picture or make a diagram.
3. Collect data and make a table or graph.
4. Make an organized list.
5. Guess and check.
6. Use or look for a pattern.
7. Work backwards.
8. Use logical reasoning.
9. Make it simpler.
10. Brainstorm ideas.

Step 3: Carry out the strategy.
1. Follow the strategy.
2. Try a second strategy if you need to.
3. Record the data you collect. Double-check your records.

Step 4: Check your results.
1. Does the solution make sense?
2. If not, try a new strategy.

If you choose to accept this mission, you'd better make a plan.

Take a Hike!

MISSION: DRAW A PICTURE, WRITE ABOUT MATH

In math, a picture *can* be worth a thousand words! Use the following activity to help students discover how helpful drawing a picture can be in solving a problem. First, share the following story with your class:

> Katie began her hike at the family campsite. The trail goes 8 miles north to a stream and then continues 4 miles west to a waterfall. From the waterfall, the trail goes south 6 miles to a large boulder, where it then turns southeast and winds along 7 miles back to the campsite. Which landmark was Katie closest to after she had hiked 14 miles?

Ask students which problem-solving strategy would be helpful in finding the answer to the above question *(drawing a picture)*. Then direct each student to draw and label a picture, including each landmark, as you slowly reread the story. When everyone has drawn the last leg of the hike, ask the question again *(answer: waterfall)*. Remind students that drawing pictures and diagrams is a helpful way to solve many types of problems.

Next, have each student make up a story like the one you read, including a question at the end. The story may include city streets, a playground, stores in a mall—any kind of trip described with directional words, distances, and landmarks. When everyone has completed his story, pair up students and have them exchange stories with each other. Give each student a 12" x 18" sheet of white construction paper. Have the student attach his partner's story to one half of the sheet. Then have him draw a picture and answer the story's question on the other half. Display the completed projects on a bulletin board titled "Take a Hike!"

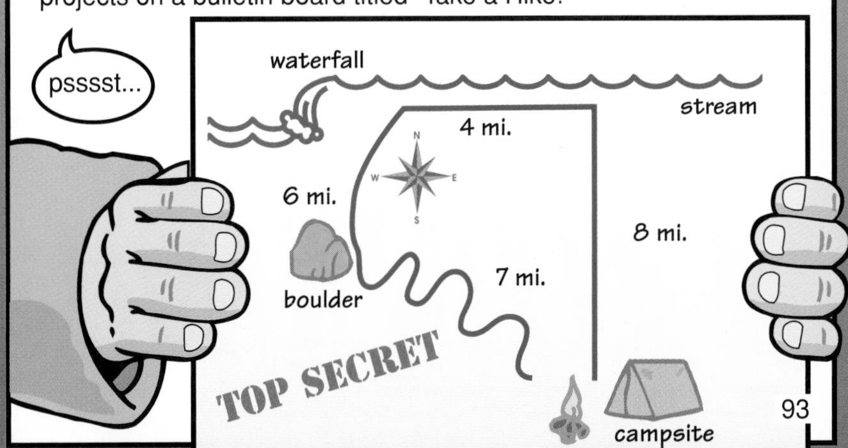

Graphing Cents

MISSION: COLLECT, DISPLAY, AND INTERPRET DATA

Problem solving often involves collecting lots of data and then analyzing that data. Send your students on a data graphing mission with this easy-to-prepare project. First, divide students into pairs. Give each twosome 50 pennies. Next, have the pair sort the pennies into decades according to the mint year on each one. Then provide each pair with a copy of page 97, a 12" x 18" sheet of white construction paper, a glue stick, a ruler, a calculator, and markers or crayons. Have each pair complete the reproducible as directed.

Rub-a-dub-dub, Compare These Tubs!

MISSION: GUESS AND CHECK, WRITE ABOUT MATH

Challenge your "spy-tacular" problem solvers with this simple-to-set-up center activity! First, collect five small margarine tubs with lids. Fill each tub with a different amount of gravel so that when any two of them are placed on a pan balance, the balance tips to one side. Code the tubs with letters; then make a key that lists the containers from lightest to heaviest. Place the tubs and a pan balance at a math center.

Challenge pairs of students to work together in the center to rank the five tubs from lightest to heaviest, using only the balance. Have each pair describe in a paragraph its strategy for ranking the tubs, using the tubs' letters in making comparisons, such as A > B, B > E, etc. When every pair has finished the activity, discuss the strategies used. Share with students that it is possible to correctly rank five different weights by making a minimum of ten comparisons; then share the key.

The tubs are here... but they're DIFFERENT WEIGHTS!
G
R
C
S
M

horses	ducks	total
1 = 4 legs	4 = 8 legs	12 legs
2 = 8 legs	3 = 6 legs	14 legs
3 = 12 legs	2 = 4 legs	16 legs

5 animals
26 legs
How many dogs?
How many beetles?

At the Zoo

MISSION: MAKE A TABLE, GUESS AND CHECK

Get problem-solving strategies out on the table with this nifty idea! Share with students the following puzzler: You have five pets; some are horses and the rest are ducks. All together the animals have 16 legs. How many horses and how many ducks do you have?

Brainstorm with students the best problem-solving strategy to use, leading them to conclude that recording guesses in a table would work well. Then draw the table shown—completing each line as students assist you—until you reach the solution: 3 horses and 2 ducks.

Extend this activity by giving each student a 9" x 12" sheet of light-colored construction paper. On her paper, have the student draw or glue cutout magazine pictures of two or three different animals, each having 2, 4, 6, or 8 legs. Then have the student label her poster with a problem similar to the one above. Have the student write her problem's solution on the back of her poster. Display the miniposters in your math center or on a bulletin board. Invite students to examine the posters and draw tables to answer several of the questions on them.

Let's Count to a Million!

MISSION: ESTIMATE, USE A CALCULATOR

How long would it take you to count to 1 million? After students have thought about this question, have each one write down an estimate. Then, based on an average of about 2.5 seconds needed to say one number, have students use calculators to determine the solution. After each calculation, have the student round up each quotient to the next whole number. Share the solution shown. Then challenge students to find out how long it would take them to count to a billion. Since most calculators can't display large numbers, students will need to perform some calculating by hand. Challenge students to solve other large calculations such as the ones below. For each calculation, have the student describe and list his strategies.

- How many pennies would be in a stack one mile high?
- How much money is a mile of quarters laid side by side?
- How many eight-inch bricks would it take to outline a football field?

One-Three-Six

MISSION: GUESS AND CHECK, MAKE EQUALITIES

This "sands-sational" hands-on activity is similar to "Rub-a-dub-dub, Compare These Tubs!" on page 94. First, prepare three weights: one-pound, three-pound, and six-pound. Place them in three similar containers labeled as shown. Also provide a pan balance, a bucket of sand, several large and small plastic zippered bags, and a cup for scooping the sand. Challenge a pair of students to determine how they can measure out exact amounts of sand from one pound to ten pounds using only the pan balance, the sand and plastic bags, and the three different weights. Have students experiment with the weights and the sand, and record each solution and how they arrived at it on a sheet of paper. (See possible solutions at the right.)

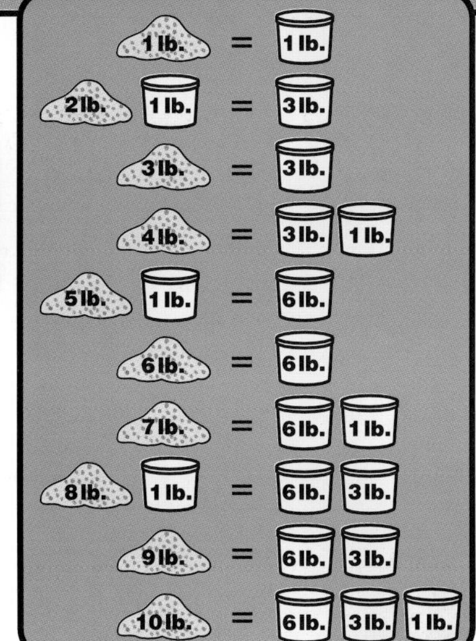

Connect 4!...in 3-D

MISSION: THINK VISUALLY, HAVE FUN!

Invite students to stretch their observation and thinking skills by trying a 3-D version of the popular game, Connect 4!. Fold an eight-inch paper square in half four times and then unfold it to reveal 16 squares. Share with students the following directions for playing the game. Then place the game and 64 checkers (32 red and 32 black) in your math center.

1. Divide the checkers. Player 1 takes all of the red ones; Player 2 takes all of the black ones.
2. Player 1 places a red checker in any square on the gameboard.
3. Player 2 places a black checker on the gameboard—either on top of Player 1's red checker or on any other square.
4. No more than four checkers can be stacked on top of each other.
5. Play continues until a player has four checkers in a row either vertically, horizontally, or diagonally in any direction on the gameboard.

(Example: Suppose a player placed a red checker in one corner of the gameboard. He could possibly make four in a row in seven different ways as shown in the illustration.)

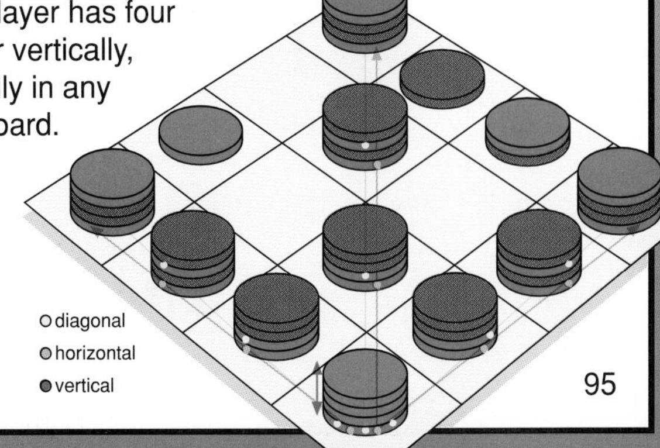

Student resource page

Name_______________

TOP SECRET

MISSION:

Make a Plan!

Step 1: Examine the problem.

1. Do you understand the problem?
2. What facts are given?
3. What conditions are given?
4. What's the goal of solving the problem?

Step 2: Choose one or more strategies.

1. Act out the problem or use objects.
2. Draw a picture or make a diagram.
3. Collect data and make a table or graph.
4. Make an organized list.
5. Guess and check.
6. Use or look for a pattern.
7. Work backwards.
8. Use logical reasoning.
9. Make it simpler.
10. Brainstorm ideas.

Step 3: Carry out the strategy.

1. Follow the strategy.
2. Try a second strategy if you need to.
3. Record the data you collect. Double-check your records.

Step 4: Check your results.

1. Does the solution make sense?
2. If not, try a new strategy.

Note to the teacher: See "It's in the Files" on page 93 for information on how to use this reproducible.

Name ______________________________

MISSION: Graphing Cents

Use the dates on your 50 pennies to complete the activities below.

1. First, organize your data. Make a tally mark beside the date in the box for each penny that has that date. If you have pennies that were minted before 1959, add those dates to the chart. (Check: Count the total number of tally marks you have made. Do you have 50?)

1959	1965	1971	1977	1983	1989	1995
1960	1966	1972	1978	1984	1990	1996
1961	1967	1973	1979	1985	1991	1997
1962	1968	1974	1980	1986	1992	1998
1963	1969	1975	1981	1987	1993	1999
1964	1970	1976	1982	1988	1994	2000

2. Fold your sheet of construction paper in half; then unfold it. Glue this page to the left half of the sheet.

3. On the right half of your sheet of construction paper, make a bar graph that shows the number of pennies that were minted in each decade (1950–59, 1960–69, etc.):
   a. Give the graph a title.
   b. Label the vertical axis.
   c. Label the horizontal axis.
   d. Color the bars.

4. Using a calculator, find the *average* year in which your pennies were minted. ______________

5. Which year is the *median,* the middle year in your set of data? ______________________

6. Which year is the *mode,* the year that appears most often in your set of data? ____________

7. What is the *range,* the difference between the earliest and most recent mint years in your set of data? ____

8. Describe another way that you could display your data besides a bar graph. ____________

____

____

9. Write three facts based on what you observe in your graph.

   a. ____

   b. ____

   c. ____

Bonus Box: Combine your pennies with those of another pair of classmates. Repeat Step 1 above. Then find the average, median, mode, and range of your data.

Note to the teacher: Use with "Graphing Cents" on page 94. Provide each pair of students with 50 pennies, a copy of this reproducible, a 12" x 18" sheet of white construction paper, a glue stick, a ruler, a calculator, and markers or crayons.

Name ____________________ Problem solving, visual thinking

MISSION: Telling Time

Telling time? Now *that* should be an easy mission!

Take a look at the two clocks below. The time on each one is shown in a digital display. The digits 0 through 9 are each formed by lighting different patterns of individual blocks. The time shown on the first clock is 3:56. The time on the second clock is 12:09.

Your mission: answer the questions below. (Don't include the colon in your answers.)

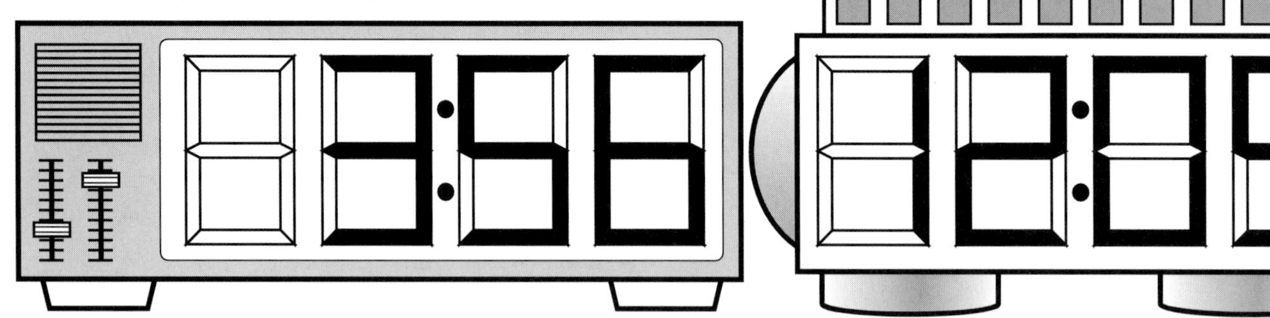

Part I: Easy-as-Pie Mission

1. How many blocks make up each place of a digital display? ______
2. How many blocks are in the entire display? ______
3. Which digit, when lit, uses the fewest blocks? ______
4. Which digit, when lit, uses the most blocks? ______
5. A digital display can also show the date. If the current month is shown on the left side of the colon and today's date is shown on the right side, how many blocks would be lit all together? ______

Part II: Average Mission

1. What is the largest digit that can be shown in the first place of the digital display—beginning on the left? (Remember: this is a clock!) ______
2. What is the largest digit that can be shown in the second place of the digital display? ______
3. What is the largest digit that can be shown in the third place of the display? ______
4. What is the largest digit that can be shown in the fourth place? ______
5. If you flip the digit 2, what digit does it become? ______
6. What do the displays for the digits 4, 5, and 6 have in common? ____________________

____

Part III: Nearly Impossible Mission (But You Can Do It!)

1. How many blocks are lit at midnight? ______
2. At what time of day are the fewest blocks lit? ______ How many blocks are lit then? ______
3. At what time of day are the most blocks lit? ______ How many blocks are lit then? ______
4. The picture at the right shows the bottom half of a digital display. What *three* times could the clock possibly be showing? ____________________

Bonus Box: Write your birthday month and date in a digital display. How many total blocks would be lit to show your birthday?

Ideas for Studying Famous Black Americans

Use the following activities to introduce your students to famous Black Americans who blazed a trail for others to follow.

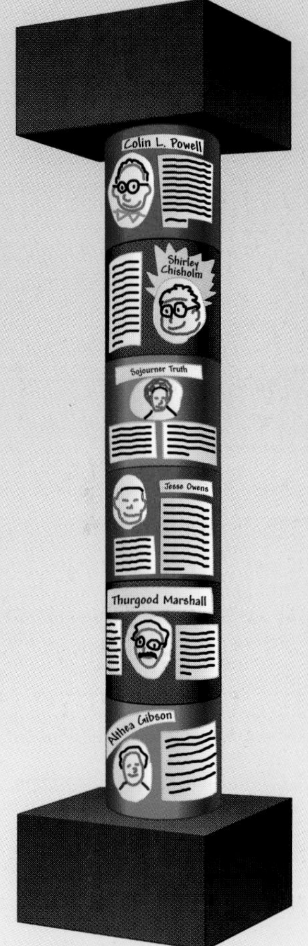

Pillars of Courage

Skills: Research skills

Honor the towering personalities in Black American history with this unique research project. In advance, ask your cafeteria staff to save a class supply of large, same-sized food cans. Have each student research a famous Black American (see the list on page 100) and write a brief report. Also direct the student to sketch or photocopy a picture of his person. After the student finishes his report, have him type it on a word processor so that it will fit (in one or several pieces) on the side of a can.

Next, measure around one can and write the measurements on the chalkboard. Give each student a ruler and a sheet of red, green, or black construction paper. Have the student measure and cut the paper to fit around his can. Then have him cut out his report and picture and glue them to his paper. Finally, have the student wrap the paper around the can and glue it in place.

After each can is finished, use hot glue to stack six or seven cans atop each other to make a pillar. At the top and bottom of each pillar, hot-glue a box that's been covered with black paper. Display the pillars in your school's lobby with a banner titled "Black History's Pillars of Courage."

Beth Patrilla—Grs. 4–5
St. Martin dePorres School
Toledo, OH

The Interview Project

Skills: Research skills, giving an oral presentation

Combine a study of famous Black Americans with a book-report assignment that focuses on biographies and autobiographies. Ask your school's media coordinator to help you gather a collection of biographies and autobiographies about famous Black Americans. Have each student select a book to read; then have her fill out a copy of the form on page 101. Direct the student to be ready to answer the form's questions in a "live" interview. During the interview, the student will pose as her famous person while you ask the questions on the form. Encourage students to dress as their famous persons for the interviews and/or bring props that represent important facets of their lives. Not only will students be introduced to some of black history's major contributors, but they'll also be more motivated to pick up a biography or autobiography on their next trip to the library.

Lisa Groenendyk—Gr. 4
Pella Christian Grade School
Pella, IA

Black History Newsletter

Skills: Research skills, writing a newspaper story

Want the scoop on how to work a study of black history into your already-packed curriculum? Try this activity that turns students' research on famous Black Americans into a newsworthy historical newsletter. First, have each student select a person to research from the list below. Then guide students through the following steps:

1. Collect details about your person. Start by answering these questions: *Who? What? Where? When? Why? How?* Then try to gather information that tells something important, unusual, or interesting about your person and his or her accomplishments.

2. After you've completed your research, write the first draft of your news story.
   a. Begin with a lead paragraph that gives an important or interesting detail.
   b. Write the main portion of your story.
   c. End your story by giving the reader something to think about.

3. Review and revise your story. Make sure you included all important information and that all facts are correct.

4. Edit and proofread your story for mistakes in spelling, capitalization, and punctuation.

5. Write the final copy.

Issue #1 Miss Cullum's 5th Grade Class March 15

Black History Chronicle

Coretta Scott King Speaks Out

Jemison Blasts Off

First for Baseball

A Man of Courage

Work with your computer lab teacher to help students type their final copies and piece them together in the format of a newsletter or newspaper. Be sure to make enough copies so that the newsletter can be shared with other classes.

Amy Rzyrkowski, Gardens Elementary, St. Clair Shores, MI

Famous Black American Achievers

Astronauts/Explorers: Ronald McNair, Guion Bluford, Mae Carol Jemison, Frederick Drew Gregory, Matthew Henson, James Pierson Beckwourth

Athletes: Jesse Owens, Jackie Robinson, Arthur Ashe, Wilma Rudolph, Althea Gibson, Jackie Joyner-Kersee

Civil Rights Leaders: Rosa Lee Parks, Fannie Lou Hamer, Coretta Scott King, Dr. Martin Luther King Jr., Jesse Jackson, W. E. B. Du Bois, Sojourner Truth, Harriet Tubman

Doctors/Nurses: Charles Richard Drew, Daniel Hale Williams, Susie King Taylor, Mary Elizabeth Mahoney

Educators: Mary McLeod Bethune, Booker T. Washington, Benjamin E. Mays, E. Franklin Frazier

Film/T.V. Personalities: Sidney Poitier, Bill Cosby, Oprah Winfrey, Lou Gossett Jr., Spike Lee, James Earl Jones

Government Officials: Shirley Chisholm, Ralph Bunche, Barbara C. Jordan, Thurgood Marshall, Thomas Bradley, Andrew Jackson Young Jr., Colin L. Powell

Musicians: Louis Armstrong, Count Basie, Dean Dixon, Duke Ellington, Dizzy Gillespie, Charlie Parker

Poets/Playwrights: Phillis Wheatley, Maya Angelou, Gwendolyn Brooks, Paul Laurence Dunbar, Lorraine Hansberry

Scientists/Inventors: Ernest Everett Just, Benjamin Banneker, George W. Carver, Garrett Morgan, Jan Ernst Matzeliger, Lewis Howard Latimer

Singers: Marian Anderson, Leontyne Price, Ella Fitzgerald, Lena Horne, Sarah Vaughan, Nat "King" Cole

Writers: Virginia Hamilton, Alice Walker, Toni Morrison, Alex Haley, Langston Hughes

Sharpen math skills during Black History Month with the **ready-to-use reproducible** on page 102.

An Interview With

____
(name of person you read about)

Now that you've read about a famous person, it's time to share your new knowledge with the rest of the world (or at least your classmates). You will be asked to pretend to be the person you read about and give a live interview in the classroom. Below are the questions you will be asked. Fill in the blanks. Then study your answers so you'll be ready to share them during the interview.

1. What is your full name? ______________________________
2. When and where were you born? ______________________________
____
3. What accomplishments are you most famous for? ______________________________
____
____
4. Tell us about your family (parents, siblings, family life, etc.). ______________________________
____
____
5. Tell us about your childhood (friends, schooling, interests, etc.). ______________________________
____
____
6. What goal did you have as a young person? ______________________________
____
____
7. Tell about a favorite or noteworthy memory you have about your adult life.
____
____
8. How did you spend the later years of your life? ______________________________
____
____
9. Why do you think you were so successful? ______________________________
____
____
10. On the back of this page, list anything else you'd like to tell the audience.

Be prepared to answer other questions from the audience.

Note to the teacher: Use with "The Interview Project" on page 99. Or use anytime you want students to research famous people, such as U.S. presidents, historical figures, authors, etc.

Name____________________ Problem solving

Famous Folks Fair

To celebrate Black History Month, Galvez School held a Black History Fair. Each booth at the fair sold an item that represented the achievements of a famous Black American. The money that was raised was used to buy books about Black Americans for the library.

Use the information on the booths to solve the problems below. In the first blank, write the equation. In the second blank, write the answer. Show your work on another sheet of paper. The first blank has been filled in for you.

Expenses: 20 pounds green peanuts at $1.89/pound
$.89 per box of salt
Sales: 98 cups of peanuts

1. How much was spent on peanuts for the booth?
   20 x $1.89 = __________
2. For every pound of peanuts boiled, the students added 1 cup of salt to the water. If each box of salt contains 2 cups of salt, how many boxes did the students use?
   __________ = __________
3. How much was spent on salt? (Use the answer to #2.)
   __________ = __________
4. What were the total expenses for this booth?
   __________ = __________
5. The booth sold 98 cups of peanuts. How much money did it make (before expenses were subtracted)?
   __________ = __________
6. How much money was left over after expenses were paid? __________ = __________
7. Each pound of peanuts filled 5 cups. How many cups were used? __________ = __________

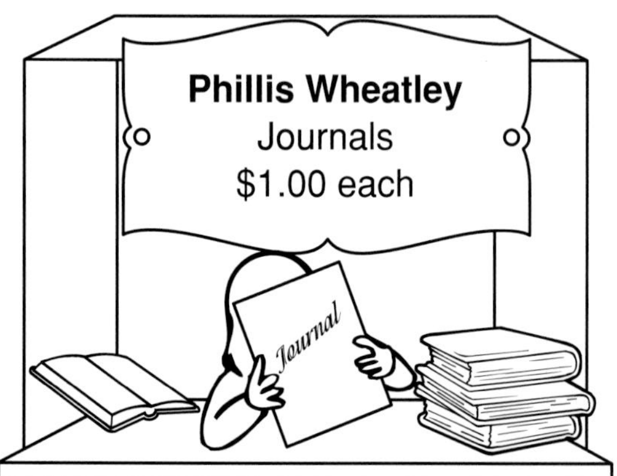

Expenses: ____ packs of 150 sheets of lined paper for $1.50 each
2 paint pens at $2.99 each
90 front covers at $.09 each
90 back covers at $.05 each
Sales: 90 journals

8. To make each journal, students stapled 25 sheets of lined paper between a front and a back cover. How many journals did 1 pack of paper make?
   __________ = __________
9. The students made 90 journals. How many packs of paper did they have to buy? __________ = __________ (Write the answer in the blank on the booth.)
10. Find the total spent for the following supplies:
    paper: __________ = __________
    front covers: __________ = __________
    back covers: __________ = __________
    paint pens: __________ = __________
    TOTAL: __________ = __________
11. The booth sold 90 journals. How much money did it make (before expenses were subtracted)?
    __________ = __________
12. How much money was left over after expenses were paid? __________ = __________

Bonus Box: How much money did the students make on the Carver and Wheatley booths combined?

Literature-Related Units

 Name ____________________

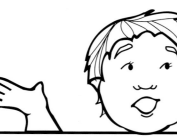

So What's the Problem?

Stories are often about problems and how the characters solve them. Understanding the problems that characters face and wondering how they solve them is part of the fun of reading. As you read the story, list each problem as you find it. Then predict how you think the problem will be solved. Later list how the problem was solved in the story. Staple notebook paper to this sheet when you run out of space.

What is the problem?	How do you predict the problem will be solved?	How was the problem solved in the story?

So What's the Message? An author sends the reader a message when he or she writes a story. What message about life and living with others did the author send in this book? As you read, list your ideas in the box. Be ready to share and explain your ideas.

Note to the teacher: Use with "So What's the Problem?" on page 107. Provide each student with a folder in which to store his copy of this page as he reads. Discuss students' charts periodically as they read or at the end of the novel.

Name ____

You "Gotta" Have Heart!

Part 1: The characters in *There's a Boy in the Girls' Bathroom* didn't always have a heart for one another. Think about the actions of each character below. Did the character treat others kindly? Write each character's name in the appropriate column. Beside the character's name, tell why you placed him/her in that column. Some characters may belong in both columns!

Bradley	Jeff	Carla	Colleen	Lori	Melinda
Claudia	Robbie	Andy	Mr. Chalkers	Mrs. Chalkers	Mrs. Ebbel

With Heart	**Without Heart**

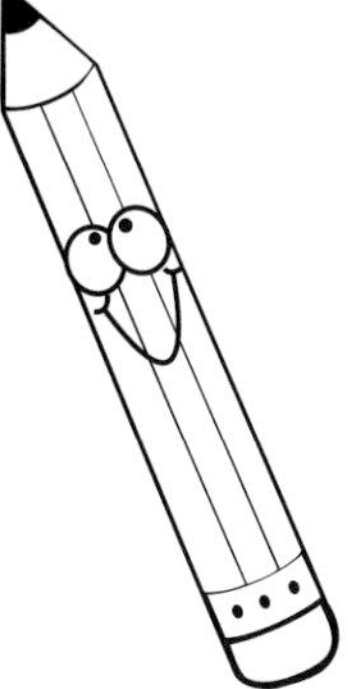

Part 2: Choose one of the characters above. On another sheet of paper, write a description of that character. What kind of person is he/she? Would you want to know this person? On the paper, draw a sketch of the character. Then share the sketch and description with your classmates.

Bonus Box: Carla suggested that Bradley give Colleen a birthday gift from the heart. So he gave Colleen a replica of the human heart. Use an encyclopedia or other reference book to help you draw a diagram of the heart. Label the parts.

After Chapter 20: **Hard on the Outside, Soft on the Inside**

While reading chapters 17–20, prominently display a plastic egg in your classroom. Don't explain its presence except to tell students that it has something to do with the story. After students have read chapter 20, reread with them the section in which Margaret realizes "…I wasn't afraid of him [Gordy] anymore." Pick up the plastic egg; then ask each student to write a sentence or two describing how Gordy is like an egg. After students share their responses, explain that an egg has a hard protective shell (like Gordy's rough exterior, caused by his horrible home life). But the inside is soft and fragile—which is just how Margaret now sees Gordy.

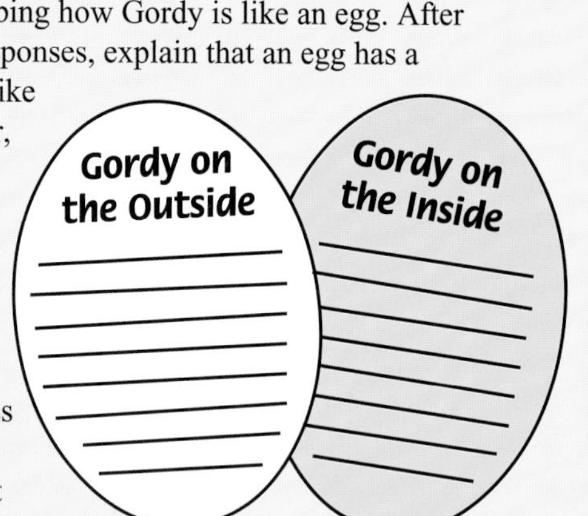

Next divide the class into groups. Give each group an egg shape cut from white paper and one cut from yellow paper. Have a recorder for the group label the cutouts as shown. Direct each group to discuss how Gordy is like an egg, then list specific examples of Gordy's rough exterior on the white cutout. Direct the group to then list examples of Gordy's soft side on the yellow cutout. After about 20 minutes, have each group share its cutouts. Adapt this idea to use with any novel that has a character similar to Gordy (rough on the outside, soft on the inside). *

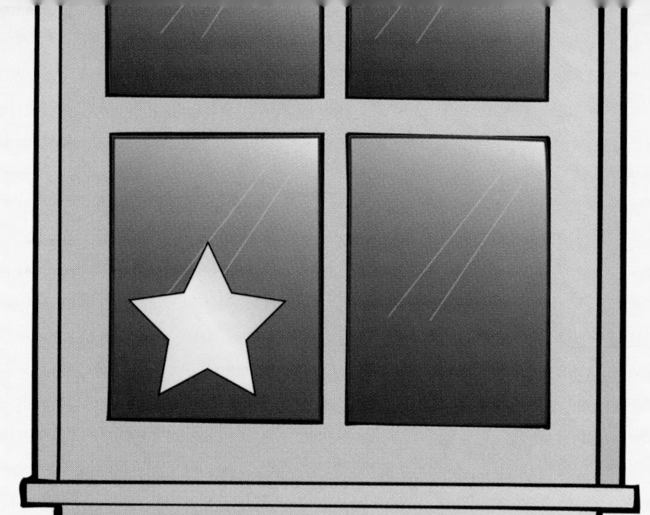

After Chapter 24: **In Memory of Jimmy**

At the end of this chapter, Margaret and her family get the dreadful news that Jimmy has been killed in action. Although readers never meet Jimmy, they learn a lot about him from Margaret's recollections, as well as the letters and cartoons he sends home. Brainstorm with students some of Jimmy's characteristics (funny, sensitive, loving, artistic, etc.). Explain to students that a *eulogy* is a speech in praise of a person who has died. Tell students to imagine that College Hill is going to hold a special memorial service to honor those who lost their lives in the war, and Margaret has been chosen to eulogize her brother. Have each student or pair of students write a short eulogy from Margaret's point of view. Provide time for each student to read her eulogy aloud. If desired, play patriotic music softly in the background as students read their eulogies.

At the End of the Book: **Make Mine Murals!**

Review the important events of this thought-provoking book with a fun art activity. With students brainstorm a list of important scenes from the book (or use the list below). Divide the class into groups of two to four students. Have each group choose a scene and draw a mural of it on a large piece of butcher paper. Encourage students to refer to the book for details about their scene. Also direct each group to describe its scene on an index card mounted somewhere on its mural. When the groups are finished, display the murals in order in your hallway. Adapt this culminating activity for any novel your class is reading. (For another great end-of-the-book activity, see the reproducible on page 117.) *

Possible Scenes:

- Chapter 4: Margaret and Elizabeth see Gordy and his friends near the hut for the first time.
- Chapter 7: Gordy and Elizabeth have a fight.
- Chapter 8: Elizabeth and Margaret get revenge on Gordy by trying to destroy the hut.
- Chapter 13: The girls go to Gordy's house for the first time and encounter the Smith family.
- Chapter 16: Elizabeth and Margaret play hooky from school to help care for Stuart in the hut.
- Chapter 17: In desperation, the girls take Barbara to the hut to help Stuart.
- Chapter 19: The girls and Gordy put Stuart on the bobsled to take him to the doctor.
- Chapter 22: Mrs. Baker confronts Mr. and Mrs. Smith at their house.
- Chapter 24: Margaret arrives home to discover her brother has been killed in action.
- Chapter 26: The girls witness the police arresting Mr. Smith.

Vocabulary List

Use with "World War II Lingo" on page 112. The number in parentheses indicates the page number on which the word can be found (taken from the paperback version of *Stepping on the Cracks* published by Avon Books, 1991).

- ★ **Hitler** *(2)*—Nazi ruler of Germany from 1933–1945
- ★ **Nazi** *(2)*—a supporter of Adolf Hitler and his beliefs
- ★ **knickers** *(6)*—loose-fitting short pants gathered at the knee
- ★ **drafted** *(14)*—enlisted in the army by the government rather than by choice
- ★ **bond** *(16)*—a certificate issued by the government that promises to pay its holder a certain amount on a certain date
- ★ **scrap** *(16)*—discarded metal collected during the war to be recycled
- ★ **foxhole** *(21)*—a pit dug to provide cover during battle
- ★ **tramp** *(22)*—a homeless person who travels on foot, and may beg for or steal food
- ★ **panzer** *(26)*—a German tank used during World War II
- ★ **pinup** *(27)*—a photo or poster of a pretty girl
- ★ **liberation** *(34)*—setting free
- ★ **oxfords** *(40)*—a type of laced shoe
- ★ **hobo** *(60)*—a homeless and usually poor person who wanders from place to place
- ★ **Victrola** *(64)*—a record player
- ★ **jitterbug** *(64)*—a type of dance popular in the 1940s
- ★ **deserter** *(70)*—one who leaves the military without permission
- ★ **furlough** *(98)*—a temporary time period during which a soldier has permission to leave the service
- ★ **conscientious objector** *(111)*—a person who refuses to serve in the military for moral or religious reasons
- ★ **Allies** *(127)*—50 nations, including the United States, China, the Soviet Union, and Great Britain; fought against Germany, Italy, and Japan
- ★ **ration** *(130)*—allow people to buy only a limited amount of food and other supplies
- ★ **AWOL** *(142)*—stands for "absent without leave"; absent from the military without permission
- ★ **Mussolini** *(152)*—Italy's leader during World War II
- ★ **Hirohito** *(152)*—Japan's leader during World War II

Pattern

Use with "Star Light, Star Bright" on page 112 and "Wish Upon a Star" on page 113.

Writing Scenarios

Use with "Not As Simple As It Seems" on page 113.

Pretend that you are Gordy. Your other brother, Don, has found out that you've been hiding Stuart. Write a letter to Don explaining why you decided to help your other brother hide out from the war.

Pretend that you are Stuart. To kill time while in the hut, you've been keeping a journal. Write a journal entry that tells about your feelings toward war.

Pretend that you are Margaret and you have just discovered Stuart in his hut. You really don't know if you should turn him in as a deserter or not. Write a letter to your brother Jimmy. Describe your problem and ask for his advice about what to do.

Pretend that you are Joe, Elizabeth's brother. You have just heard about Stuart being a deserter. Write a letter to Elizabeth explaining how you feel about war and Stuart's choice to desert.

Name ____________

Stepping on the Cracks
Cause and effect

Effects on Everyone

The people of College Hill are all affected by the war—even though it's taking place thousands of miles away! In the spaces below, write how each character is being affected by the war. Where the circles overlap, write one way that both characters are affected.

Margaret

Gordy

Now, on the back of this page, draw a diagram like the one above. Label one circle "Barbara" and the other "Stuart." Then fill in the diagram.

Bonus Box: Because there were shortages during the war, Margaret and Elizabeth had to give up certain things they loved. On the back of this page, list ten items you'd hate to have to give up.

Note to the teacher: Use with "Touched by War" on page 113.

Name ____________________

A Top-Notch Title

Like many great books, *Stepping on the Cracks* has chapters that do not have titles. Pretend that author Mary Downing Hahn has asked you to come up with a great title for one of the book's chapters. After your teacher assigns a chapter to you, follow these directions:

1. Write the chapter number in the blank below.
2. Reread the chapter.
3. Write a title for that chapter and your reasons for choosing it in the blanks below.
4. Draw and color a scene from that chapter in the large space below.
5. Color a design in the border of your square.
6. Cut out the square and give it to your teacher.

Chapter ________

Chapter title: ______________________________

I chose this title because ______________________________

____

Name ______________________________

Note to the teacher: After the class has finished the book, duplicate a copy of this page for each student. Assign a chapter to each student. Then provide students with scissors and markers, crayons, or colored pencils. Glue or tape students' finished squares in sequential order on a large piece of bulletin-board paper to make a book quilt. Display the quilt in your room as a great review of a super book!

Mrs. Frisby and

Activities For Robert C. O'Brien's Newbery Winner

Mrs. Frisby, a widowed mouse, is in a precarious situation: her son Timothy is sick and too weak to be moved. But if she and her four children don't move soon, they'll be killed by the farmer's plow. Her only hope lies with the mysterious rats of NIMH. Introduce your students to this classic Newbery tale that has captivated readers for years; then follow up reading with the creative activities and reproducibles that follow.

ideas by Jane Robinson, Joy Kalfas, and Elizabeth H. Lindsay

Before Reading: Rats, Mice, and Intelligence

Before beginning this novel, share the book's cover with students. Have them use the cover to predict possible characters, settings, and plot events. Then write each of the following phrases on a different envelope as shown:

Rats are animals that…
Mice are animals that…
Rats and mice are different because…
Being intelligent means…
Animals and people are different because…

Rats and mice are different because…

Place each envelope—along with five index cards and a pencil—at a different area in the room. Next divide students into five groups, directing each group to a different envelope. Have group members discuss how to best finish the envelope's phrase; then have the group write its response on an index card and place the card in the envelope. After rotating each group to every envelope, share the responses from each one. Discuss with students their perceptions of rats and mice and how they think they were formed. Also talk about what they think are characteristics of someone who is intelligent.

After Chapter 1: Putting Predictions to the Test

Put prediction skills to the test with this ongoing activity! Guide students to understand that when they ask questions, use clues, and guess answers while reading, they are making *predictions*. Model this strategy by reading aloud chapter 1. Stop to ask questions about what you're reading (for example,"Why is Timothy sick? What is moving day? What will Mrs. Frisby do about Timothy's sickness?"). Think aloud about each question, verbalizing clues and possible answers. Afterward ask students what questions they asked themselves. As you record their responses on the chalkboard, have them identify clues and suggest possible answers. Then give each student a copy of page 121 to complete as she reads the book. Throughout the story, have students share the thoughts they have recorded on their sheets.

Mice are animals that…
Rats are animals that…
means…
ferent…

the Rats of NIMH

After Chapter 1: Building a Better Mouse House

Challenge students to put on the hard hats and build their thinking skills with this nifty homework activity! First have students describe Mrs. Frisby's house (see chapter 1). Discuss how she uses the things she finds around her to furnish it. Then ask, "If you were a mouse, from what materials would your home be made and furnished?" For homework, instruct each student to create a mouse house using materials found in her home. The following day let each student hide her house in the classroom. Then invite students to go "mousing" for the hidden houses. Finally have each student share her house. Extend the activity by challenging each student to choose a classmate's house and write a tale about the mouse who lives in it.

During Reading: Brain Busters

While reading the story, continue building thinking power with these fun-filled brain busters:

- After Chapter 1: Pick a period in history, such as the colonial period, the Egyptian period, or the future. Brainstorm items from that period that a mouse might use in its house, such as a quill pen for a bed.
- After Chapter 14: Brainstorm alternative solutions to Mrs. Frisby's moving-day dilemma. For example, the Frisby family could have moved in with the rats.
- After Chapter 18: Brainstorm a list of imaginary books the rats might want to read, such as *Miniature Gardening* and *Dollhouse Furnishings*.
- After Chapter 18: NIMH is an *acronym* that stands for the *National Institute of Mental Health.* Brainstorm other acronyms and their meanings, such as *NASA* (National Aeronautics and Space Administration) and *ZIP* (Zone Improvement Plan).

After Chapter 16: "A-maze-ing" Mazes

A *maze* is a place or puzzle with many confusing paths and passageways. They are often used to test skill in problem solving or to test reactions in animals. Provide each student with an 8½" x 11" sheet of drawing paper and a fine-tipped black marker. Direct the student to first use a pencil to draw his design on a sheet of loose-leaf paper. Then have the student use the black marker to carefully trace his maze onto the drawing paper. Laminate the completed mazes. Then give each student a classmate's maze and have him solve the puzzle using a wipe-off marker. If desired, give students a time limit for solving the mazes. Reward each student who finds his way out of a maze with a small prize or treat.

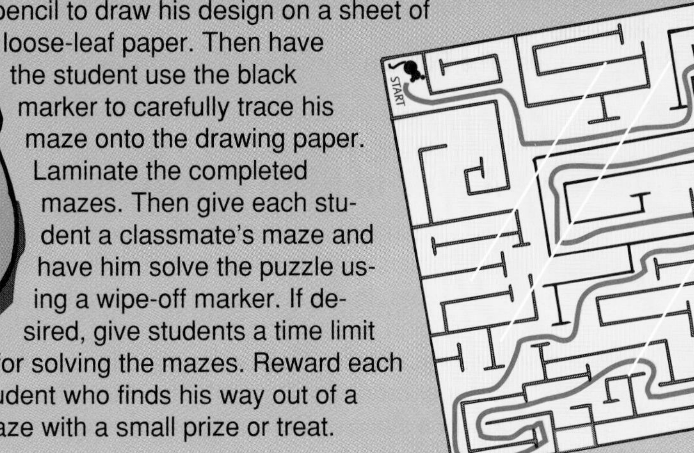

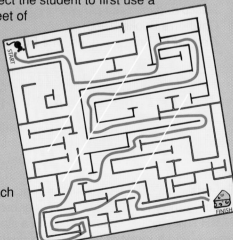

Pattern

Use with "Power Prescriptions"
on page 120.

Symptoms:

Rx:

Prescribed by:

Name ______________________________ *Mrs. Frisby and the Rats of NIMH*

Journal writing

What Do You Think?

After reading the story, choose _____ of the journal topics listed below. Write your responses in a special journal or notebook of your own.

1. What characteristics would rats need to have to be considered respectable creatures? Explain.
2. Mr. Frisby said to his wife, "All doors are hard to unlock until you have the key." What do you think he meant?
3. After receiving injections at NIMH, the rats became highly intelligent and stopped aging. If you could choose either of these qualities, which would you choose and why?
4. *Intelligence* is the ability to understand, think, and learn. Give three examples from the story that show the rats' intelligence.
5. Jenner and a few others left the main group because they didn't agree that the rats should stop stealing from humans. Which rats do you agree with, and why?
6. Think about the qualities of a good leader. If Nicodemus could no longer be the rats' leader, which rat should replace him? Explain.
7. Many characters in the story show great courage. Which character do you think is the most courageous, and why?
8. Dr. Schultz conducted experiments on the rats and mice in his lab at NIMH. Make a list of the pros and cons of using animals in medical and scientific experiments.
9. Choose one of the situations below. Write what you think happened.
   - why the toy tinker was in the woods
   - which rats died in the tunnel
   - what happened to the six mice lost in the air ducts at NIMH
   - why the seven rats were in the hardware store
   - how the rats will live at Thorn Valley
10. After their experience at NIMH, the rats felt they didn't fit in anywhere. Sometimes people feel this way. Write three things you could do to help a person who feels left out to fit in.
11. Many animals in the story help one another. Write about a time when you and a friend, neighbor, or family member helped each other.

Note to the teacher: Fill in the blank before duplicating.

Our Readers Write

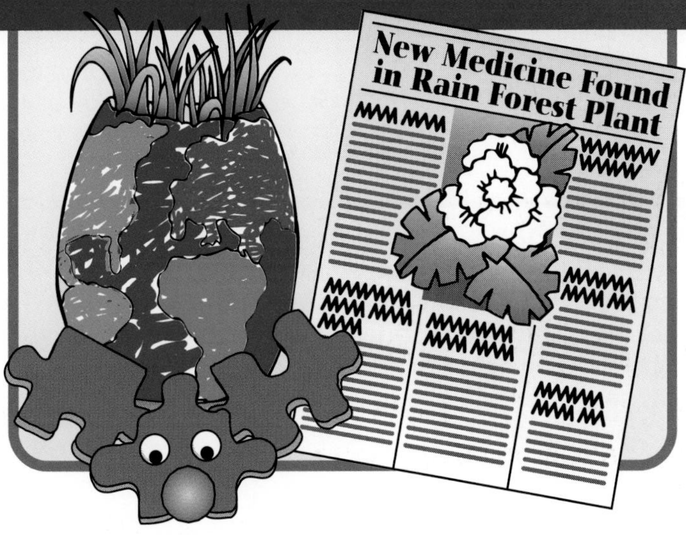

New Medicine Found in Rain Forest Plant

Our Readers Write

Love Those Labels!

Help students keep track of their school supplies with this great tip. For each child, program two sheets of name labels with a permanent marker, or type them on your computer. Give one sheet to each student to use for labeling his personal school supplies. File the other sheet to use throughout the year for nametags, seating charts, or gift labels. Keeping track of students' supplies will no longer be a sticky issue!

Bonni Teplitz
Gordon Day School
Miami, FL

Billy Barnes

Billy Barnes

Pocketful of 100s!

Motivate students to study their spelling words while boosting self-esteem with this "denim-ite" display. First, hang an old pair of overalls on a bulletin board. Then keep track of students who receive 100s on weekly spelling tests. When a student earns five 100s, write her name on an index card and place it in a pocket of the overalls. Then reward the student by exempting her from the following week's spelling homework. What a great way to add a pocketful of improved spellers to your classroom!

Donna DeRosa—Gr. 4
Good Shepherd Academy
Nutley, NJ

Class Photographer

Catch every Kodak moment as it happens by assigning the weekly job of class photographer. Bring in an old camera, or purchase several disposable ones. Direct the photographer to take the camera with him wherever he goes during school hours. Limit the pictures taken to two per day so the photographer will learn to choose his photos wisely. When the pictures have been developed, have the photographer put them into a class scrapbook and add a caption to each one. By June, you'll have a picture-perfect scrapbook of the school year—created entirely by your kids!

Tammy Brown—Gr. 6, Midway Elementary, Cleveland, MO

Traveling Tuesdays

Send students on a journey around your state with this fun geography project. During the first week of school, have each child write a letter to the Chamber of Commerce or a travel bureau in a specific county, asking for brochures and other information. On "Traveling Tuesdays" throughout the year, have selected students share the information they've received, marking their counties with pushpins on a state map. At the end of the year, celebrate your last Traveling Tuesday with a party featuring foods and activities from different counties.

Sister Pat Madden—Gr. 4
Corpus Christi School
Lansdale, PA

Road to Success

Start students on the road to success early in the year with this goal-setting activity. On the first day of school, hang a picture of your college or university on a bulletin board titled "Road to Success." (If you don't have a picture, ask your college alumni office for a brochure that includes a photo.) Then discuss planning for the future and goal setting with the class. Refer to your college picture and share with students the goals you set for yourself. Finally, have each child add a brief paragraph about her goals for the future to the display.

Kimberly Minafo—Gr. 4
Tooker Avenue Elementary
West Babylon, NY

My Goals

Your Work Is Monumental!

Show off your students' accomplishments with this monumental display! On a bulletin board titled "Your Work Is Monumental!" post pictures of famous monuments, such as the ones listed. Then fill the display with your students' best papers. To extend the board's use, divide the class into teams and assign one monument per group. Instruct each group to research interesting facts about its monument to share with the class. Display the facts on the board along with students' monumental papers.

Sample Monuments
Statue of Liberty
Eiffel Tower
Great Sphinx
Stonehenge
Great Wall of China

Stephanie Fowler, Bixby Middle School, Bixby, OK

Place-Value Necklaces

Use the following hands-on activity to teach place value to students. Provide each student or group with food coloring, uncooked pasta noodles, and string. Have students color the pasta with the food coloring. Allow time for the pasta to dry. Then assign values to the different colors of pasta (for example: blue = 1, red = 10, yellow = 100, and so on). Direct each student to string the pasta, then calculate the value of her necklace. How's that for using the ol' noodle?

David Reitz—Gr. 4
Glenwood Elementary
Virginia Beach, VA

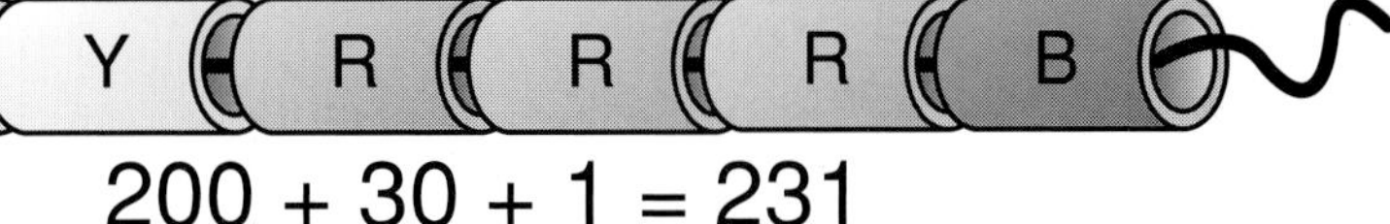

200 + 30 + 1 = 231

Tabletop Treasure

Have students create a keepsake for the year with this simple idea. Place a vinyl tablecloth on a classroom table. Have each student autograph the tablecloth with a permanent marker on the first day of school. Each time the class does something special throughout the year, have a student record the event on the tablecloth with a small picture and caption.

Julie Eick Granchelli—Gr. 4
Towne Elementary, Medina, NY

Nouns to Know

Create a back-to-school bulletin board that also reviews nouns. Cover a board with inexpensive back-to-school fabric. Make three columns on the board with the headings "People," "Places," and "Things." Under each heading, list actual people, places, and things that relate to your school. What a great way to review nouns *and* help students become more familiar with their new environment!

Marilyn Davison—Grs. 4–5, River Oaks School, Monroe, LA

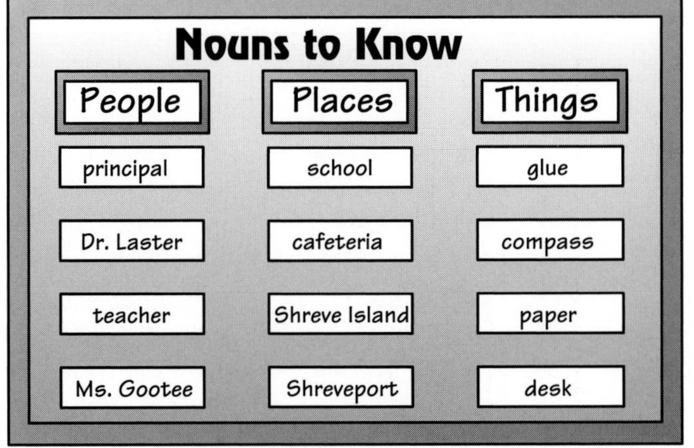

Nouns to Know
People
Places
Things
principal
school
glue
Dr. Laster
cafeteria
compass
teacher
Shreve Island
paper
Ms. Gootee
Shreveport
desk

The Perfect 10!

Turn your class's behavior in line into a "perfect 10" with the following idea. Explain to students that a perfect 10 means "1 line with 0 noise." After arriving at your destination, decide as a class whether a perfect 10 was maintained throughout the journey. Add a plastic dime to a jar every time the class maintains a perfect 10. When the class earns \$1.00, reward students with ten extra minutes of recess or free time. When the class earns \$10.00 (100 perfect 10s), reward students with a Perfect 10 Party. You'll find that students will love the rewards as well as the rave reviews from other teachers, parents, and administrators!

Chuck Yeager—Gr. 5, Priceville School, Decatur, AL

Hospitality Hosts

Let your students take charge of Open House! Have each child place his books, folders, and portfolio on his desk at the end of the school day. Provide each student with a copy of a hospitality checklist (see the illustration) to use as an outline when his family arrives. On the night of Open House, have students greet parents, describe important aspects of the classroom, and answer questions. You can sit in the background with parents and help when the need arises.

Phyllis Ellett—Grs. 3–4
Earl Hanson Elementary
Rock Island, IL

Open House

Make sure you see…

__ Daily journal
__ Reading folder
__ Portfolio
__ Art projects
__ Computer room
__ Science exhibit

Recycled Timeline

Don't junk those preprinted envelopes from junk mail! Use them to create a timeline in your classroom. Simply have students donate unused envelopes from junk mail. Next, have them write important facts and dates on the backs of the envelopes. Then hang the envelopes over a piece of string and seal tightly.

Sr. Margaret Xavier, Mother Seton Academy, Baltimore, MD

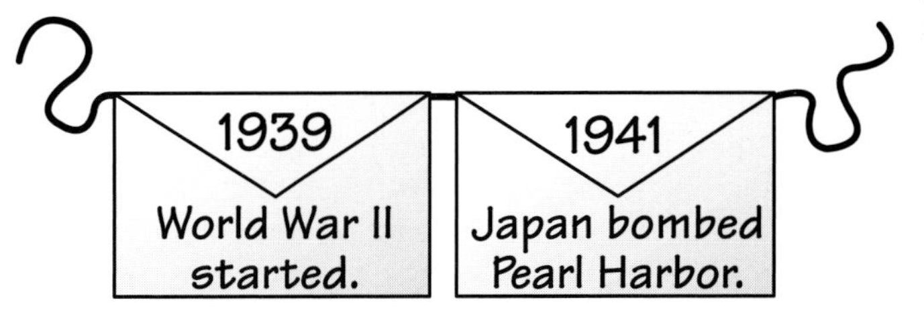

World War II started.

Japan bombed Pearl Harbor.

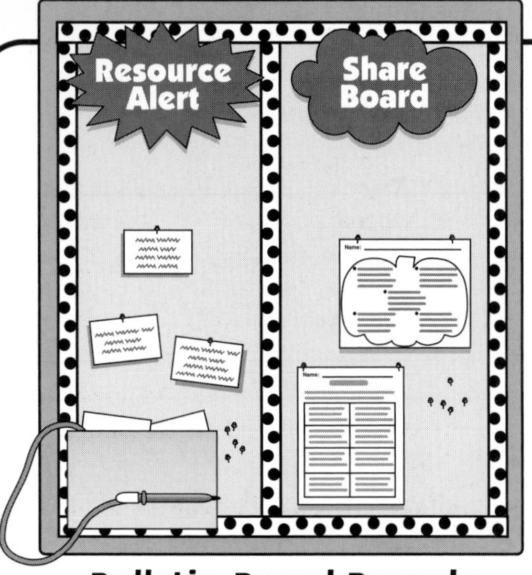

Bulletin-Board Remedy

Never have an empty hallway bulletin board again! Cover the board; then label half "Resource Alert" and the other half "Share Board." Attach a pen, an envelope containing index cards, and a supply of pushpins to the board. Invite teachers to request supplies such as empty baby-food jars or egg cartons on the "Resource Alert" side and post their favorite ideas from *The Mailbox®* magazine and other resources on the "Share Board" side.

Cheryl Althouse—Gr. 4,
Kralltown Elementary, East Berlin, PA

A Values Auction

Find out what your students value most with this thought-provoking activity. Tell each student that he has $4,000 to spend at an auction for values. Direct the student to write down how much he would be willing to pay for each value listed below. Then compare student bids for every item and award that value to the highest bidder. Follow up the activity by having each student write his reflections in a journal. *(Values: freedom, high-school education, college education, marriage, family, religious freedom, a good paying job, lots of friends, one good friend, respect for parents, happiness, being left alone, fancy car, having everything I want, service to others.)*

Diane Ptak, Albany, NY

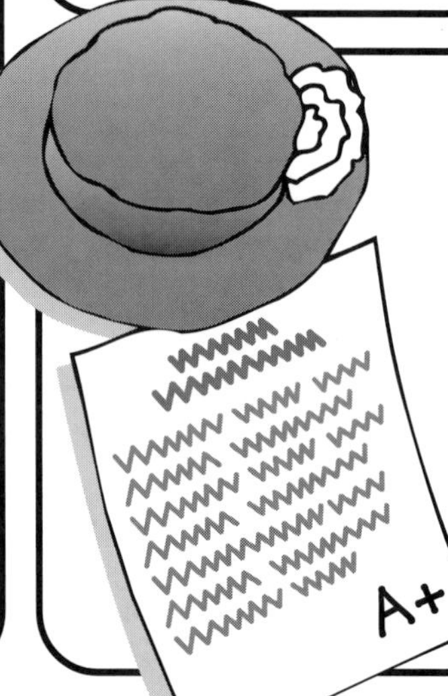

Hats Off!

Tip your hat to great student work with this attractive bulletin board. Have each student contribute her favorite hat to display on a board titled "Hats Off to Great Work!" Post samples of a few students' work next to their hats for about a week. Then return the hats to their owners and refresh the display with a new group of work and hats.

Jennifer Bruce—Gr. 5
East Sparta Elementary, Canton, OH

Self-Esteem Mural

Shower your students in compliments and boost their self-esteem! Assign each student a two-week period to be featured on a classroom bulletin board. Cover the board and label it with the name of the featured student. Keep a supply of markers nearby and invite classmates to visit the board to add as many compliments about the featured student as they choose. Each child in your classroom is guaranteed to feel special!

Judy Foley—Gr. 4, Howe-Manning School, Middleton, MA

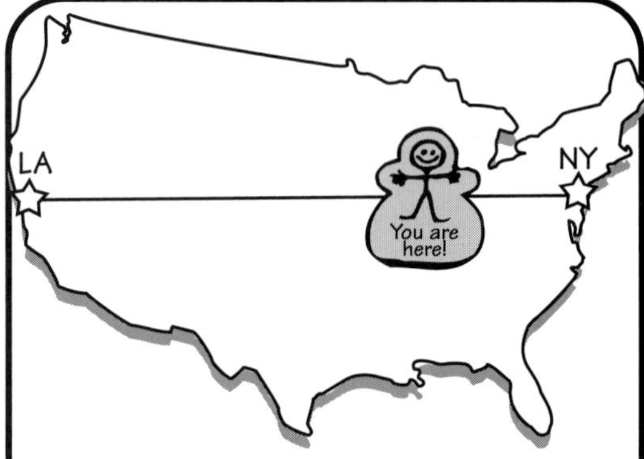

Walkers' Club

Ensure physical exercise for your students by starting a Walkers' Club. Measure a distance around the school for students to walk during recess. Then have your club calculate the distance to a chosen city on a map and set a club goal to walk that same distance around the school. Create a display in the classroom to chart your students' daily or weekly progress. Once your club reaches its goal, reward it with a special treat.

Patricia E. Dancho—Gr. 6
Apollo-Ridge Middle School
Spring Church, PA

In the News

Expand your students' study of science and social studies beyond the classroom walls. Award extra-credit points to students who bring in newspaper or magazine articles that relate to your current units of study. Have each student summarize his article for the class, then post it on a bulletin board titled "In the News." This simple idea helps students see that what they learn in the classroom is also part of the world outside our school.

Debra Garrett—Gr. 4
El Dorado Springs R-2 Elementary
El Dorado Springs, MO

Why Was It Invented?

Begin a unit on inventions with the following ingenious idea! Bring in several different household inventions, such as a peeler, a fitted sheet, or a screwdriver. Have students identify the problem solved by one of the inventions and suggest ways that the invention might be improved. Next, display a transparency of the form shown. As a class, evaluate another invention using the form's questions. Then give each pair of students a copy of the form and have them evaluate another invention. For an inventive homework assignment, send a form home for each child's family to complete together.

Jan Drehmel—Gr. 4
Parkview Elementary, Chippewa Falls, WI

Why Was It Invented?

Invention: ____________

1. Why was this invention invented? What problems does it solve? ____________
2. How have people benefited from this invention? ____________
3. How might this invention be improved? ____________

   Draw a diagram of your improvements on the back of this form.
4. How would you rate this invention?

   Useful   Not important

   Why did you rate it as you did? ____________

Adjective Family Portraits

Promote teamwork, review adjectives, and have lots of fun with this quick-and-easy activity. Divide the class into small groups. Have each group decide on an adjective that describes its "family" (for example, *gloomy, nervous, joyful,* etc.). Then have each group pose for a make-believe family portrait in their stage faces. Challenge the class to guess the type of family (adjective) each group is portraying. Change groups and repeat the activity with different adjectives. Say cheese!

Marsha Schmus—Gr. 4, Ypsilanti, MI

"Tee-rrific" Books

Line up a "tee-rrific" bulletin board this November to celebrate National Children's Book Week! For each student, fold a large sheet of white construction paper in half widthwise. Place a T-shirt pattern on the fold as shown; then trace and cut out the shirt, leaving the shoulder seams uncut. Have each student write his book report inside one of the T-shirts. Next, have him decorate the shirt's front with his book's title and author, and an illustration. Hang the shirts over a clothesline that's been strung across a bulletin board. Title the board "Line Up for a 'Tee-riffic' Book!"

Terry Healy—Gifted K–6
Eugene Field Elementary
Manhattan, KS

Math Bumper Stickers

Celebrate math with this easy-to-do art activity! Give each student a white sentence strip (or "bumper sticker"). Have the student create an original slogan promoting math. Next, have him use markers to write his slogan on his bumper sticker and add colorful illustrations. Attach the completed bumper stickers to a bulletin board titled "Stick With Math!"

David Reitz—Gr. 4
Glenwood Elementary
Virginia Beach, VA

Pencil Dice

Turn broken pencil stubs into dynamite dice with this nifty recycling idea! Use a black permanent marker to draw a dot on one side of a short, hexagonal pencil. Rotate the pencil and draw two dots on the next side. Continue increasing the number of dots until you have six dots on the last side. Demonstrate for students how to gently roll the pencil on a table or desk. You'll have no more games with missing dice!

Shirlee Angerame
Roxboro Road Middle School
Brewerton, NY

Math Points

Help students see the point to math homework with this easy-to-play game! Divide the class into two teams. Call on a student from Team 1 to answer the first problem from the homework assignment. If she answers correctly, award Team 1 a point. Continue asking Team 1 questions until a student answers incorrectly. Then call on a student from Team 2. Keep awarding points for correct answers until all homework problems have been answered. The team with the most points wins!

Shannon Popkin—Gr. 4, Heritage Christian School, Brookfield, WI

A "Piece-ful" Holiday Art Project

Piece together a great art project with this activity involving puzzle pieces. Spray-paint large puzzle pieces brown; then provide each student with any three pieces. Have the student glue the puzzle pieces together to make a reindeer, using two puzzle pieces as antlers and one as a face. Give each student two small wiggle eyes and a red pom-pom nose to attach to the face. Then glue a string or ribbon onto the reindeer to use for hanging it on a Christmas tree.

Sonya Franklin, Springville Elementary
Springville, AL

Reach for the Stars

Keep up with current events using this star-studded activity! Have each student bring in a newspaper article detailing a recent news event. Provide each student with a copy of the star pattern shown. Direct the student to complete each section of the star using information from her news article. Then have the student summarize the news-making event in a paragraph with the help of her star organizer. Display the completed stars and paragraphs on a bulletin board titled "Star-Studded Current Events."

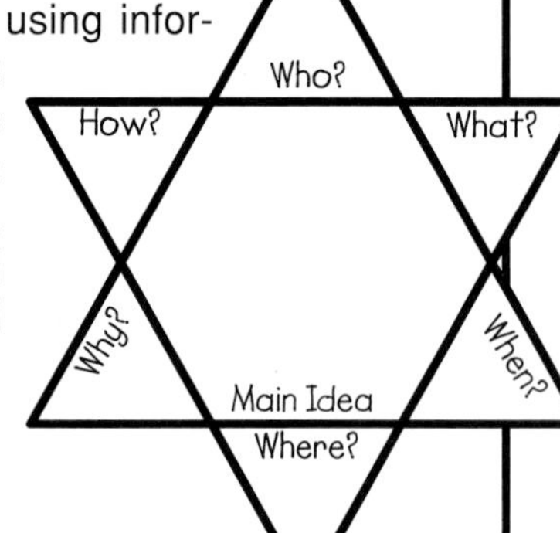

Jane Cooney—Gr. 5
Guion Creek Elementary
Indianapolis, IN

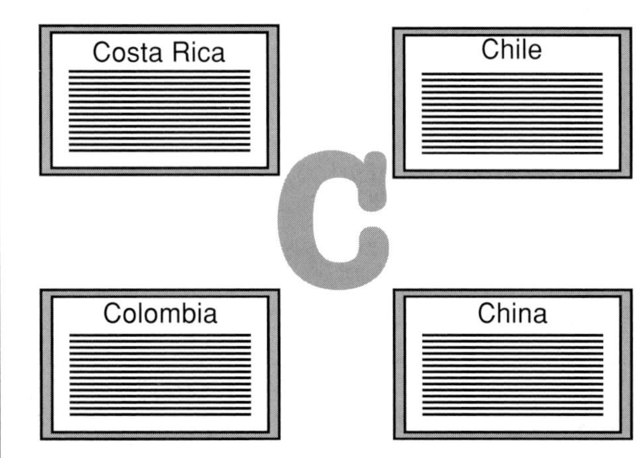

Christmas Around the World

This eye-catching wall display and research project makes a great addition to your holiday lesson plans. Write the letters from *Christmas* on nine 11" x 14" construction-paper sheets, writing one letter on each sheet. Then divide your class into eight groups (since the letter *s* appears twice). Assign one letter to each group; then direct the group to research the holiday customs of as many countries as possible that begin with its assigned letter. Have the group find out how each country celebrates the holidays and record that information on an index card. Mount each index card on colorful paper and display it around the letter to which it corresponds.

Pat Thames, Ivor, VA

Christmas-Card Quilt

Make a quilt with a Christmas theme by cutting the fronts from an assortment of Christmas cards (use either only ones with horizontal designs or only ones with vertical designs). Punch a hole in each of the four corners of each card.

Thread four-inch lengths of green or red yarn through the punched holes; then tie the yarn into bows to connect the greeting cards in a quilt formation. Hang the Christmas-card quilt on the wall as a festive holiday decoration.

Andrea Troisi—Librarian
LaSalle Middle School
Niagara Falls, NY

Crystal-Clear Storage

Avoid spending your valuable teaching time searching for frequently used supplies with the help of this practical suggestion. Store all of your small supplies—such as tape, scissors, and markers—in clear, plastic shoeboxes. Stack the boxes on top of one another in a convenient location in your classroom. How's that for an easy way to save time and stay organized?

Sharon Abell
Mineral Springs Middle School
Winston-Salem, NC

Covering All Bases

Keep all your bases covered the next time your class makes salt-relief maps. Before your map-making project, locate the person in charge of stocking your school's soda machine. Request that the cardboard soda trays used to ship soda be saved for you to use as map bases. Then have each student use one of the sturdy trays as a base for his salt-relief map. What a great way to keep dough from getting all over your room!

Susan Sandman—Gr. 5
Parkview Middle School
Creve Coeur, IL

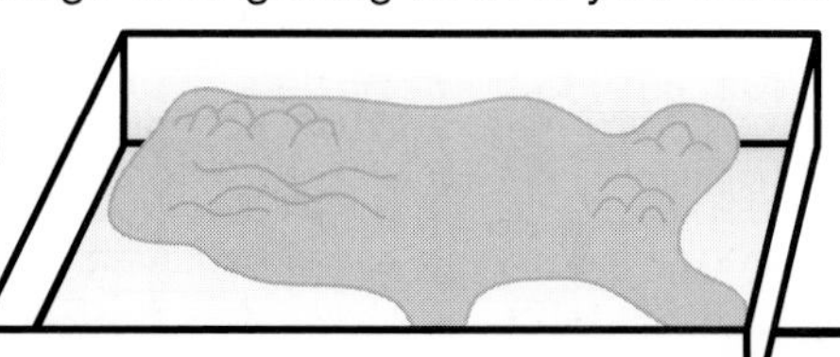

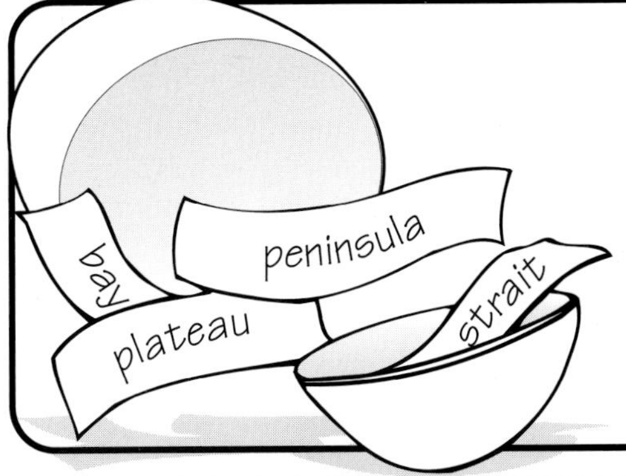

Crack a Word

One of my favorite spring activities is our annual Easter egg hunt. I buy plastic eggs that are readily available during this season. Inside each egg I place a slip of paper labeled with a vocabulary word. I hide the eggs outside; then I send students on a search for the eggs. When all the eggs have been found, we return to class. Each student reads and defines the words hidden inside her eggs. For each correct definition, a student wins a piece of Easter candy.

Dawn Partin, Lugoff Elgin Middle School, Lugoff, SC

Classroom Museum

Don't throw out the old study carrel that no one seems to want—turn it into a classroom museum instead! Select a student each week to display items on the carrel that tell about himself and are special to him. Once everyone has had a turn to prepare an individual display, select a museum committee to be responsible for setting up special-topic exhibits. What a great way to recycle that study carrel and learn about one another at the same time!

Phyllis Ellett—Grs. 3–4 Multiage
Earl Hanson Elementary
Rock Island, IL

It's in the Mail!

Make keeping in touch with parents a little easier this year! Have parents, grandparents, and/or other caregivers send large, preaddressed and stamped envelopes to school. Let each student put her favorite papers or artwork in her envelope; then mail the envelopes. It's an easy way to make sure a great paper actually makes it home in one piece!

Melinda Salisbury—Grs. 4–6
Baldwin North Intermediate
Quincy, IL

Earth Eggs

Conclude your celebration of Earth Day with an "eggs-ellent" art activity! Provide each student with an egg. Help him carefully poke a dime-sized hole in the top narrow end of his egg and remove its contents. Have the student rinse and dry the eggshell, then use permanent markers to decorate it to resemble Earth. Finally, direct the student to fill the egg $^{2}/_{3}$ full of potting soil and sprinkle rye grass seeds on top. With a little water and sunlight, students' Earth eggs will grow full heads of grassy hair!

Holly Bowser—Gr. 6
Cork Elementary
Geneva, OH

Category Challenge

Challenge students to use their brain power with the following group game. Choose a category such as prefixes, occupations that end in *er,* or words that begin with *qu.* Divide the class into groups. Have each group brainstorm words that belong to the category within a time limit. When time is up, have a student stand and read her group's list of words. Instruct each of the other groups to look at its list and cross off any word listed by another team. The group with the most words at the end of the game is the winner.

Sandra Bartman
Waterloo, Ontario
Canada

Blooming Poetry

Brighten your room with a display that's abloom with student poetry! Have each student cut out a flower shape from loose-leaf paper and write a short poem about spring on it. Then have him color the flower with pastel colored pencils. Mount the poems on a bulletin board decorated with colorful construction-paper flowers. Add cut-out clouds and a sun for a cheerful finishing touch.

Jeannette Freeman—Resource, The First Lady Educational Program, San Juan, Puerto Rico

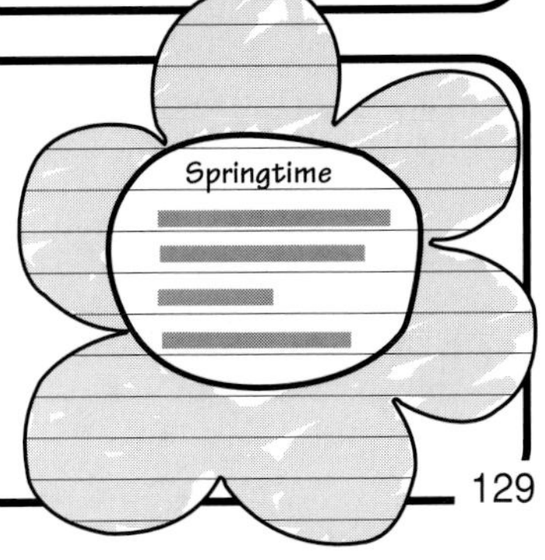

Charming Chimes

Charm students into giving you their undivided attention with this idea. Hang wind chimes from the ceiling. Instead of raising your hand, clapping, or turning off the lights, gently move the chimes. What a soothing way to remind students, "I need you!"

Sue Mechura—Gr. 4
Ebenezer Elementary
Lebanon, PA

Beauty Is...

A camera and one roll of film is all you need for a writing lesson that's a real beauty! Ask students to discuss the question, "What is beauty?" Then walk with students around your school and school grounds to observe. Have each student select one item or scene that he finds beautiful; then have him photograph it. After the film is developed, have each child write a paragraph explaining why he thinks the item he photographed is beautiful. Display the photos and paragraphs with the title "In the Eye of the Beholder."

Julia Alarie—Gr. 6
Essex Middle School
Essex, VT

Awards Breakfast

Complete the year on a tasty note with an end-of-the-year awards breakfast. Reserve your school cafeteria or another meeting place before the start of a selected school day. Contact a few parents to provide coffee, juice, doughnuts, and paper goods. Award special student awards or plan the breakfast to coincide with the school's award program. The breakfast takes little preparation and provides a great ending to a successful year!

Karen Martino
Oxford, OH

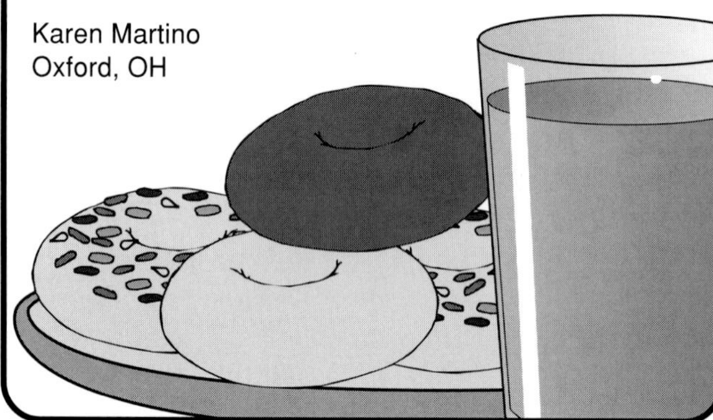

Watch This Sign

An index card and a drinking straw can make mundane math practice a fun game! Provide each student with one card and a straw. Have the student fold the card in half, then write "Yes" on one side and "No" on the other side. Next, have the student staple the folded card onto the straw. Write a review problem on the chalkboard, including a correct or an incorrect answer. Have each student work the problem and hold up the appropriate side of her sign. This is a great way to encourage students to check problems carefully!

Julie Eick Granchelli—Gr. 4
Towne Elementary
Medina, NY

Cheap Chart Stand

Transform an inexpensive clothing rack into a chart stand for your classroom. Purchase a clothing rack from a local discount store's housewares department. Add two metal shower-curtain rings for the hangers. Simply punch two holes in the top of each item you want to hang on the stand. What an easy way to display charts and posters!

Susan Lynnette Perkins
Halifax County Middle School
South Boston, VA

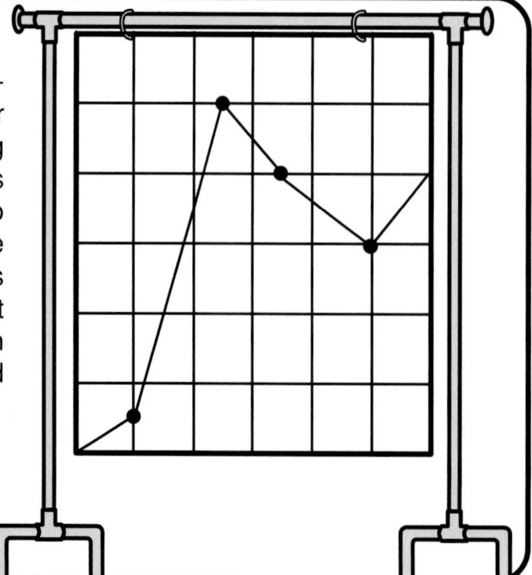

A Year in Review

Throughout the year I use large sheets of chart paper to record class discussions. During the last week of school, I take down all of my bulletin boards and hang the charts from the year's studies. Then the students and I discuss all of the wonderful things they learned during the year. On the last day of school, I take the charts down, roll them up, and award them to students as prizes.

Shari Medley—Gr. 5
Lakeshore Elementary
Fond du Lac, WI

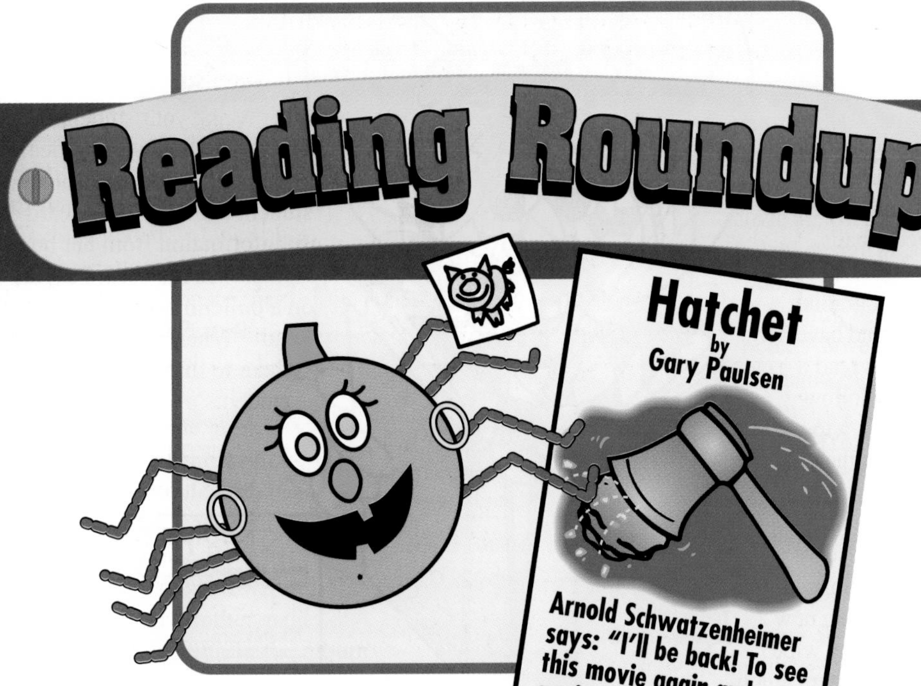
Reading Roundup
Hatchet
by
Gary Paulsen
Arnold Schwatzenheimer says: "I'll be back! To see this movie again and again..."

Mission: Possible!

Skill: Reviewing basic grammar skills

Give your students the scoop on grammar skills with this nifty newspaper activity! Create a skeletal reproducible on your computer that includes the following: "Your mission, should you choose to accept it (and you will), is..." Complete the sentence with directions for each student to find such grammatical items as helping verbs, direct objects, proper nouns, or prepositional phrases. Give a copy of the assignment and one page from the local newspaper to each student; then have him circle or highlight examples of the assigned grammar term on his news page. In no time your students will be reporting higher grammar grades!

Teena Andersen—Grs. 4–6, Hadar Public School, Hadar, NE

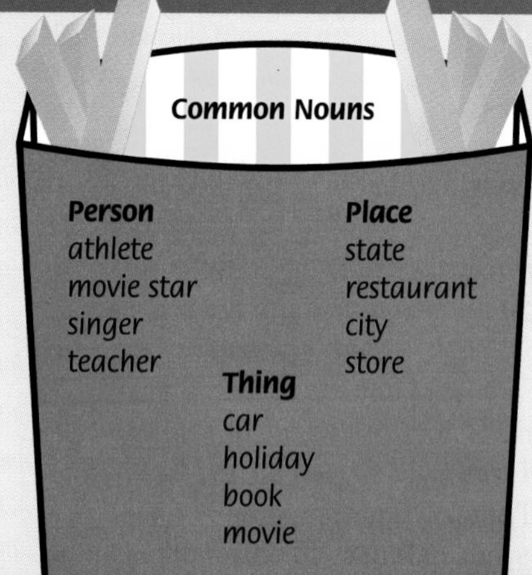

Common Nouns
Person
athlete
movie star
singer
teacher
Place
state
restaurant
city
store
Thing
car
holiday
book
movie

The Name Game

Skill: Common and proper nouns

There's nothing common about this great way to review common and proper nouns! Divide your class into teams of four or five students each; then have one person from each team go to the chalkboard. Call out a category of common nouns, such as restaurants. Have each student at the board write a proper noun relating to that category, such as McDonald's® or Pizza Hut®. After he writes his proper noun on the board, the first player sits down. Then the next student on his team goes to the board and writes a second example. The team that lists the most proper nouns in one minute wins a point. Play as many rounds as there are team members; then tally the scores. Award the winning group bonus points on your next grammar test!

Kimberly J. Branham—Gr. 5, Wateree Elementary, Lugoff, SC

Preposition Poster

Skill: Prepositional phrases

Several years ago, professional basketball players Michael Jordan and Larry Bird appeared in a commercial together. They challenged each other to make amazing basketball shots, describing them using only prepositional phrases, such as "over the backboard" and "around the scoreboard." Discuss this commercial with your class, noting that "over the backboard" and "around the scoreboard" are prepositional phrases. Then pair students and give each pair a 12" x 18" sheet of white construction paper. Direct each pair to describe your classroom, grade level, or school using only prepositional phrases. Have each pair write and illustrate its prepositional phrases on the sheet of construction paper. Display the completed posters on a bulletin board titled "Preposition Pizzazz!"

Jana S. Whinrey—Gr. 6, Westlake Elementary, Indianapolis, IN

Nursery Rhyme Sentences

Skill: Four kinds of sentences

Reinforce the four kinds of sentences with an activity that features favorite nursery rhymes. Ask student volunteers to recite popular nursery rhymes for the class. Or read aloud rhymes from a collection such as *The Arnold Lobel Book of Mother Goose* (Alfred A. Knopf, Inc.; 1997). After hearing the rhymes, have each child write and label four sentences—one declarative, one interrogative, one exclamatory, and one imperative—about his favorite rhyme. Then have the student copy his sentences onto drawing paper and add a picture that illustrates the rhyme. Surely Mother Goose would approve!

Christine Sforzo—Gr. 5, P.S. 204, Brooklyn, NY

Declarative: Humpty Dumpty sat on a high brick wall.
Interrogative: How did Humpty Dumpty lose his balance?
Imperative: Please help Humpty Dumpty.
Exclamatory: Look out, Humpty Dumpty!

Catalog Helper

Skill: Punctuation

Put old catalogs to work in a way that strengthens punctuation skills! Scan catalogs for items whose descriptors contain the punctuation marks your students need to review. Make transparencies of these pages. Then use them to review punctuation rules with your class. Next have each student cut out a catalog picture of an item and glue it to a sheet of white paper. Instruct the student to write a descriptor of the item next to its picture. If desired, require that the descriptor contain a given number and type of punctuation (for example, one period, two commas, and two exclamation marks). Compile the finished pages into a class book titled "A Catalog Just for Kids!"

Kimberly Minafo—Gr. 4, Tooker Avenue School, West Babylon, NY

Between now and January 31, get this nifty neon yellow yo-yo for only $4.95! While quantities last, you'll also receive a terrific booklet that shows you how to do dozens of tricks. What are you waiting for? Order today!

How Are You Feeling, Frosty?

Skill: Adjectives

Let students turn alliterative adjectives into frosty faces this winter! List the adjectives shown on the chalkboard. Have each student choose one word from the list to use in a descriptive name for Frosty the Snowman, such as "Flirty Frosty" or "Funky Frosty." Next, give each child a white paper plate, scissors, glue, markers, and paper scraps. Have the student use the materials to make the head of a snowman whose facial expression, clothes, and accessories depict his new name. Display these cool characters on a bulletin board titled "How Are You Feeling, Frosty?" Then challenge students to use the adjectives in their spelling sentences, journal entries, or writing pieces.

Julia Alarie—Gr. 6, Essex Middle School, Essex, VT

Adjectives: funny, flirty, furious, forgetful, fearful, freezing, frustrated, freckled, funky, foolish, fashionable, feeble, filthy, frizzy, fretful, futuristic, frisky, forlorn, factual, flabbergasted, floral, fastidious, fancy, fluorescent, fiendish, fidgety

Blooming Adjectives

Skill: Identifying adjectives

Send students on an adjective hunt that blooms into a bed of flowers! After reviewing adjectives, instruct each student to search any piece of fiction for a sentence containing one or more adjectives. Direct her to copy the sentence onto a sentence strip and highlight each adjective. Then have her stack eight tissue-paper squares, fanfold them, and wrap one end of a green pipe cleaner around the middle of the fan as shown. Direct the student to separate the folds by gently pulling the edges toward the middle. Finally, have the child post the resulting flower with her sentence strip on a bulletin board titled "Sentences BLOSSOM With Adjectives!" Follow up by placing materials for additional flowers and sentences near the board. Then challenge the class to fill the board with blooming adjectives!

Brandi Lampl—Gr. 4, W. A. Fountain Elementary, Forest Park, GA

dear	night	further	sit
hare	deer	close	farther
heard	reign	clothes	scene
knight	weak	set	you're

Bingo Blast

Skill: Word usage

Everybody wants to use the *right* words—right? Have students list commonly misused word pairs on the board and identify the correct use of each word. Then instruct each student to write a sample sentence for one of the words on a strip of paper. Place the strips in a container. Next, give each student a 16-square bingo sheet and bingo markers. Direct the student to write one word from the list on each square of his card. (If desired, have the student choose 15 words, then fill in a free space.)

To play, pull a strip from the container and read its sentence. If the student has the correct word on his bingo sheet, have him cover the word with a bingo marker. End the game when someone covers four vertical, horizontal, or diagonal squares in a row and calls, "Bingo"; then check the child's answers and start a new game.

Team Up!

Skill: Reviewing parts of speech

Team up for this fun parts-of-speech review! Label 26 paper squares with a different letter of the alphabet. Put the squares in a zippered plastic bag. Next, group students into four teams: nouns, verbs, adjectives, and adverbs. Have one player from each team draw a letter from the bag. Then instruct each team to choose a word that both matches its assigned part of speech and begins with the letter on its square. Have each team call out its word for you to record on the board. Then challenge each team to suggest a sentence that uses all four words correctly (adding additional words if needed). Collect the squares and replace them in the bag. After four rounds, rotate the teams' assignments so that each group practices a different part of speech.

JoAnn Henn, Brightwaters, NY

Write On!

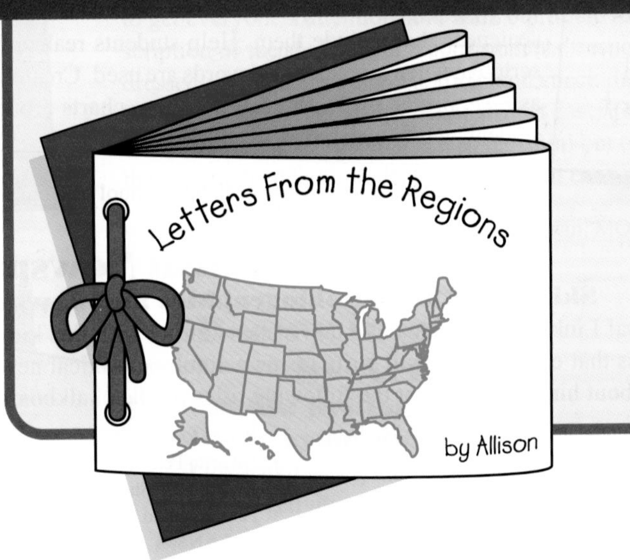

Celebrate the Season
Holiday and Seasonal Activities for the Classroom

Back to School:
Getting-to-Know-You Poll

Use this ice-breaking activity to help your students appreciate how they are alike and different. Begin by writing five yes-or-no questions on the board, such as the ones shown on the graph. (Avoid questions that would group students by gender or along racial or cultural lines.) Ask each student to number his paper from 1 to 5; then have him answer the questions. After collecting the papers, display the results of the poll in a simple double-bar graph as shown. Next, have students help you label a large sheet of chart paper with several statements based on the poll. (For example, "Most of us were born in this state. Five students don't consider pizza their favorite food.") Then have each student write a paragraph describing the benefits of having classmates who are both alike and different. ***Lisa Waller Rogers, Austin, TX***

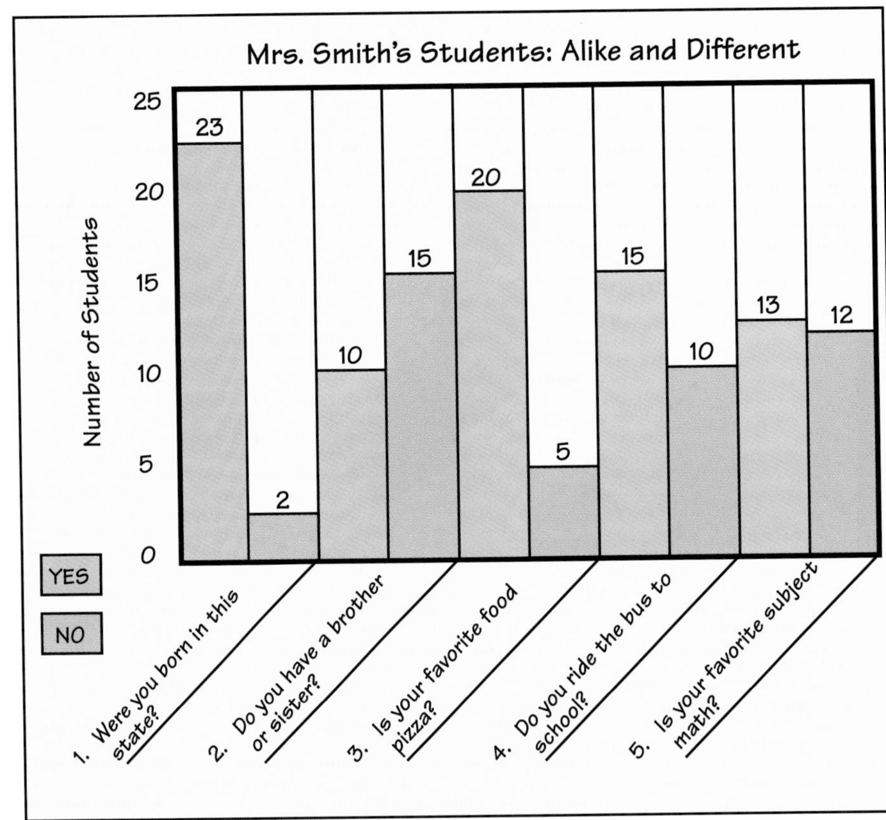

2. Do you have a brother or sister?

4. Do you ride the bus to school?
5. Is your favorite subject math?

All-About-Me Key	
Subjects I like (body): Math = yellow Social Studies = purple Science = green Reading = red	**Family (scales—one per item):** Sister = pink triangle Brother = blue triangle Cat = orange circle Dog = black circle Other Pet = green triangle
Hobbies (tail): Computer = pink Sports = brown Music = blue Art = orange	**Food Favorites (fins):** Pizza = red Fries = yellow Tacos = green Burgers = brown

Back to School:
Into the Swim of Things

Dive into a new school year with this fishy art project! Give each student a sheet of 8½" x 11" white paper. Have the student draw a large fish shape; then have her write her name in bubble or block letters inside the outline before cutting out the fish. Post a color key as shown. Have the student use markers and crayons to personalize her fish according to her choices from the key. Display each student's fish and the key on a bulletin board that you've covered with blue paper and titled "We're Back Into the Swim of Things!"
Joan M. Macey, Binghamton, NY

Back to School:
Guessing-Game Bulletin Board

Arm yourself with a camera to produce a winning bulletin board that helps students get to know their classmates. Take a snapshot of each child during the first week of school; then have him copy and complete the information shown at the right on an index card. Mount each photo and its card on a bulletin board titled "Who Am I?" Next, staple a paper flap over each snapshot to conceal it. No student will be able to resist reading the clues, taking a guess, and lifting the flap to see if his guess is right! ***Lisa Waller Rogers, Austin, TX***

Who Am I?

Who Am I?

My first and last names have a total of ______ letters.
I've attended this school for ______ years. (Write the number as a math sentence.)
My favorite TV show is __________________.
My favorite food is __________.
My favorite day of the week is ______________.
My favorite fast-food restaurant is _____________.
My favorite commercial is __________________.
My first name comes ______ alphabetically on the class roll.

Back to School:
Toilet-Paper Tattle

This getting-to-know-you activity is a real attention grabber! Distribute one roll of toilet paper to every group of four to six students. Without any explanation, direct each student to take as many sheets as he thinks he needs and then pass the roll to the next child in his group. Have each student count his sheets and write that number of little-known facts about himself—such as having seen the *Star Wars* video 56 times—on loose-leaf paper. Have students share their completed lists. Then follow up with questions such as the following: What new things did you learn about your classmates? Would you like to do any of the things you heard about? What funny (happy, surprising, sad, etc.) things did you learn? With this fun-filled activity, your students will be rolling in information about one another! ***Lisa Waller Rogers***

Back to School:
Stand Up and Be Recognized!

Spark new friendships and build camaraderie with this easy getting-to-know-you activity. Have each student complete a copy of the half-page reproducible on page 160; then have him cut out the clues, fold them in half, and place them in a container provided by you. Each day during the first week of school, gather students in a large circle on the floor and read aloud 10–20 clues one at a time. After you read each clue, direct its writer to stand. As clues are read, your students will quickly identify classmates with whom they share something in common. What an uncommonly great icebreaker! ***Joy A. Kalfas, Palatine, IL***

Columbus Day: Charting a Course to Comprehension!

Help your students chart a course to comprehension with this story-mapping activity! First, make a transparency of page 161. Then review with students the elements of a good story and their definitions, shown in the chart on the right. The next time you discuss a story or novel that you're currently reading, list its elements on the transparency as students describe them. Then, when you read your next story or novel, provide students with copies of page 161 to complete independently. After completing their story maps, have students color and cut them out. Post the completed ships on a bulletin board titled "Charting a Course to Comprehension!"

Setting: the place and time during which a story's action occurs

Characters: the people or animals in a story

Plot: the problem that needs to be solved, including the sequential events that lead to its solution

Climax: the event that brings about a solution to a story's problem

Ending: the conclusion of a story

Theme: the main idea of a story

Halloween: Top Banana!

Try this "ap-peel-ing" contest as a fun and creative way for your bunch to celebrate October's top holiday. First, challenge each student to design a costume for either a real or a plastic banana. Suggest that students use a variety of materials, such as paper, cloth, paint, glue, markers, glitter, and yarn. In addition, have each student create a setting and a nameplate for his banana. Have students bring their completed projects to school on the day of your Halloween party. Invite other classes to parade by your display of costumed bananas. Also ask a few staff members to choose the five "top bananas."

For a language arts connection, have each student write a story featuring his banana as the main character. Then, during your Halloween party, have students share their stories while they enjoy banana splits—with new bananas, of course! ***Marianne Bush—Grs. 5 and 6, Our Lady of Lourdes School, Toledo, OH***

Halloween: Dying to Read a Good Book?

Turn October book reporting into an issue of "grave" importance with this fun idea! Have each student draw a tombstone shape on a 12" x 18" sheet of gray construction paper. Direct the student to cut out this shape, write his book's title on it, and illustrate it. Then have him trim lined paper to fit the tombstone's shape. On the lined paper, have the student write his book report. Then have him staple the report behind the cutout. Display the completed projects on a board titled "Just Dying to Read a Good Book?" ***Terry Healy—Gifted K–6, Eugene Field Elementary, Manhattan, KS***

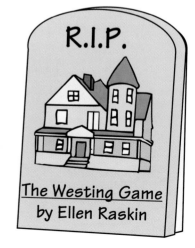

Fall: Famous-People Pumpkins

To wrap up a study of biographies, have your students make famous-people pumpkins. Provide each child with a large sheet of orange construction paper. Have the student study a picture of the famous person she read about and then make a pumpkin to resemble him or her. Encourage students to use scrap materials and a variety of art supplies, such as pipe cleaners, ribbon, lace, and yarn. When each student shares her biography book report, be sure she shows off her pumpkin person! ***Shea Lauria, Center Street School, Williston Park, NY***

Harriet Tubman Pumpkin

Babe Ruth Pumpkin

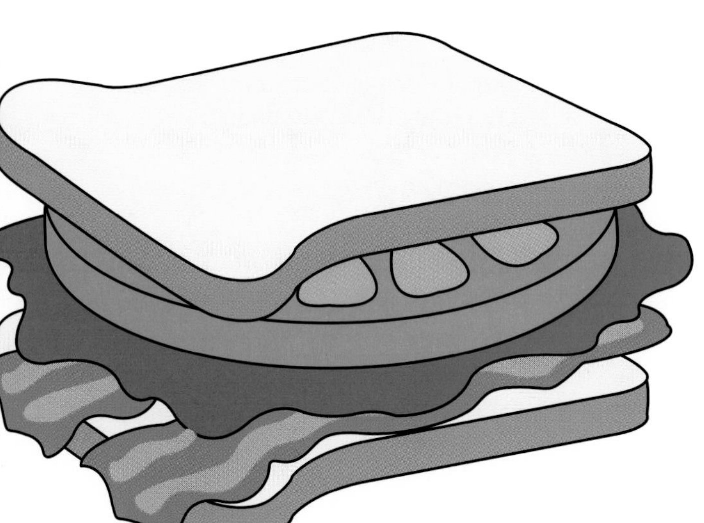

Sandwich Day: Picnic Pictograph

Celebrate Sandwich Day (November 3) with a graphing activity that's a real picnic for everyone! In advance, invite each student to bring his favorite sandwich to school on November 3. When the big day arrives, read aloud John Vernon Lord's *The Giant Jam Sandwich* (Houghton Mifflin Company, 1987). In this delightful picture book, a small village's citizens try to trap a mass of wasps using a giant jam sandwich. After discussing the book, have each student use art materials to make a paper version of his sandwich. Next, direct students to work together to sort their paper sandwiches into different categories; then have them pin the sandwiches to a bulletin board to create a pictograph. Help students label the graph, add a key, and draw conclusions from its data. Conclude your Sandwich Day celebration with a picnic that includes the sandwiches students brought to school. ***Leasha Segars and Lindy Hopkins—Gr. 5, Saltillo Elementary, Saltillo, MS***

Thanksgiving: Thankful Thoughts

Fill a November bulletin board with a bountiful supply of thankful thoughts! Give each student a colorful leaf cutout. On the cutout, have the student write and illustrate a brief thank-you note to a friend, a family member, or a staff member at your school. Display the cutouts on a bulletin board titled "Thinking Thankful Thoughts." Just before Thanksgiving break, return each cutout to its author in time for her to deliver it to its recipient. ***Cari Lott—Gr. 4, Roosevelt-Lincoln Middle School, Salina, KS***

Dear Mrs. Olsen,
You are the best school nurse ever! The ointment you put on my scraped knee didn't hurt or burn. I liked the way you signed my bandage! I'll never forget you!
Love,
Kristin

December Holidays: Festive Estimation

Help your students' estimation skills measure up with this fun holiday center! Wrap several boxes of various sizes in colorful gift wrap; then use a marker to number the boxes. Place the boxes on a table along with a supply of ribbon or yarn, scissors, and rulers or tape measures. When visiting the center, each student estimates the amount of ribbon needed to tie around each gift and records it on his paper. The student tests his guess by cutting the estimated length of ribbon and attempting to tie it around the box. Then he calculates how much more (or less) ribbon he needed to adequately wrap the box. For an added challenge, have students estimate the length of ribbon needed to tie two or more boxes together. ***Amy Polcyn—Substitute Teacher, South Lyon Community Schools, South Lyon, MI***

Christmas: Sock Snowman

Help students trim their holiday trees with "snow-dorable" ornaments fashioned from white socks! Stuff a toddler-sized white tube sock with Poly-Fil stuffing all the way up to the ribbing. Wrap a rubber band around the sock to make a snowman. Fold the ribbing down, then up, to form a cap; then use a hot glue gun to glue a pompom atop the cap. Next, tie a strip of plaid flannel fabric around the rubber band for a scarf. Poke a round wooden toothpick that's been painted orange and cut to a one-inch length into the snowman's head to make a nose; then secure the toothpick with a little hot glue. Finally, use a black fine-tipped marker to add eyes, a mouth, and buttons to the snowman. To turn the project into a snowy ornament, hot-glue a loop of narrow ribbon to the back of the snowman. ***Marilyn Davison—Grs. 4 and 5, River Oaks School, Monroe, LA***

Hanukkah: Hope on Hand

Spread the spirit of hope this Hanukkah with a lovely holiday display. Have each student trace his hands on construction paper and cut out the tracings. After he paints his cutouts with thinned glue, have the student place them in a cardboard box and sprinkle construction-paper confetti onto them. Then direct the student to lift the cutouts from the box, tap off any loose confetti, and set them aside to dry. Meanwhile, discuss the history of Hanukkah with the class, focusing on the hope that the Jewish people must have felt after the miracle of the lamp that stayed lit for eight days. Give each student an index card and have him write a narrative paragraph describing a time in his life when he was given hope, felt very hopeful, or saw a hope come true. Staple the hand cutouts on a bulletin board in a large circle, making sure that the hands touch each other slightly. Above the circle add the title "Joining Hands for Hanukkah!" Then staple the students' paragraphs inside the circle of hands.

Stepping on the Cracks
by Mary Downing Hahn
by
Ali

New Year's Day:
Betcha Can't Read Just One!

Start the new year with a resolution to read! When students return from the holiday break, ask them to donate emptied potato-chip bags. Staple the bags around the perimeter of a bulletin board titled "Betcha Can't Read Just One!" Then have each child cut a potato-chip shape from yellow construction paper. On his chip cutout, have the student write a brief book recommendation, including the title and author of his recommended book. Staple the chip cutouts to the board. Finally, challenge each student to resolve to read at least one book from the display by the end of February. When a student turns in a brief review of the book he has read, let him tear a "bite" off the chip that recommends that book. Betcha can't read just one!

Birthday of Dr. Martin Luther King Jr.:
Birthday Banners

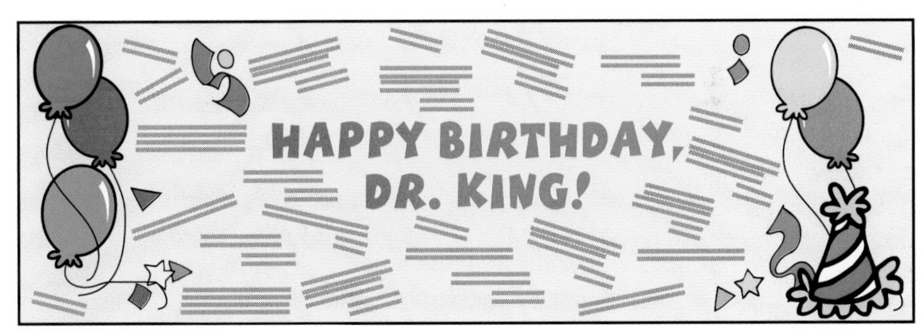

Celebrate the birth of a great American this January with an activity that invites the entire school to join the party! Divide your class into several groups (one per grade level in your school). Have each group decorate a large sheet of butcher paper to resemble a giant birthday banner in honor of Dr. Martin Luther King Jr. Challenge each group to title its banner with a birthday greeting, such as "Happy Birthday, Dr. King—A Powerful Peacemaker!" Then post each banner in your hallway. Invite each class in your school to come by and write their birthday wishes to this great man. If desired, have your students serve birthday cookies and punch when each class comes to add to its grade-level banner. ***adapted from an idea by Benita Mudd—Grs. 4 and 5, Losantiville School, Cincinnati, OH***

National Soup Month: Super Soup

What goes together like soup and a sandwich? This "soup-er" creative-thinking activity and January, which is National Soup Month! Tell students that the country's leading maker of tasty, nutritious soups has just asked each of them to invent a new recipe. This soup must appeal to a lot of people, yet be different from anything that's already sitting on grocery-store shelves. Display a variety of canned soups for students to examine. Then give each child a 4" x 7" piece of white paper on which to design a label that will go on his soup can (looking at the sample cans for ideas). Be sure the student includes the following:

- the name of his soup
- the ingredients listed in order of quantity
- any catchy phrase or slogan that will help sell the soup
- the net weight of the contents
- the name and address of the manufacturer
- directions for preparing the soup
- any recipes or special tips on using the soup so that people will buy more of it

After students write and color their labels, post the projects on a bulletin board titled "Mmmm, Good!" ***Ann Fisher, Constantine, MI***

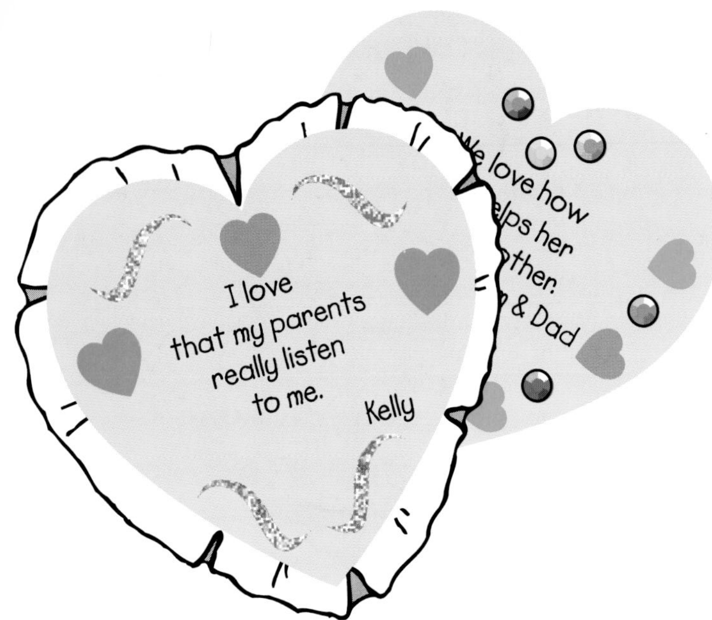

Valentine's Day:
That's What I Love About You

Invite your students' parents to become part of your February lesson plans with this heartwarming activity! Give each student two large heart shapes cut from construction paper. On one heart, the child writes a sentence that describes something he loves about his family. Then he takes both hearts home and asks his parent to label the blank cutout with something she loves about him. Next, the parent and child work together to decorate both hearts. The following day, display each pair of hearts on a bulletin board or in a hallway.

If a student has a difficult home situation, have him label his heart with something he loves about your class; then label another cutout with a quality you appreciate about him. Finally, set aside a few minutes for you and the student to decorate both hearts together. ***Teena Andersen—Grs. 4–6, Hadar Public School, Hadar, NE***

Valentine's Day:
Heartbreak!

If you love an idea that's adaptable to just about any subject, then you're in luck! This fun-to-play game is easy to make and can be used to review a variety of skills. To prepare the game, cut one heart-shaped card for each student from a folded piece of construction paper as shown. Set aside two cards; then write "HEARTBREAK!" on the inside of each one. Label the inside of each remaining card with a point value from 200 to 1,000.

To play, arrange the cards on a chalk tray or table. Divide the class into two teams. Write a math problem on the board; then have a player from each team come to the board and try to solve the problem. Let the first player to determine the correct answer choose a heart card. If the card contains a point value, add it to the player's team score. If the student selects a HEARTBREAK! card, erase all points earned by her team so far. Continue playing until each student has had a turn. The team with the higher score at the end of the game wins. Make additional cards for other holidays, such as egg cards for Easter and pumpkin cards for Halloween. ***Theresa Roh Hickey—Grs. 4 and 5, Corpus Christi School, Mobile, AL***

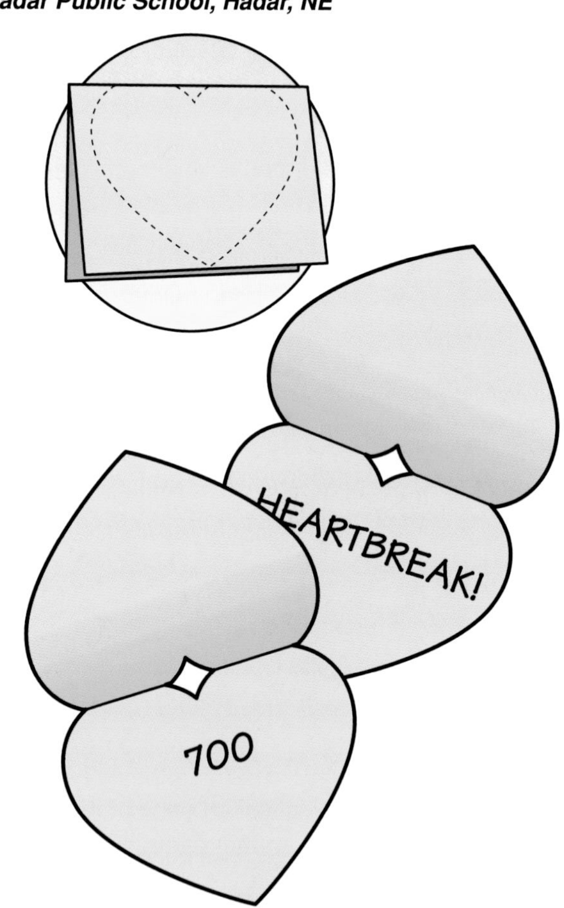

Black History Month: Guess Who?

Combine art and famous African-Americans for a game that's both informational *and* fun! First, assign each student a different African-American. Require the student to research to find ten facts about his person. Next, have the student illustrate one of his facts on a 12" x 18" sheet of drawing paper. On the back of the drawing, have the student list all ten facts he researched—without mentioning the famous person's name in any of the facts. To play, divide students into two teams. Have a member of Team 1 come to the front of the room, hold up his drawing, and read the list of facts on the back. Give one point to Team 2 if it guesses the person's identity in three tries or less. If Team 2 guesses incorrectly, give Team 1 the point. Alternate teams until all students have shared. (See also pages 99–102.)

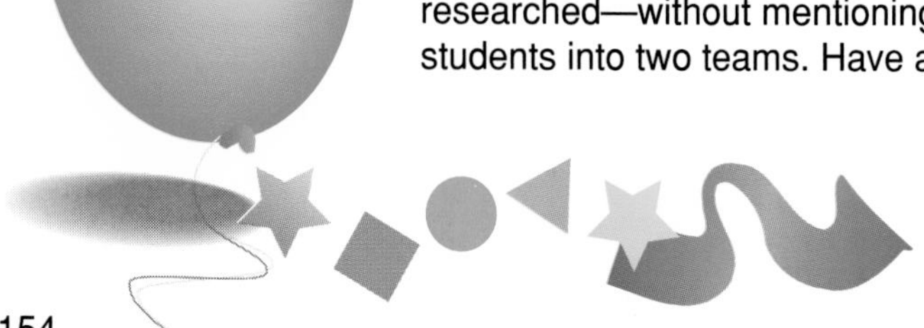

Presidents' Day:
Presidential Promises

Practice writing paragraphs this February by asking students to take a walk in the president's shoes! Give each student an index card. On his card, have the student write a paragraph describing a promise he would make to the American people if he were president of the United States. Then give each student a large red heart cut from red construction paper. Direct each student to use old magazines and other art materials to decorate his heart with a collage that illustrates his promise. After each student shares his paragraph and collage, mount the projects on a bulletin board that's covered with blue paper. ***Louella Nygaard—Gr. 5, Isabell Bills Elementary, Colstrip, MT***

As president, I promise to do everything I can to make our country a place where different people get along without fighting or prejudice.

St. Patrick's Day:
Lucky Shamrocks

You won't need a leprechaun around to benefit from the good luck in this St. Patrick's Day activity! Duplicate a supply of the booklet page shown. Label the shamrock on each page with a different letter of the alphabet; then give one to each student. Ask each child to think of something she's lucky to have that begins with her shamrock's letter. On the shamrock, have her write a paragraph describing her item and add illustrations. Bind students' completed pages into a booklet titled "Not Just the Luck of the Irish!" Or tape the papers together end-to-end to form a long mural. ***Theresa Roh Hickey—Gr. 5, Corpus Christi School, Mobile, AL***

booklet page

St. Patrick's Day:
Somewhere Over the Rainbow I Found...

You don't have to look over the rainbow for a great poetry activity! After reviewing several different forms of poetry with students, discuss the St. Patrick's Day legend about finding a pot of gold at the end of a rainbow. Ask students, "If you traveled to the end of the rainbow, what would you want to find there?" Let students brainstorm a list of ideas; then ask each child to choose a favorite form of poetry and write a poem that describes his own special rainbow reward. While students work on their poems, let small groups color a large rainbow that you've drawn on a bulletin board. Post the finished poems on the board. ***Melissa A. McMullen—Gr. 5, Saint Patrick School, Newry, PA***

Spring:
Match the Hatch!

Hatch a matchless descriptive writing activity with this idea! Spray-paint a supply of craft sticks white. After the sticks dry, glue them around the perimeter of a flat box to resemble a fence. Line the box with green Easter grass and add a cardboard sign as shown. Next, give each child a plastic egg and ask him to imagine something unusual that could have hatched from it. Instruct the student to decorate the outside of his egg with a clue about the hatchling. Then collect the eggs and arrange them in the box.

Next, have each student write a descriptive paragraph about his hatchling, keeping its identity a mystery until the last sentence. Have each student read his description aloud (except for the last sentence) and challenge the class to guess what hatched from his egg. Follow up by posting students' paragraphs near the box of eggs. During free time, challenge students to match the eggs to the corresponding descriptions. ***Maria Di Benedetto—Gr. 6, Tilden Middle School, Philadelphia, PA***

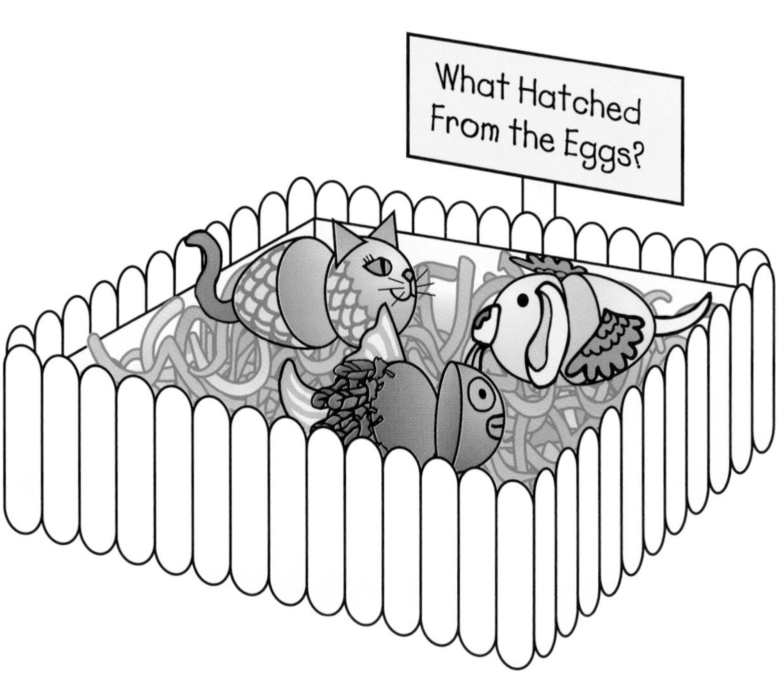

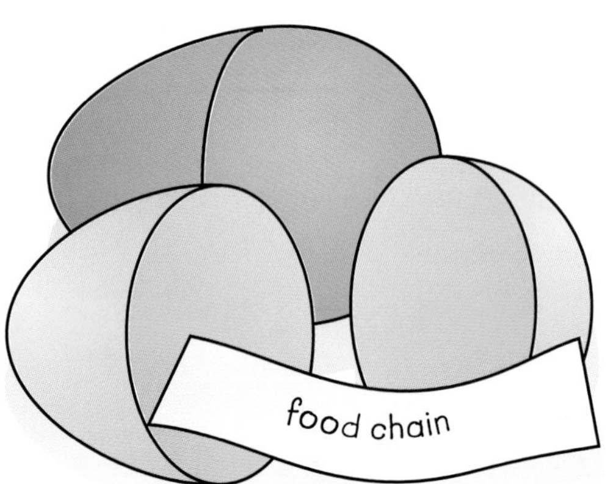

Easter:
Reviewing Over Easy

Turn a review of any subject into an "eggs-tra" special treat! Fill plastic eggs with paper strips that have been labeled with words from a unit you want students to review. Nestle the eggs in a basket filled with Easter grass. Carry the basket around the room, stopping at each student's desk to have her choose an egg. After distributing the eggs, ask one child at a time to open hers and state a fact or ask the class a question using the word inside. With this fun format, you may never have to egg students on to review again! ***Jaimie K. Hudson, Pace, FL***

Easter:
Couldn't You Just "Dye"?

Let students practice the scientific method with an experiment they'll really "dye" for! Ask parents to contribute various egg-dyeing kits and other materials for the experiment on page 162. Divide students into groups of four. Give each group a copy of page 162 and the materials listed on it. Then have the group complete the activity as directed. If desired, have each group write to the manufacturers of the kits it tested to make a suggestion or give a compliment based upon the group's findings. Or have each group create a bar, circle, or line graph to display the class's combined data. ***Kelly Blessey, Redding Elementary, West Redding, CT***

Earth Day:
Prescription for Planet Earth

What threatens our planet's health? Challenge students to find out and to suggest remedies with this Earth Day activity! Have students brainstorm a list of threats to our planet as you record their ideas on the board. Then assign each child a topic from the board to research. After the research is completed, give each student a large unlined index card, a 1" x 4 1/2" strip of white paper, a glue stick, and an empty 35 mm film container. Instruct the student to write on the card (as shown) a prescription for the ailment he has researched. Have him fill out his paper strip to resemble a prescription bottle's label and glue it to his film container. Then have him glue the container to the upper right corner of the card as illustrated. After students share their remedies, place the projects in the media center under a banner titled "Prescriptions for a Healthy Planet Earth."

Mother's Day:
"Pinning" a Card for Mom

Help students remember Mom or another special lady on Mother's Day with this heartfelt gift! Have each child paint a small wooden heart and allow it to dry. Use a glue gun to attach a large pin back to the back of each child's heart cutout. Have the student use a fine-tipped black marker to write a simple message on the heart. Then have her glue on tiny silk flowers in an attractive design. Next, direct the student to fold a 5 1/2" x 8 1/2" piece of card stock and write a message inside. After the child pins the heart to the front of the card and adds decorations, have her wrap the gift with tissue and ribbon. ***Merrill Watrous, Eugene, OR***

Memorial Day:
Memorial Day Tributes

Make Memorial Day memorable with this interviewing and writing activity. Ask each student to interview family members to learn about a loved one who died while serving our country in time of war. After the interviews, give each student one white and two slightly larger blue stars cut from 9" x 12" sheets of construction paper, two 5 1/2" x 7" pieces of construction paper (one white, one red), a ruler, scissors, and a glue stick. Then have him complete the steps below. Display the finished projects on a bulletin board titled "Memorial Day Tributes."

Steps:

1. On the white star, write a tribute to the individual you learned about.
2. Glue the white star atop a blue star.
3. Make 1/4-inch-wide cuts, or streamers, in the red paper, stopping about one inch from the end. Then cut off the even-numbered streamers.
4. Repeat Step 3 with the white paper, cutting off the odd-numbered streamers.
5. Glue the strips of streamers together at the top. Then glue them between the blue stars so they hang down as shown.

Captain Robert J. Smyre
1930–1968
Captain Robert J. Smyre was killed in action during the Vietnam War on January 30, 1968, in Saigon. He was a courageous man who had served his country since joining the Army in 1948.

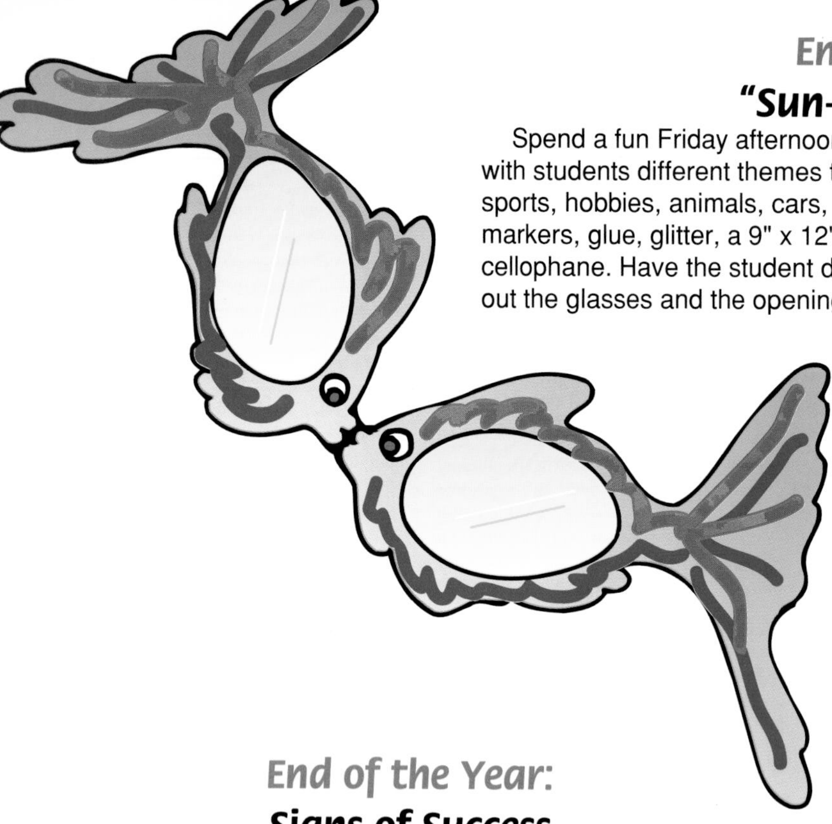

End of the Year:
"Sun-sational" Shades

Spend a fun Friday afternoon making "sun-sational" shades! First, brainstorm with students different themes that could be used for their designs, such as sports, hobbies, animals, cars, etc. Then give each student scissors, clear tape, markers, glue, glitter, a 9" x 12" piece of oaktag, and a 9" x 12" piece of colored cellophane. Have the student draw and color his design on the oaktag, then cut out the glasses and the openings for the eyes. Finally, have him tape the cellophane to the back and trim off the excess. After students add details with markers and glitter, display the decorative sunglasses on a bulletin board titled "'Sun-sational' Shades!" ***Joan M. Macey, Binghamton, NY***

End of the Year:
Signs of Success

Get a jump on August by having your students prepare a display that will head next year's class in the right direction! First, discuss with students different types of road signs (stop, yield, railroad crossing, speed limit, road work, etc.). Point out how such signs help people move about more safely and successfully. Together, brainstorm words of wisdom that this year's students could give your next class; then assign each student a different letter of the alphabet and give him a sheet of oaktag, scissors, and colored markers. Direct the student to design a road sign and label it with a piece of advice that begins with his assigned letter. Post the signs; then save them to display at the beginning of the next school year. ***Margaret Zogg—K–6 Substitute, Liverpool School District, Liverpool, NY***

STOP
Focus on doing your best.
YIELD
Listen thoughtfully to the ideas of others.

End of the Year:
Lunch Bag Publishing

Turn plain paper lunch bags into memory books that help students reminisce about their super school year. Have each child fold a lunch bag in half; then have her reinforce the unfolded edges by covering them with clear tape. Direct the student to fold four sheets of plain white paper in half two times, then cut out the resulting sections to make 16 pages for her book. Next, have the student staple the pages inside the cover at the fold and glue the first and last pages to the covers. Finally, have her title her book "Food for Thought About a Fun Year" and decorate the cover. Direct students to use the suggestions below for writing and illustrating the first few pages of their books, leaving the remaining pages for classmates' autographs. What a treasured keepsake this will become! ***Ingrid Wolf—Gr. 5, Catholic Central School, Appleton, WI***

Suggestions:
My favorite memory about this school year is…
The funniest thing that happened this year was…
How could I forget…
The best field trip this year was…

Food for Thought About a Fun Year

End of the Year:

And the Days Go Marching On…

"Ant-ticipate" a fun ending to a terrific year with a display that counts down the days 'til school's out! Cover a bulletin board with an inexpensive, red-checkered plastic tablecloth. Staple on paper plates and napkins, empty drink boxes, and other picnic items. Enlarge an ant pattern such as the one shown; then duplicate one ant for each remaining school day. Have students color and cut out the ants; then post them among the picnic items. Each day let a student remove an ant from the board. Before you know it, summer vacation will be here! ***Teena Andersen, Hadar Public School, Hadar, NE***

Flag Day/Independence Day:

Life, Liberty, and Happiness

Create an eye-popping patriotic display with this easy-to-do activity. Together, discuss the Declaration of Rights found in the Declaration of Independence (see the illustration); then have students share their interpretations of "life, liberty, and the pursuit of happiness." Next, give each student old magazines, scissors, glue, and a 9" x 12" sheet of red construction paper. Guide students through the steps below to make a large American flag. ***Jan Kneessi—Gr. 5, Trinity Christian School, Northridge, CA***

Steps:

1. On his red paper, have each student create a collage of pictures representing his thoughts about "life, liberty, and the pursuit of happiness."
2. Tape the collages together side by side as shown to form five red horizontal stripes.
3. Write each part of the Declaration of Rights on a separate 4-inch-wide banner of white paper as shown.
4. Have students cut out and glue 50 white stars to a 26" x 36" blue rectangle.
5. Tape the field of stars and the stripes together to make a giant flag as shown.

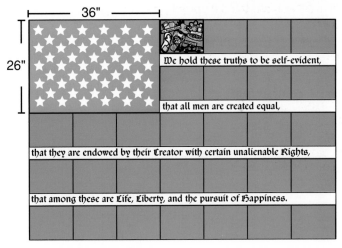

36"

26"

We hold these truths to be self-evident,

that all men are created equal,

that they are endowed by their Creator with certain unalienable Rights,

that among these are Life, Liberty, and the pursuit of Happiness.

Father's Day:

Magnetic Frame

Want a gift idea that's sure to attract a lot of attention? Then this magnetic frame should do the trick! Give each student four craft sticks and several different shapes of dried pasta. Direct the student to glue the sticks together to make a square. When the glue has dried, have him paint the square and pasta pieces with paint. After the sticks and pasta have dried, have the student glue the pasta onto the sticks in an attractive arrangement, adding glitter if desired. Finally, have the student attach two pieces of self-sticking magnetic tape to the back of the frame. Let students take their frames home to surprise their dads. Or present them at the end of the year to your parent volunteers. ***Sherri Kaiser—Gr. 4, Walnut Grove Elementary, Suwanee, GA***

Name________________________ Personal attributes and opinions

☆ ☆ ☆ Introducing Me! ☆ ☆ ☆

Clue others in on what makes you tick by completing the sentences below. Next, cut the clues apart on the dotted lines. Fold the clues in half and place them in the container provided by your teacher. Then get ready for a fun getting-to-know-you activity for the whole class!

1. What I look forward to most about the first day of school is ________________________.
2. I can't ____________, but I'm really good at ________________________.
3. All it takes to make me happy is ________________________.
4. The way I spend free time is ________________________.
5. If I were planning my favorite meal, it would include ________________________.
6. If I were giving an Emmy for the best TV show, I'd award it to ________________________.
7. My most prized possession is ________________________.
8. If I could be like another person, I'd choose ____________.
9. If I could own only one book, I'd want it to be ________________________.
10. To cheer myself up, I ________________________.

Name________________________ Personal attributes and opinions

☆ ☆ ☆ Introducing Me! ☆ ☆ ☆

Clue others in on what makes you tick by completing the sentences below. Next, cut the clues apart on the dotted lines. Fold the clues in half and place them in the container provided by your teacher. Then get ready for a fun getting-to-know-you activity for the whole class!

1. What I look forward to most about the first day of school is ________________________.
2. I can't ____________, but I'm really good at ________________________.
3. All it takes to make me happy is ________________________.
4. The way I spend free time is ________________________.
5. If I were planning my favorite meal, it would include ________________________.
6. If I were giving an Emmy for the best TV show, I'd award it to ________________________.
7. My most prized possession is ________________________.
8. If I could be like another person, I'd choose ____________.
9. If I could own only one book, I'd want it to be ________________________.
10. To cheer myself up, I ________________________.

©The Education Center, Inc. • *The Best of* The Mailbox® • *Intermediate* • Book 4 • TEC894

Note to the teacher: Use "Introducing Me!" with "Back to School: Stand Up and Be Recognized!" on page 149. Provide students with scissors.

Charting a Course to Comprehension!

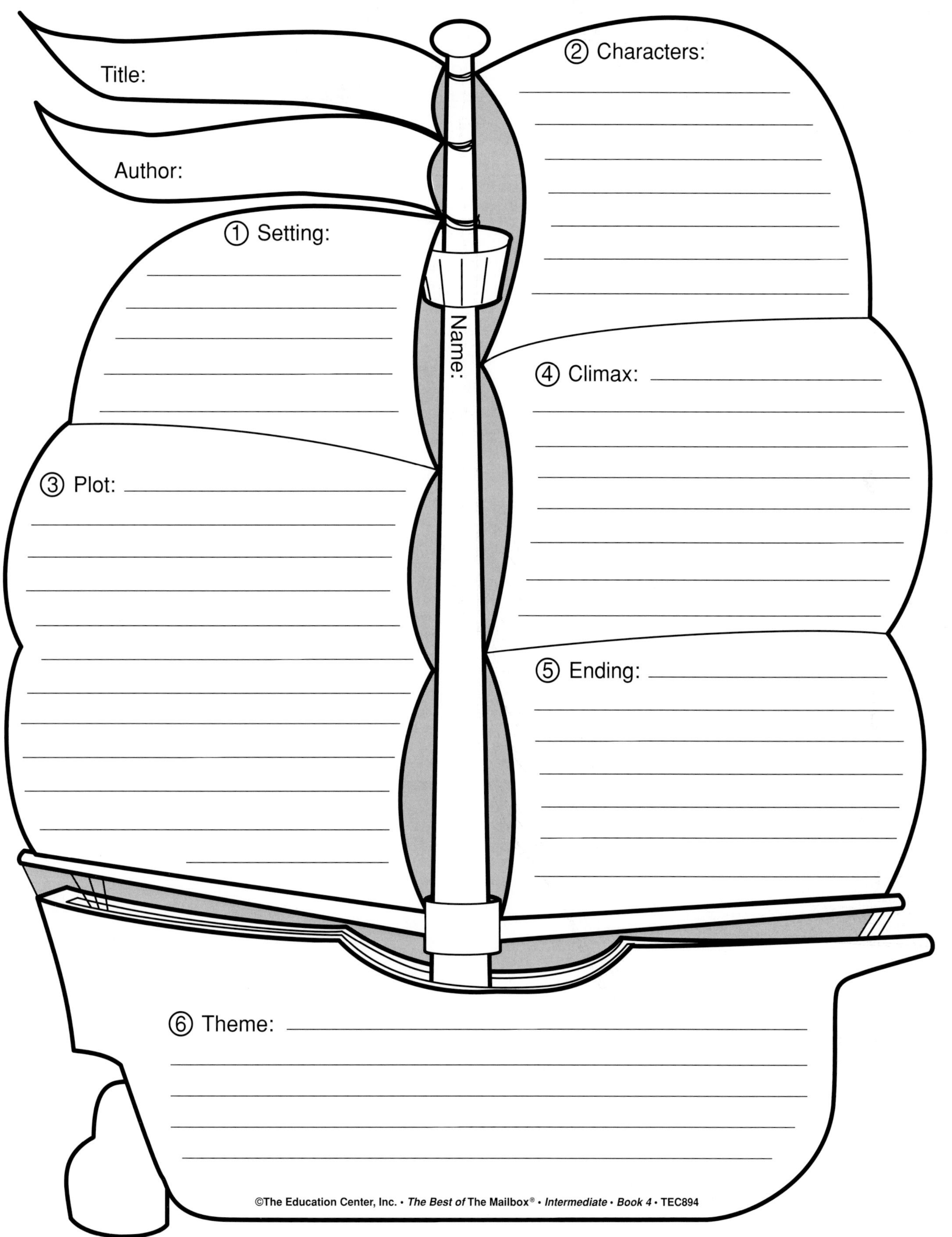

Note to the teacher: Use with "Columbus Day: Charting a Course to Comprehension!" on page 150.

Names ____

____

Couldn't You Just "Dye"?

Reggie Rabbit has a special job this Easter. The Easter Bunny has asked him to dye all the eggs! Reggie knows how particular the Easter Bunny is about the appearance of his eggs. Help Reggie find out which kit will do the best job.

Materials: 3 different egg-dyeing kits (see packages for additional materials needed), 1 dozen hard-boiled eggs, newspaper, pencil

Steps:

1. Cover your work area with newspaper.
2. Record the name of each kit in the chart.
3. For each kit, follow the directions on the package to dye four eggs.
4. Use the rating scale below to record your observations for each kit in the chart.
5. Find the total score for each kit. Then find the average score for each kit. Round to the nearest whole number.
6. Based on your findings, complete the sentence that tells which kit Reggie should use for dyeing the eggs.

Name of kit	Brightness of color	Easy to use	Directions are clear	Includes extra decorations	Total score	Average score

Rating Scale

1 = No way! 2 = Kind of yucky 3 = Okay 4 = Pretty good 5 = This is it!

Reggie should use ______________________ because ______________________

____.

Bonus Box: Create an advertising slogan for the dye kit Reggie should use: ______________________

____

Note to the teacher: Use with "Easter: Couldn't You Just 'Dye'?" on page 156. Duplicate one copy for each group of students. Students' answers will vary based upon the kits used and their ratings.

Seasonal and Holiday Reproducibles

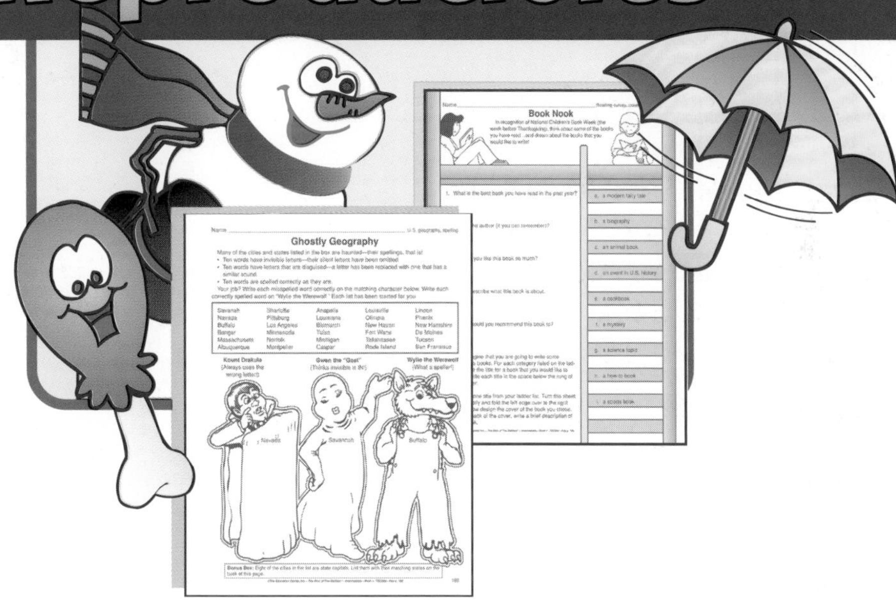

Name ____________________

Miss Pickwell's Puzzlers

Priscilla Pickwell takes great pride in creating puzzles to perplex students during the first days of school. See if you can solve the puzzles she's giving this year's class!

Puzzle #1

Solving this puzzle will let you in on a little secret! Start reading from one of the letters in the top row. Move to the right, left, up, or down to discover this secret. Hint: You can't move diagonally!

I	N	B	K	S
N	G	O	O	A
R	T	S	E	R
A	O	Y	T	H
E	L	E	K	E

The secret:

______
______
______
______
______
______

Puzzle #2

Some schoolchildren visited the chimpanzee section at the city zoo. They gave the zookeeper this challenge: Name ten three-letter words that are chimpanzee body parts. The keeper had no problem coming up with ten words. Can you?

_____ _____ _____ _____ _____

_____ _____ _____ _____ _____

Puzzle #3

Use the grid on the right to rearrange the numbers in the other grid so that the same number does not appear twice in any row, column, or diagonal. If the numbers are arranged correctly, each row and column totals 100. Good luck!

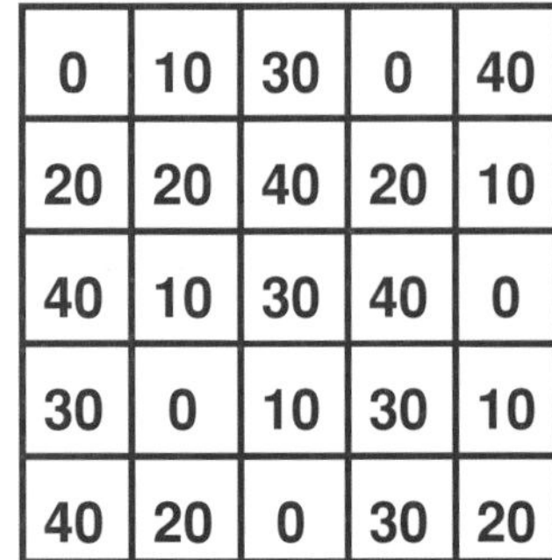

0	10	30	0	40
20	20	40	20	10
40	10	30	40	0
30	0	10	30	10
40	20	0	30	20

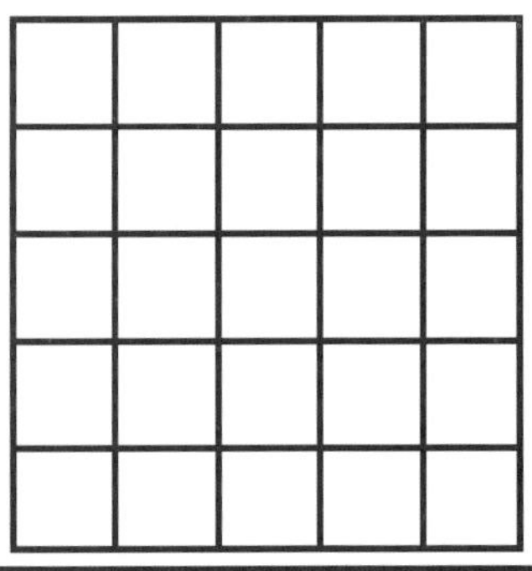

Puzzle #4

Hidden in this puzzle is a word that completes Miss Pickwell's advice about homework. Compare each pair of numbers. Then circle the number that is greater. Write the letter above the circled number in its corresponding blank below to read the message.

	T		B
①	1,610	or	1,601
	W		A
②	27,770	or	27,707
	D		I
③	4,500	or	4,550
	J		O
④	36,005	or	36,050
	H		J
⑤	580,070	or	508,070
	T		H
⑥	882,222	or	822,882
	U		E
⑦	55,489	or	54,895

DON'T
LEAVE
HOME

__ __ __ __ __ __ __
2 3 6 5 4 7 1

IT!

Bonus Box: When is the only time that two fours make one?

Name____

Oh, Be "Cents-ible"!

How are you going to solve the problems on this page? By being "cents-ible," that's how!
Directions: Pretend that each letter of the alphabet is worth $.05 more than the letter before it: A = $.05, B = $.10, and so on until Z = $1.30. Show your work on the back of this page or another sheet of paper. Then write your answers on the lines.

1. What is the total value of your school's name? ____________

2. Calculate the total value of your first, middle, and last names. ____________

3. How many of your classmates have first names that are equal in value to yours?____________
List them. ____________

4. Guess which of your classmates has the most valuable first name. ____________
Why did you pick this person?____________
Check your prediction by calculating the value of that classmate's name. Were you right?
____

5. Write the name of the classmate seated on your right (or left). ____________
Find the difference in the values of your first names. ____________ Next, find the difference in your last names. ____________ Then find the difference when both the first and last names are combined. ____________ Which difference is greatest: first names only, last names only, or both names together? ____________

6. Which school supply below do you think has the highest value? ____________
The lowest? ____________ Find out by calculating the value of each item.

a. pencil ________	e. eraser ________
b. crayons ________	f. bookbag ________
c. scissors ________	g. calculator ________
d. glue ________	h. sharpener ________

7. How much would your first name be worth if you multiplied the value of each of its letters by 5? ____________ By 10? ____________

Bonus Box: Whose name is worth more: your teacher's or your principal's?

Note to the teacher: To complete this activity, students may need a copy of the class roster. Use as a back-to-school activity or anytime you want students to practice computing money.

Name ____

CAPTAIN CRAYON TO THE RESCUE!

Help! Someone has hidden your teacher's supplies! The start of the school year will have to be postponed unless you and Captain Crayon can crack this mystery.

Each question below contains one of the school supplies written on the crayons. Find and circle each hidden word, and color its crayon. Then write an answer on the line to show that you understand the question. Use a dictionary to find the meanings of any unfamiliar words. Let the search begin!

Example: Could a bri(de sk)ip gleefully down the aisle? (desk)
Answer: Yes, a bride could skip gleefully if she didn't mind looking silly.

1. Would you dampen cilantro with salad dressing or motor oil? ______________________
2. Can rocks be shaped by running water as erosion occurs? ______________________
3. Can a clock erratically tick and become undependable? ______________________
4. Is it possible for a plastic ray on a toy starfish to break off? ______________________
5. Could you catch Al King trying to make a kite ascend? ______________________
6. Can a drum's tap lessen in frequency? ______________________
7. Can someone's papa steadily rise out of a chair that he has been sitting in? ______________________
8. Could a worksheet include a mark erroneously made by your teacher? ______________________
9. Should a rule resolutely remain the same for all students in a class? ______________________
10. Can music from a melodious harp energize people? ______________________
11. Can a baby play peek-a-boo keenly with his mommy or daddy? ______________________
12. Can a dog's rear appendage tap excitedly on the floor? ______________________
13. Would a person gape nonchalantly if he were about to step on a snake? ______________________
14. Would it be ethical for a taxi driver to dump a person in a chasm? ______________________

L
paper
O
sharpener
book
V
A
crayon
D
marker
staples
E
eraser
C

Bonus Box: Rearrange the letters from the crayon tips above to spell the name of Captain Crayon's hometown and state.

___ ___ ___ ___ ___ ___, ___ ___ ___ ___ ___ ___ ___ ___

Take the "Prime-ary" Path!

Find your way through this pumpkin maze, from start to finish. Sounds easy, right? There's one catch though: Your path can cross *only* prime numbers. Remember that a *prime number* is a number that has exactly two factors: itself and 1. Use a pencil to draw your route.

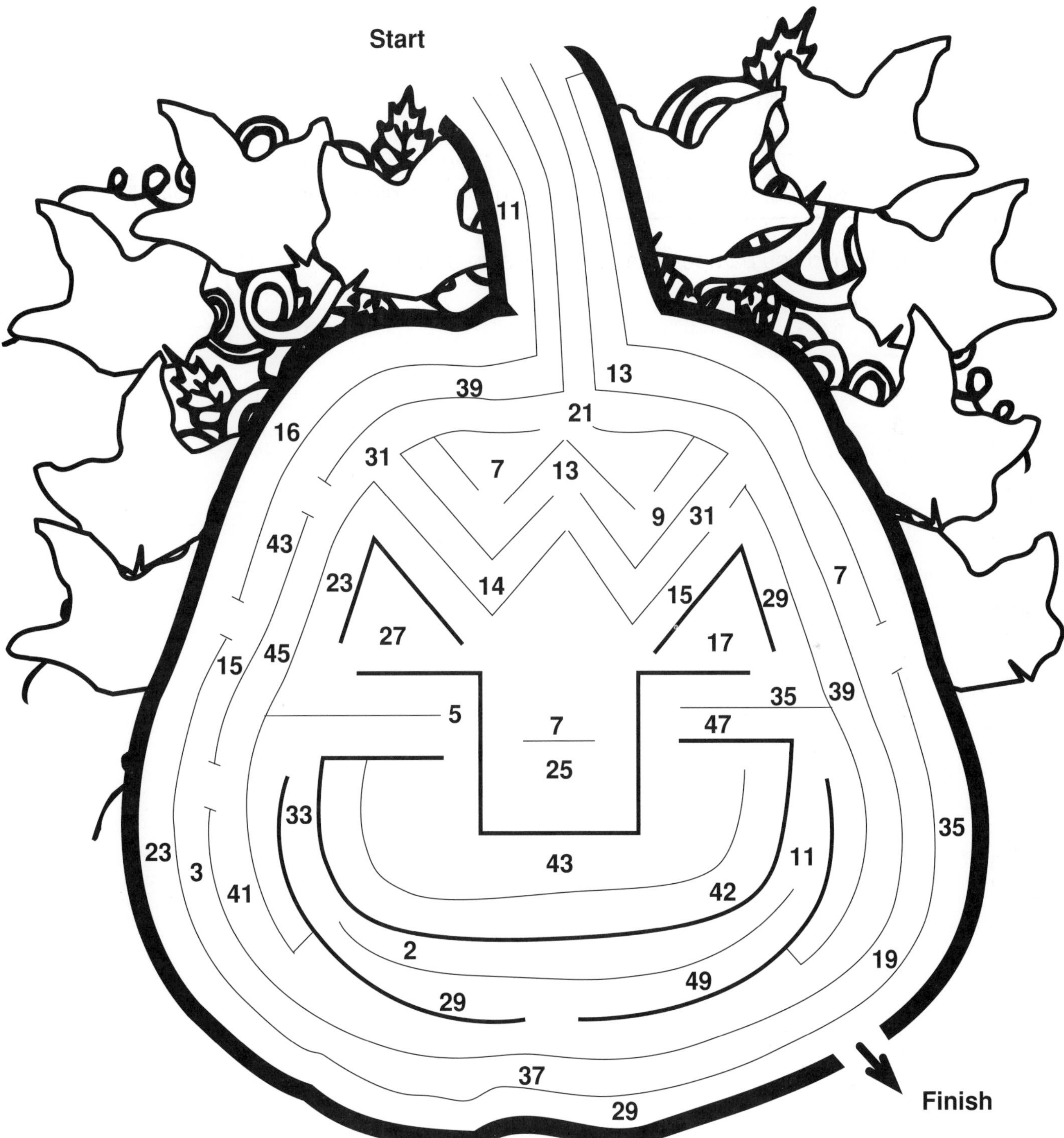

Now that you've made your way through the maze, list the ten prime numbers between 50 and 100 on the leaves, one number per leaf.

Bonus Box: Multiply the following prime factors to find the weight of the largest pumpkin ever grown: 2 x 3 x 3 x 5 x 11 = __________ pounds.

Name ________________________________ Recognizing fact and opinion

Man, What a Month!

October's here...a time of football, Halloween, raking leaves, and sweets. Sweets? Yep, October is National Cookie Month *and* National Dessert Month! Take a look at some of the other interesting goings-on in October listed in the calendar below.

Directions: Read each statement. If the statement is a fact, outline its box in red. If the statement is an opinion, outline its box in blue. Remember:

- A **fact** is a statement that can be *proven* to be true.
- An **opinion** is what someone *believes* is true.

October

S	M	T	W	TH	F	S
				1	2	3
4	5	6	7	8	9	10
11	12	13	14	15	16	17
18	19	20	21	22	23	24
25	26	27	28	29	30	31

October
October is one of seven months that has 31 days.

Month Of The Dinosaur
An asteroid probably caused the dinosaurs to die out.

National Dessert Month
Americans eat more ice cream than do the people of any other country.

National Pizza Month
Pizza is the Italian word for *pie.*

National Popcorn Poppin' Month
The United States grows almost all the world's popcorn.

Child Health Month
Chicken pox affects more children than adults.

Computer Learning Month
Every family should own a computer.

Healthy Lung Month
Smoking is the most important health problem we should solve today.

National Communicate With Your Kid Month
Communicating with a parent isn't a hard thing to do.

National Dental Hygiene Month
The world's first dental school was founded in Baltimore.

National Cookie Month
Chocolate-chip cookies are much better than oatmeal cookies.

National Roller Skating Month
Roller skaters shouldn't skate on sidewalks.

National Stamp Collecting Month
A *philatelist* is a person who collects or studies stamps.

National Car Care Month
It's important to spend time each week taking care of your car.

Halloween
People in England and Ireland once carved out beets, potatoes, and turnips to use as Halloween lanterns.

Bonus Box: If you could designate October as "_______ Month," how would you fill in the blank? On the back of this page, draw the front of a greeting card that someone might send to celebrate this special October happening.

Name ______________________________ U.S. geography, spelling

Ghostly Geography

Many of the cities and states listed in the box are haunted—their spellings, that is!

- Ten words have invisible letters—their silent letters have been omitted.
- Ten words have letters that are disguised—a letter has been replaced with one that has a similar sound.
- Ten words are spelled correctly as they are.

Your job? Write each misspelled word correctly on the matching character below. Write each correctly spelled word on "Wylie the Werewolf." Each list has been started for you.

Savanah	Sharlotte	Anapolis	Louisville	Lincon
Navada	Pittsburg	Louisiana	Olimpia	Phenix
Buffalo	Los Angeles	Bismarch	New Havan	New Hamshire
Banger	Minnesoda	Tulsa	Fort Wane	De Moines
Massachusets	Norfolk	Mishigan	Tallahassee	Tucson
Albuquerque	Montpelier	Caspar	Rode Island	San Fransisco

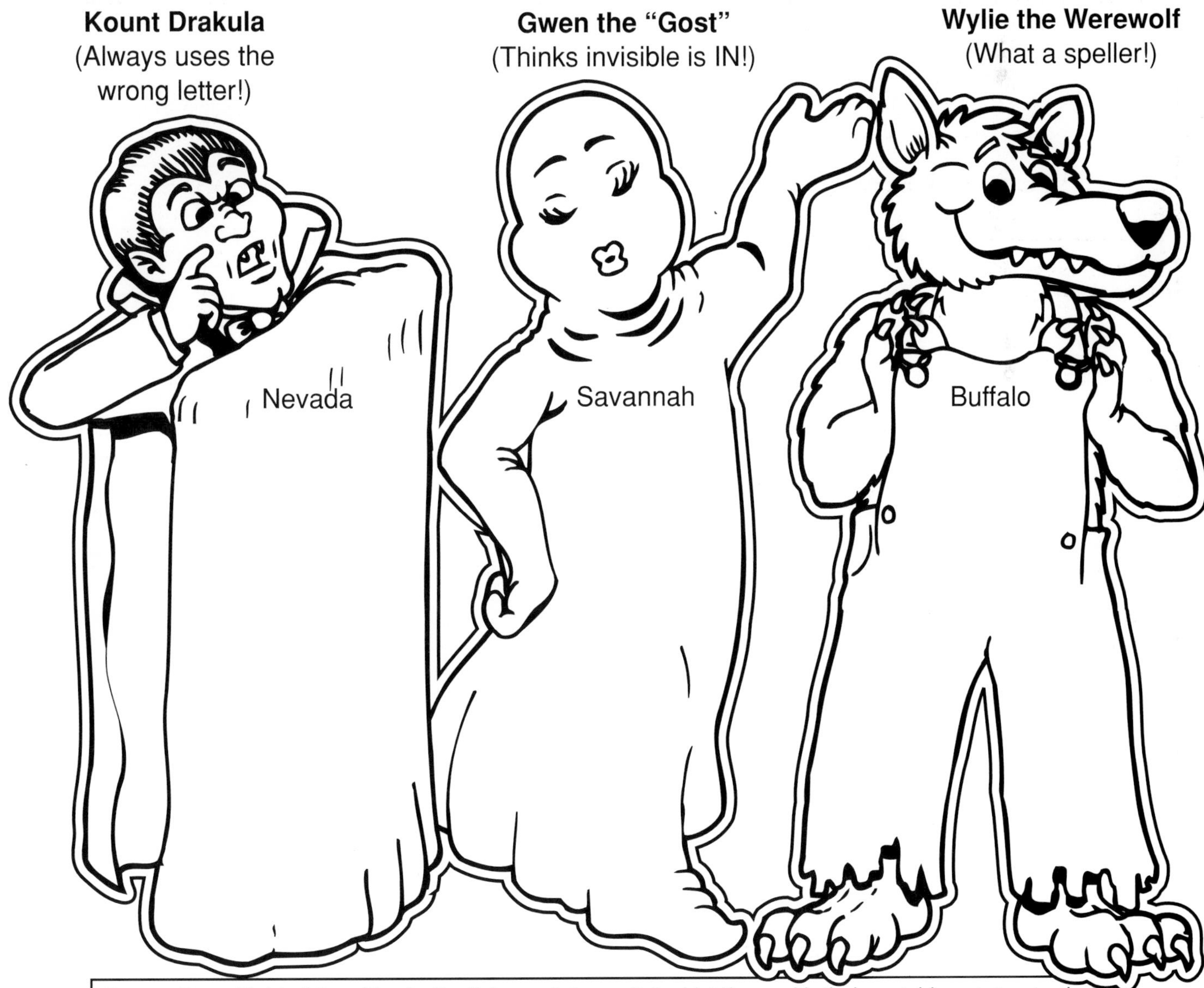

Bonus Box: Eight of the cities in the list are state capitals. List them with their matching states on the back of this page.

Name____ Reading survey, creative thinking

Book Nook

In recognition of National Children's Book Week (the week before Thanksgiving), think about some of the books you have read…and dream about the books that you would like to write!

1. What is the best book you have read in the past year?

2. Who is the author (if you can remember)?

3. Why did you like this book so much?

4. Briefly describe what this book is about.

5. Whom would you recommend this book to?

6. Now imagine that you are going to write some children's books. For each category listed on the ladder, write the title for a book that you would like to write. Write each title in the space below the rung of the ladder.

7. Choose one title from your ladder list. Turn this sheet horizontally and fold the left edge over to the right edge. Now design the cover of the book you chose. On the back of the cover, write a brief description of your book.

a. a modern fairy tale

b. a biography

c. an animal book

d. an event in U.S. history

e. a cookbook

f. a mystery

g. a science topic

h. a how-to book

i. a sports book

Name____

Eating in the Dark

When the *Mayflower* set sail on September 6, 1620, its 102 passengers included more than 20 children. During that first hard winter in Plymouth, nearly half the adults died. But almost all the children survived!

What was life like for the Pilgrims? Remember: They were real people—just like you—who lived long ago. Below are some fascinating facts about the Pilgrims. Each one is the effect of a cause-and-effect statement. Read each effect; then see if you can provide its cause in the blank. Use what you already know about the Pilgrims to help you, plus try to make some good guesses!

Remember:
An *effect* tells *what happened.* A *cause* tells *why it happened.*

____ 1. On the *Mayflower,* some Pilgrims preferred to eat at night because ____________________

____ 2. In the main cabin, anyone over five feet tall had to walk bent over because ____________________

____ 3. No one could eat the pigs, goats, and sheep aboard the *Mayflower* because ____________________

____ 4. The Pilgrims took lots of spices to the New World because ____________________

____ 5. Cooking wasn't allowed on the ship due to ____________________

____ 6. The *Mayflower* could not go too close to the land because ____________________

____ 7. The Pilgrims were astonished when they met Samoset because ____________________

____ 8. The Pilgrims were not very good hunters due to ____________________

____ 9. Pilgrim families had chickens but rarely ate them because ____________________

____ 10. The Pilgrims didn't like vegetables because ____________________

____ 11. The Pilgrims often stood and ate right out of the cooking pot because ____________________

____ 12. Some children had to stand at the table at mealtimes because ____________________

Causes

a. there was often nothing for them to sit on.
b. they couldn't see the bugs crawling on their food.
c. he could speak English.
d. the ceiling was so low.
e. eggs were so important.
f. the Pilgrims hoped they would be the parents of large herds and flocks in America.
g. they were just too busy for regular meals.
h. the danger of starting a fire.
i. they didn't consider vegetables real food.
j. spices could cover up the bad taste of rotting food.
k. it would get stuck in the sand.
l. noisy and inaccurate guns.

Note to the teacher: After duplicating this page, cut it along the first dashed line. Have students complete each statement with a reasonable cause. Then distribute the bottom section of the reproducible so that students can match each effect to its actual cause. Have students write the letter of each cause in the blank in front of its matching effect. See the answer key on page 190.

Name ________________________________ Adjectives, alliteration

A Descriptive Thanksgiving

Who you calling problematic?

How would you describe the pie you had last Thanksgiving? Was it *pulpy, priceless,* or *problematic?* These three descriptive words are all *adjectives*. An adjective is a word that describes a noun.

Listed below are nouns that are related to Thanksgiving. Above each noun, write two adjectives that could describe it *and* that begin with the same letter. Use a dictionary if you need help.

Example: pulpy, priceless pie

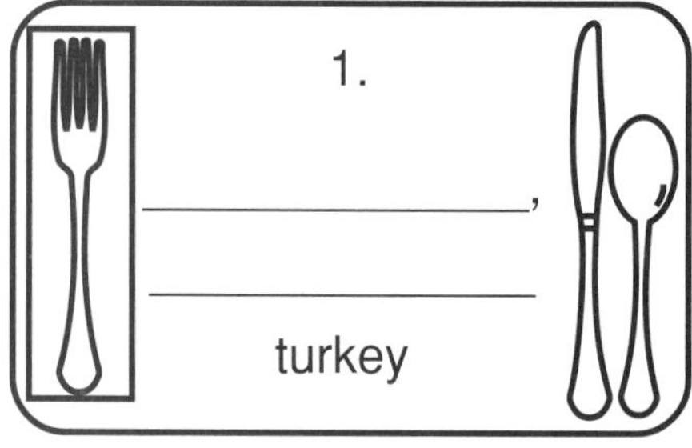

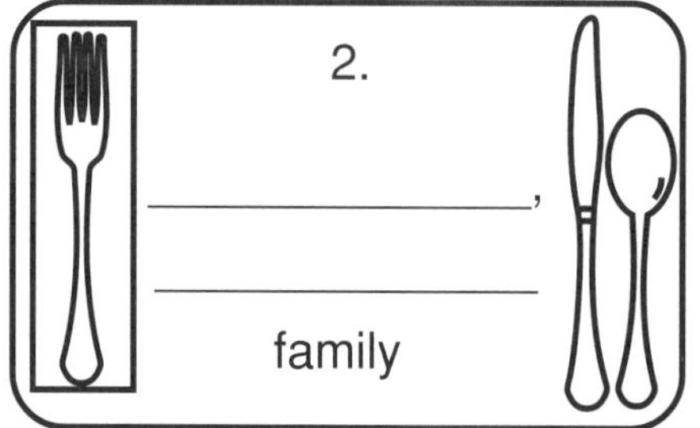

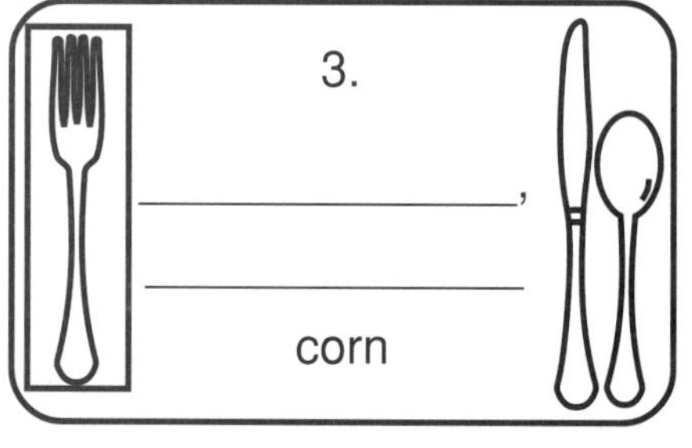

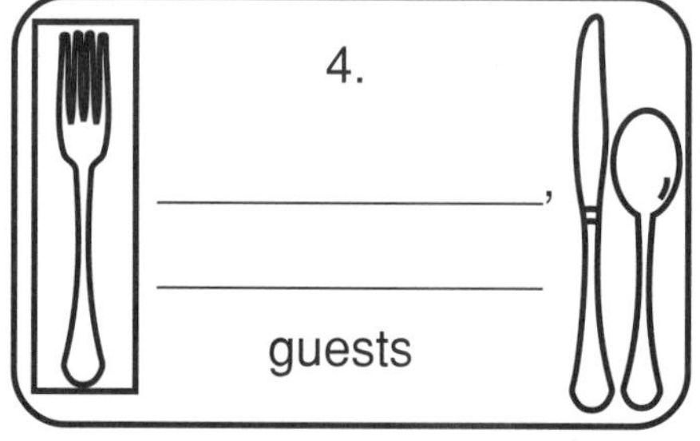

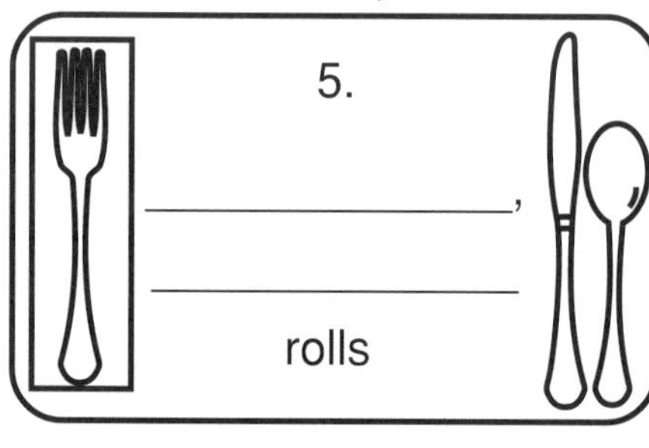

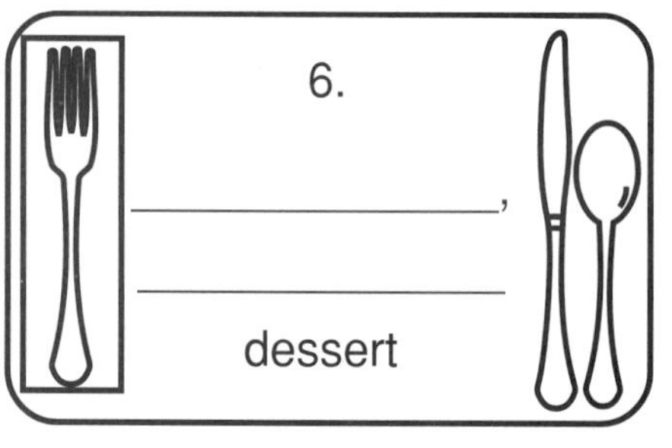

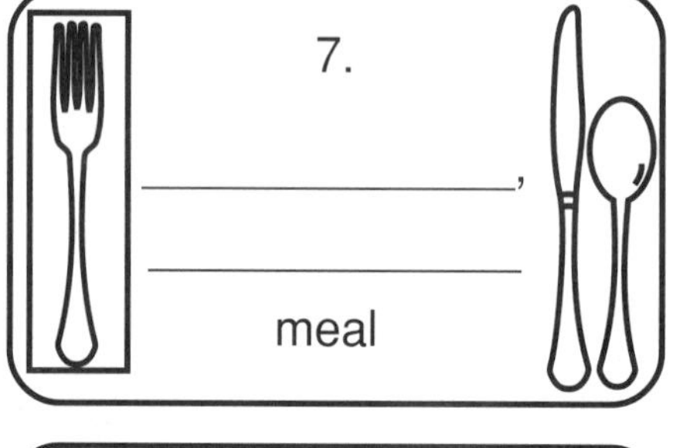

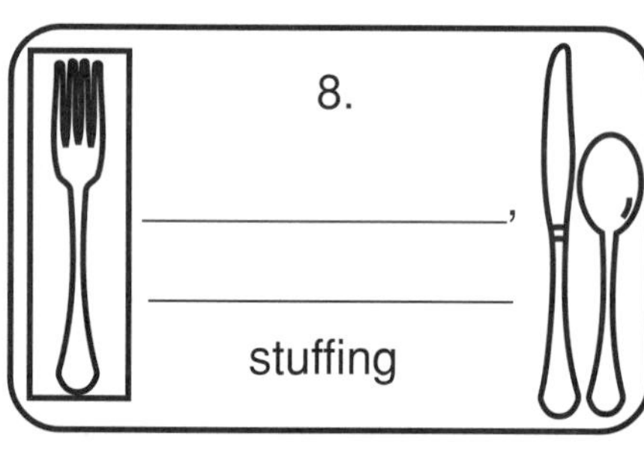

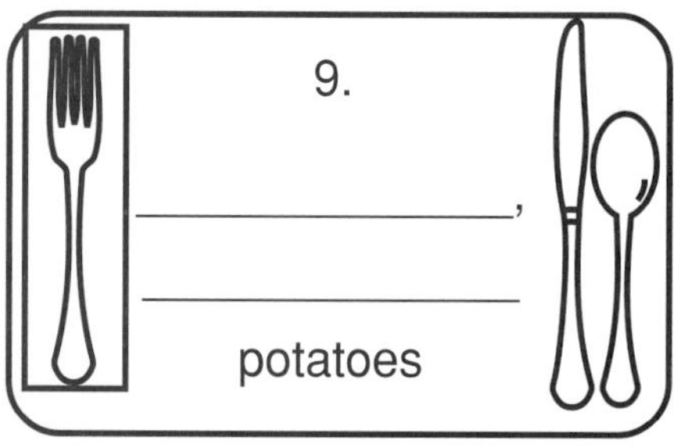

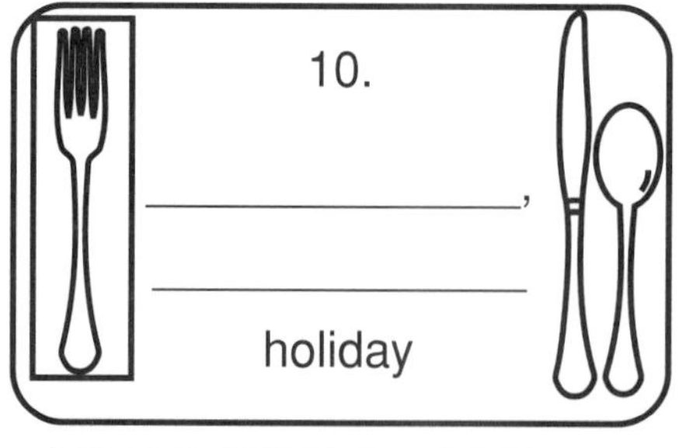

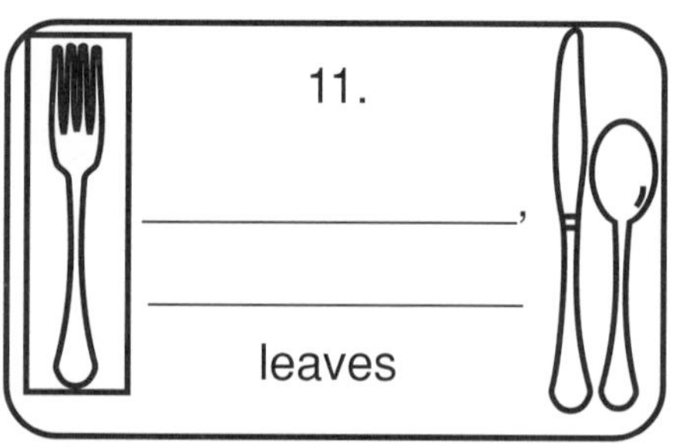

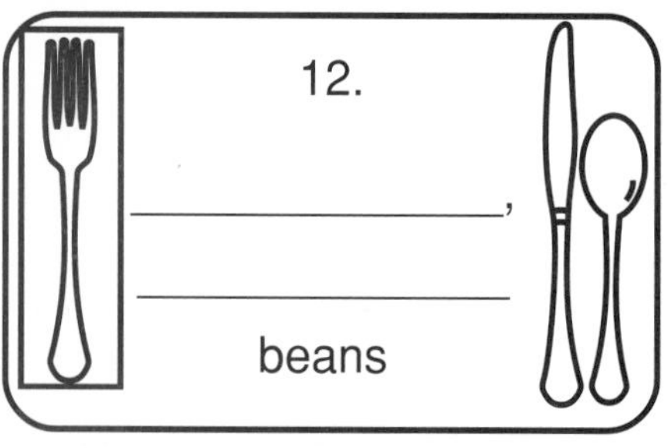

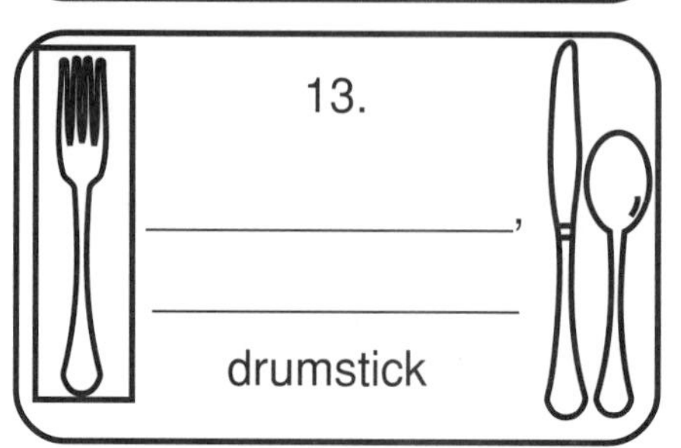

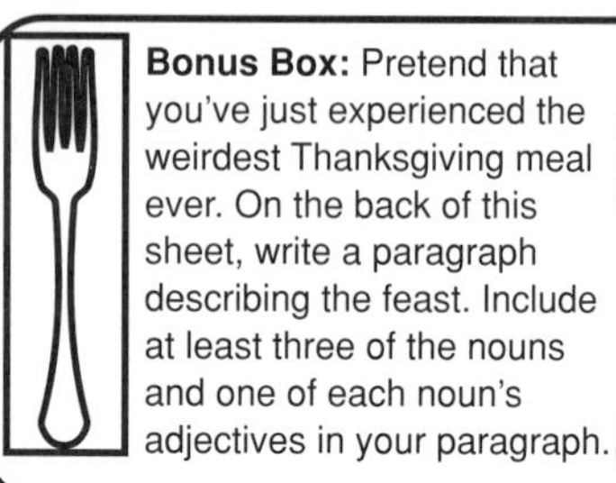

Bonus Box: Pretend that you've just experienced the weirdest Thanksgiving meal ever. On the back of this sheet, write a paragraph describing the feast. Include at least three of the nouns and one of each noun's adjectives in your paragraph.

Name____________________ Mental math, multiplying decimals

Bright and Beautiful Star

Celebrate Hanukkah with the glow of this colorful Star of David! First, complete the problems below by mentally multiplying. Write your answers on the blanks. Then follow the code at the bottom of the page to color the star.

a. 0.4 x 4 = __________
b. 0.1 x 0.1 = __________
c. 0.01 x 0.1 = __________
d. 0.1 x 0.2 x 0.3 = __________
e. 2 x 0.2 = __________
f. 0.2 x 0.02 x 0.3 = __________
g. 0.5 x 0.5 = __________
h. 5 x 0.5 = __________
i. 6 x 0.7 = __________

j. 0.06 x 0.7 = __________
k. 0.3 x 2 x 0.2 = __________
l. 0.01 x 0.01 = __________
m. 0.4 x 2 x 0.7 = __________
n. 0.5 x 0.05 = __________
o. 0.6 x 0.02 x 0.3 = __________
p. 5 x 0.05 = __________
q. 0.05 x 0.05 = __________
r. 0.3 x 0.3 x 3 = __________

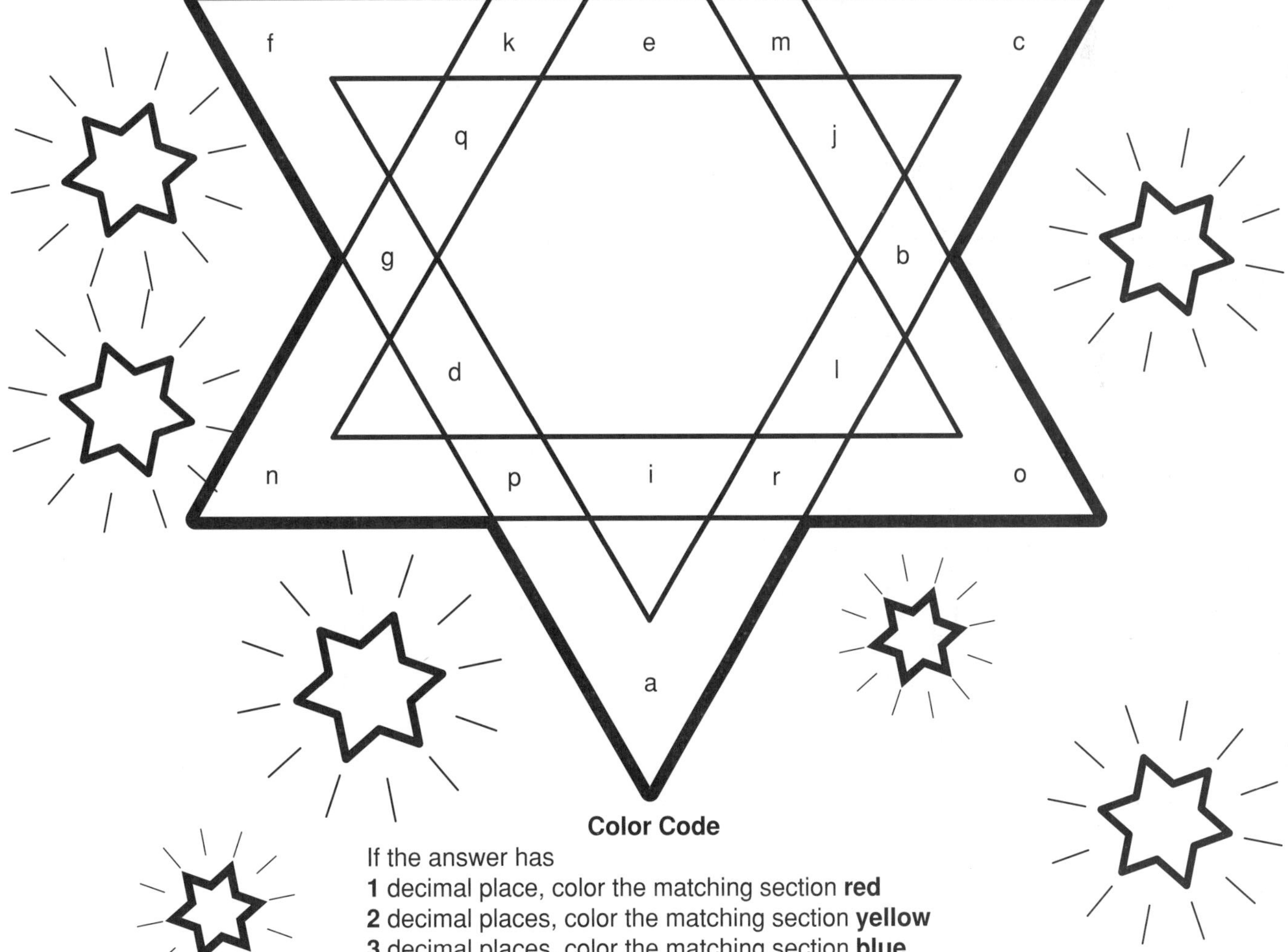

Color Code

If the answer has
1 decimal place, color the matching section **red**
2 decimal places, color the matching section **yellow**
3 decimal places, color the matching section **blue**
4 decimal places, color the matching section **green**

Bonus Box: Cut out your Star of David on the bold outer lines. Carefully cut out the sections that you didn't color. Then glue the completed star onto a black sheet of construction paper.

Note to the teacher: Provide each student with glue, scissors, and an eight-inch-square sheet of black construction paper.

Christmas Hideaways

Can you find the hidden Christmas words? Each word on a gift contains a four-letter word related to Christmas. The four letters are in the correct left-to-right order. Your job? Read the clue below for each word. Decide what the word is and find it in the corresponding word on a gift. Circle the letters of the hidden word; then write it on the gift and beside its clue. The first one is done for you.

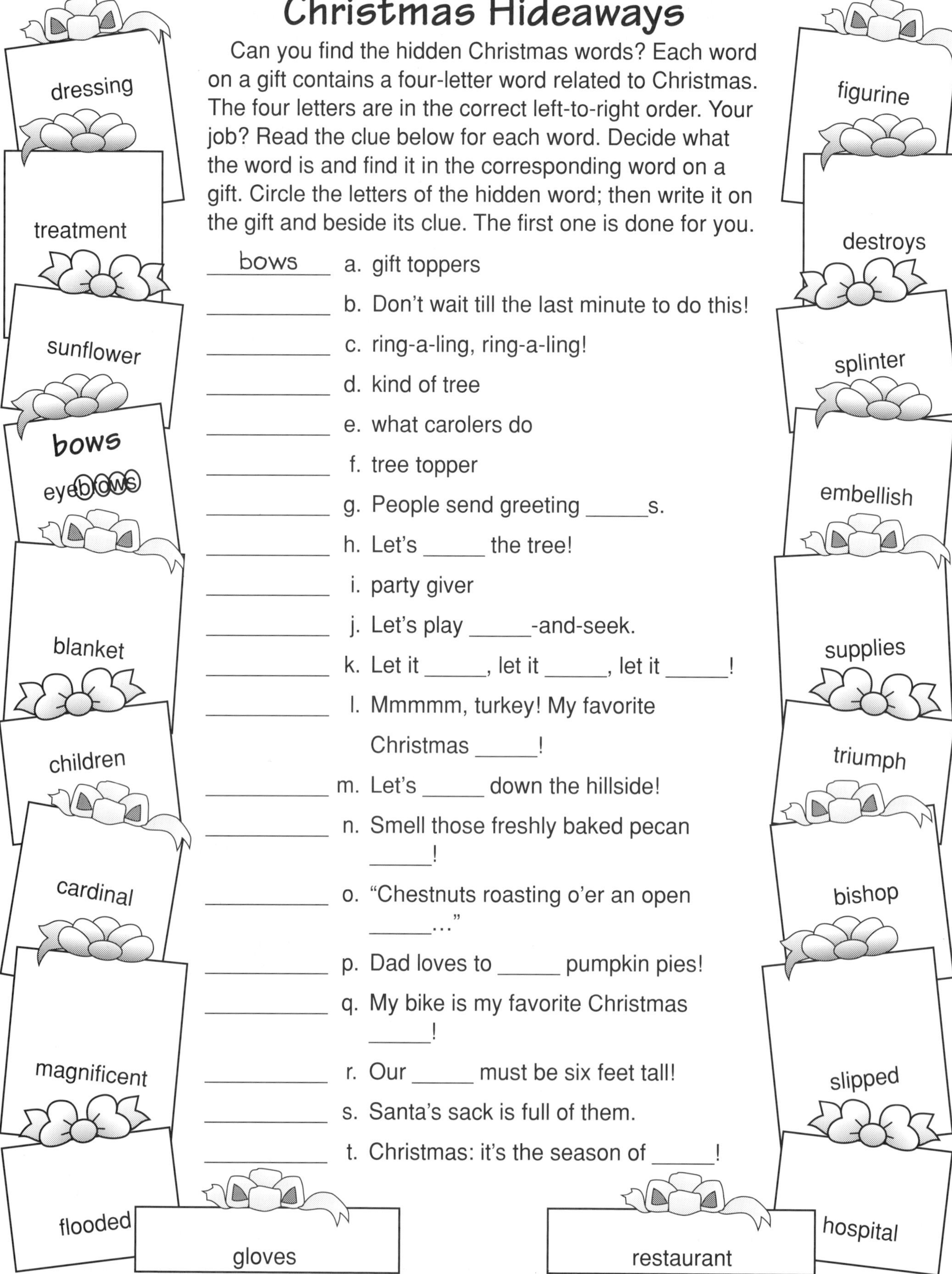

bows a. gift toppers

______ b. Don't wait till the last minute to do this!

______ c. ring-a-ling, ring-a-ling!

______ d. kind of tree

______ e. what carolers do

______ f. tree topper

______ g. People send greeting _____s.

______ h. Let's _____ the tree!

______ i. party giver

______ j. Let's play _____-and-seek.

______ k. Let it _____, let it _____, let it _____!

______ l. Mmmmm, turkey! My favorite Christmas _____!

______ m. Let's _____ down the hillside!

______ n. Smell those freshly baked pecan _____!

______ o. "Chestnuts roasting o'er an open _____..."

______ p. Dad loves to _____ pumpkin pies!

______ q. My bike is my favorite Christmas _____!

______ r. Our _____ must be six feet tall!

______ s. Santa's sack is full of them.

______ t. Christmas: it's the season of _____!

Bonus Box: How many four-letter words can you make using the letters in *Christmas?* Don't use plurals, and don't use a letter more times than it's used in *Christmas*. Write your words on the back of this sheet.

Name ____________________ Spelling

Santa's Not-So-Super Spellers

Santa's reindeer are busily checking over some lists before handing them over to Santa. Only one of the reindeer spelled all of the items on its list correctly; the other seven need a little help! Can you lend a hand?

Read the items in each list. Circle each item that is spelled *correctly.* Write the number of items you circled in the box at the top of the list. You will use the numbers 1–8 one time each. Make sure you don't circle any mispelled items. Oops...make that *misspelled.*

Book Gift Ideas
Treasure Island
Manaic Magee
Hatchet
A Rinkle in Time
Call It Courege
Island of the Blue Dolfins
Sarah, Plane and Tall
Where the Sidewalk Ends
U.S. Cities to Visit
Cincinati, OH
Colombia, SC
Raliegh, NC
Baton Rogue, LA
Sacremento, CA
Baltimore, MD
Bismark, ND
Albuquerque, NM
Bodies of Water to Fly Over
Lake Mishigan
Saint Lawrance River
Mississippippi River
Lake Tahoe
Great Salt Lake
Gulf of Mexico
Colarado River
Monongahela River
Sports Gift Ideas
basketball
football helmet
baseball glove
soccer ball
badmitten set
croquet set
ski equiptment
roller skates
Foreign Countries to Visit
Packistan
Brazil
Colombia
Zaire
Thialand
New Zealand
Austrailia
Switzerland
Musical Gift Ideas
violin
picolo
trumpet
compact discs
set of drums
trombone
saxophone
stereo system
Clothing Ideas
ski jacket
cap
blue jeans
mittens
shirt
sneakers
warm-up pants
sweater
More Gift Ideas
telphone
mall gift cerfiticate
stuffed panda bare
jewerly
computer
camara
minature golf passes
movie theater tickits

Bonus Box: On the back of this sheet, write the correct spelling of each item that you *did not* circle.

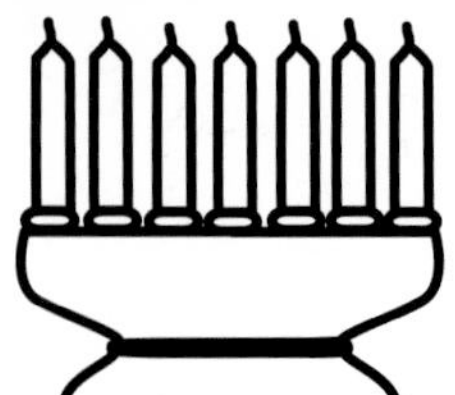

The Heart of Kwanzaa

Each year from December 26 until January 1, many Black Americans celebrate the joyous season of Kwanzaa. *Kwanzaa* means "first fruits of the harvest." The term comes from the East African language of Swahili.

Seven candles are placed in a wooden candleholder: a black candle in the middle with three red ones on its left and three green ones on its right. They stand for the seven principles of Kwanzaa. A candle is lit during each day of Kwanzaa.

Day 1: The black candle is lit to celebrate (oo-**moe**-jah), which means "unity."
Day 2: The first red candle on the left of the black one is lit. It represents (koo-jee-cha-goo-**lee**-ah), which means "self-determination."
Day 3: The first green candle on the right of the black one is lit. It represents working together and (oo-**jee**-mah), or "responsibility."
Day 4: It's time to celebrate (oo-jah-**maah**), or "cooperative economics." The next red candle is lit.
Day 5: The fifth Kwanzaa principle is (**nee**-ah). The next green candle is lit to represent "purpose." This is a time to think about the future.
Day 6: The last red candle is lit for (ku-**oom**-bah), which means "creativity."
Day 7: The last green candle is lit for (ee-**mahn**-ee), or "faith."

Directions: Cut out the candle puzzle pieces below. Use the pronunciation key below and the respellings above to help you figure out the correct spellings of the seven Kwanzaa principles. Place the completed candles in order on a sheet of construction paper; then glue them to the paper. To complete the project, color each candle and add a candleholder.

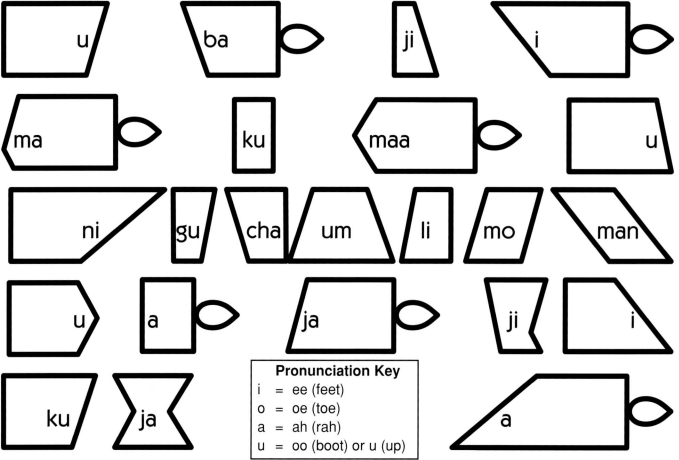

u ba ji i

ma ku maa u

ni gu cha um li mo man

u a ja ji i

ku ja a

Pronunciation Key

i = ee (feet)
o = oe (toe)
a = ah (rah)
u = oo (boot) or u (up)

 Note to the teacher: Provide each student with a 6" x 9" sheet of white construction paper, scissors, crayons or markers, and glue.

Name ____________________

In Other Words

Writers often look in a thesaurus to find a more exact synonym for a word. A thesaurus alphabetically lists words and their synonyms. Look at the sample page of synonyms for **good.**

Notice that the synonyms of a word may not all be synonyms of each other. For example:

- good means "beneficial" in: Carrots are *good* for you.
- good means "profitable" in: We made a *good* deal on the sale.
- good means "adequate" in: Jody received *good* care in the hospital.

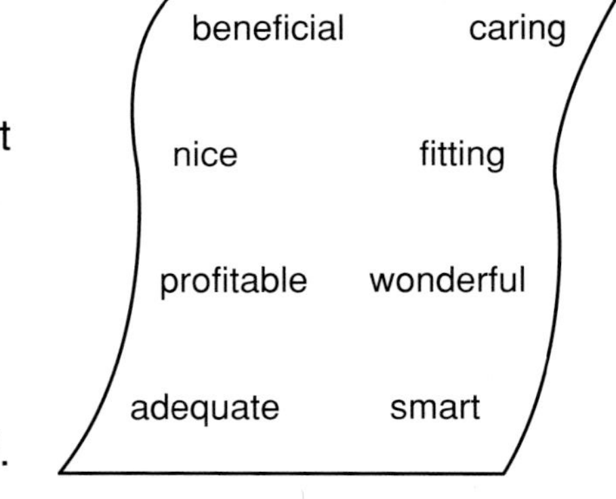

beneficial
caring
nice
fitting
profitable
wonderful
adequate
smart

A. Read the following story about Dr. Martin Luther King, Jr.

As a young man, Martin Luther King was a **good (1)** student. He was so **smart (2)** that he **bypassed (3)** the 9th and 12th grades in school! He **began (4)** college when he was 15 years old. Martin later **obtained (5)** a doctorate degree and became a minister.

Dr. King was a **good (6)** speaker. He became the **foremost (7)** leader of the civil rights movement in the United States during the 1950s and 1960s. Even after his home was bombed, he **maintained (8)** that nonviolence was the way to end discrimination. He **directed (9)** more than 200,000 Americans in the March on Washington. During this march, Dr. King gave his **acclaimed (10)** "I Have a Dream" speech.

Dr. King **worked (11)** to get the Voting Rights Act of 1965 passed. He also worked to increase job opportunities for blacks. He wanted to **better (12) bad (13)** housing and poor schools. Dr. King was arrested many times. He was jailed for protesting unfairness and discrimination.

In 1964, Dr. King **earned (14)** the Nobel Peace Prize. Sadly, he was assassinated at the age of 39. After his death Congress passed the Civil Rights Act of 1968. This act **bars (15)** racial discrimination when persons buy or rent most homes. Dr. King's birthday is now a federal holiday celebrated on the third Monday in January.

B. In each group of words below, circle the best synonym for the boldfaced word in the story. To help you decide, reread the sentence in the story that has that word.

1. **good:** nice, useful, excellent
2. **smart:** stylish, intelligent, witty
3. **bypassed:** detoured, skipped, jumped
4. **began:** initiated, started, created
5. **obtained:** caught, earned, acquired
6. **good:** pleasant, helpful, superb
7. **foremost:** good, main, star
8. **maintained:** believed, conserved, serviced
9. **directed:** led, commanded, managed
10. **acclaimed:** famous, great, primary
11. **worked:** performed, strived, satisfied
12. **better:** improve, enhance, exceed
13. **bad:** evil, ill-behaved, inferior
14. **earned:** gained, won, profited
15. **bars:** excludes, slows, prevents

Bonus Box: Some synonyms of *bad* include: *tough, naughty, evil, rotten, defective, wrong,* and *unpleasant.* Choose five of these synonyms and write a sentence for each one on the back of this page.

Choices of the Heart

Take a chance on love! Solve the ratio and probability problems below. One example of each type has been done for you. How sweet it is!

If you reached into the candy jar for a candy heart, what is the probability that you would choose one with the following:

1. I LUV U 7 out of 29 (or $\frac{7}{29}$)
2. OOOH BABY! ______
3. KISS ME ______
4. BE MINE ______
5. I'M YOURS ______
6. KISS ME or BE MINE ______
7. OOOH BABY! or I LUV U ______
8. I'M YOURS or BE MINE ______
9. I LUV U, OOOH BABY!, or KISS ME ______
10. I'M YOURS, BE MINE, or I LUV U ______

Write a ratio for each of the following:

11. I LUV U to I'M YOURS 7 : 4
12. KISS ME to BE MINE ______
13. I'M YOURS to OOOH BABY! ______
14. OOOH BABY! to KISS ME ______
15. BE MINE to I LUV U ______
16. I LUV U to OOOH BABY! ______
17. KISS ME to I LUV U ______
18. BE MINE to OOOH BABY! ______
19. I'M YOURS to KISS ME ______
20. KISS ME to BE MINE ______

Bonus Box: Suppose another "BE MINE" candy heart was added to the jar. Answer questions 1–5 with this new heart included. Write your answers on the back of this sheet or on your own paper.

Name ______________________________

Many adjectives are formed by adding different endings to nouns and verbs. Read the following story of the Exodusters. Decide which boldfaced adjectives are formed from nouns and which ones are formed from verbs. Some adjectives are formed from words that can be *either* nouns or verbs. Write each adjective in the correct newspaper column along with its base word. Use a dictionary to help you. The first one has been done for you.

THE EXODUSTERS

The Civil War (1861–1865) was a **horrible** event for all Americans. It was especially bad for Black Americans held in **crippling** slavery. Many slaves left the South and traveled north in search of freedom. These **escaped** slaves were known as "Exodusters." The word *Exodusters* comes from the **biblical** book of Exodus. Exodus tells the story of the **fascinating** flight of the Israelites from slavery in Egypt.

Many blacks went to the **bustling** cities of the North, such as Chicago and Detroit. Others traveled west and started their own **farming** communities. One such settlement was Nicodemus, Kansas. Nicodemus was the first all-black community west of the Mississippi River.

In Kansas, white citizens had **mixed** reactions to these crowds of **"colored** refugees." Most of them were **penniless.** Many were sick. The Exodusters were given **nourishing** food and other help. But they were also asked to move on. The **crowded** towns had unemployed people of their own. People said there was no room for more!

By starting their own towns, the Exodusters tried to find a place for their **visionary** idea of the **American** dream: a home of their own.

ADJECTIVES formed from nouns:	**ADJECTIVES** formed from words that are either nouns or verbs:	**ADJECTIVES** formed from verbs:
horrible - horror		

Bonus Box: One adjective in the story (not boldfaced) is formed from a verb that has both a prefix and a suffix added to it. Can you find it? What does this word mean?

Name ____________________

Votes for Women!

If you were a woman who lived in the United States before 1920, you probably didn't have the right to vote. In 1869, the legislature of the territory of Wyoming granted women the right to vote, hold office, and serve on juries. This new law was the first of its kind in the United States. The 19th Amendment to the Constitution was passed later in 1920. It guaranteed women *suffrage* (the right to vote) in all states.

Color each box in the key. Then color each state in the map to match the time during which women were given the right to vote.

1860–69 [yellow] 1870–79 [orange] 1890–99 [green] 1910–19 [blue] 1920 [red]

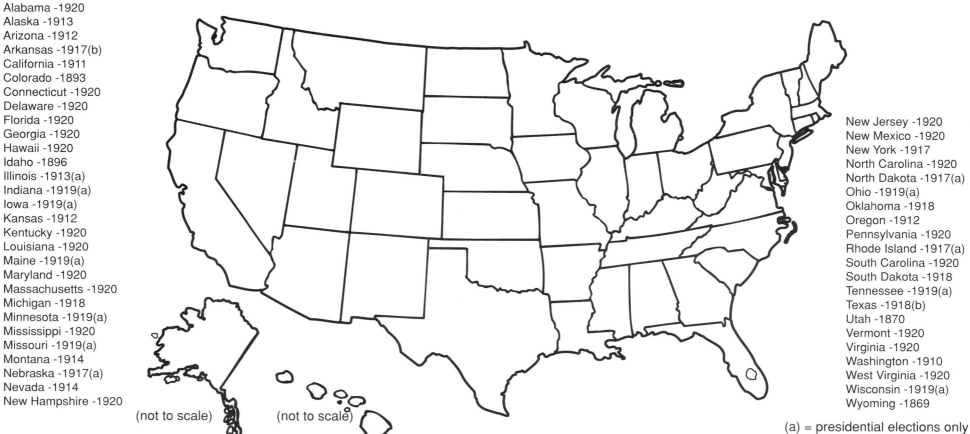

Alabama -1920
Alaska -1913
Arizona -1912
Arkansas -1917(b)
California -1911
Colorado -1893
Connecticut -1920
Delaware -1920
Florida -1920
Georgia -1920
Hawaii -1920
Idaho -1896
Illinois -1913(a)
Indiana -1919(a)
Iowa -1919(a)
Kansas -1912
Kentucky -1920
Louisiana -1920
Maine -1919(a)
Maryland -1920
Massachusetts -1920
Michigan -1918
Minnesota -1919(a)
Mississippi -1920
Missouri -1919(a)
Montana -1914
Nebraska -1917(a)
Nevada -1914
New Hampshire -1920

(not to scale) (not to scale)

New Jersey -1920
New Mexico -1920
New York -1917
North Carolina -1920
North Dakota -1917(a)
Ohio -1919(a)
Oklahoma -1918
Oregon -1912
Pennsylvania -1920
Rhode Island -1917(a)
South Carolina -1920
South Dakota -1918
Tennessee -1919(a)
Texas -1918(b)
Utah -1870
Vermont -1920
Virginia -1920
Washington -1910
West Virginia -1920
Wisconsin -1919(a)
Wyoming -1869

(a) = presidential elections only
(b) = primary elections only

Name ______________________________

The Luck of the Irish...and of You!

Think about all of the people and things you're lucky to have in your life. Then write a rainbow poem about them! Write your poem in the pattern below. Begin each line with the first letter of the color in each rainbow band: red, orange, yellow, green, blue, indigo, and violet. When you've completed your poem, lightly color the rainbow.

Note to the teacher: Have each student cut out his completed poem and glue it to a sheet of construction paper. Then have the student cut out the rainbow, leaving about a half-inch construction paper border around it. Post the completed poems on a bulletin board titled "What Luck!"

Would You Repeat That?

Waldo Woodpecker thinks his favorite comedian's jokes are sooooooo funny! To find out who Waldo's favorite comedian is, use a calculator to change the fractions below to decimals: divide the numerator of each fraction by its denominator. The resulting quotient will contain a repeating decimal. Put a bar over the digits that repeat instead of writing them several times, such as $0.\overline{3}$ for 0.3333… and $0.\overline{37}$ for 0.373737…. Then use the code to match each repeating decimal with a letter to fill in the blanks of the message.

Tell that joke to me one more time!
HA
HA
HA
HA
HA
HA

1. $\frac{5}{9}$ = ______
2. $\frac{1}{3}$ = ______
3. $\frac{5}{12}$ = ______
4. $\frac{1}{9}$ = ______
5. $\frac{7}{9}$ = ______
6. $\frac{3}{9}$ = ______
7. $\frac{2}{11}$ = ______
8. $\frac{4}{9}$ = ______
9. $\frac{1}{12}$ = ______
10. $\frac{8}{9}$ = ______
11. $\frac{2}{3}$ = ______
12. $\frac{7}{11}$ = ______
13. $\frac{8}{11}$ = ______
14. $\frac{3}{11}$ = ______
15. $\frac{2}{9}$ = ______

$\overline{1}$ = C	$\overline{3}$ = S	$\overline{5}$ = L	$\overline{7}$ = T	$\overline{18}$ = P	$\overline{63}$ = L
$\overline{2}$ = Y	$\overline{4}$ = I	$\overline{6}$ = O	$\overline{8}$ = B	$\overline{27}$ = I	$\overline{72}$ = B

__ __ __ __   __ __ __ __ __   __ __   __ __ __ __!

10 14 1 12   4 3 2 13 15   8 9   5 11 7 6

Bonus Box: On the back of this page or on another sheet of paper, write the joke that you think is making Waldo laugh so hard.

Name ____________________ Addition, division, interpreting remainders

One Stuffed Bunny!

All that candy! This stuffed bunny needs to do some serious exercising to get rid of all those calories. Follow these steps to complete each problem:

1. Use the information in the first chart to find the total number of calories in the candies listed on each egg.
2. Find out how many minutes of each activity the bunny needs to do to get rid of those calories. (Hint: If a quotient has a remainder, *round up* to the next whole number.)
3. Complete your work on another sheet of paper.
4. Write your answers in the blanks provided.

Candy	Calories
10 malted-milk eggs	230
1 chocolate bunny	900
5 Gummy Worm candies	215
10 jelly beans	410
1 bag of candy-coated chocolates	236
1 peanut-butter egg	220

Activity	Calories Burned Per Minute
dancing	6
cycling	3
golf	5
horseback riding	2
running	12
swimming	9
tennis	7
walking	4

1.

1 chocolate bunny
10 jelly beans
total calories: ________

minutes needed to burn those calories:

cycling: ________
horseback riding: ________
tennis: ________

2.

10 malted-milk eggs
5 Gummy Worm candies
total calories: ________

minutes needed to burn those calories:

dancing: ________
golf: ________
running: ________

3.

1 bag of candy-coated chocolates
1 peanut-butter egg
total calories: ________

minutes needed to burn those calories:

swimming: ________
walking: ________
dancing: ________

4.

10 jelly beans
10 malted-milk eggs
total calories: ________

minutes needed to burn those calories:

cycling: ________
running: ________
walking: ________

5.

1 bag of candy-coated chocolates
1 chocolate bunny
total calories: ________

minutes needed to burn those calories:

golf: ________
horseback riding: ________
swimming: ________

6.

1 peanut-butter egg
5 Gummy Worm candies
total calories: ________

minutes needed to burn those calories:

dancing: ________
cycling: ________
tennis: ________

Bonus Box: The bunny decided that he definitely needs to cut back on his sweets. So for a snack, he had 5 malted-milk eggs, $\frac{1}{2}$ of a chocolate bunny, and 5 jelly beans. How many total calories was that?

Name ______________________________

Recycled Words

Celebrate Earth Day by doing some recycling, but not with trash—with words!

Directions: Use the letters in each recyclable item listed below to spell a word that fits each clue. Write one letter in each blank. Use a dictionary if you need help.

newspaper

Example: a game piece used to play chess → p a w n

1. a section of glass in a window or door
2. to trade or barter
3. a flying insect that can sting
4. a long, sharp-pointed weapon
5. a large water bird with a long, graceful neck

plastic bag

6. a plaster covering that supports a broken arm or leg
7. an explosion
8. a series of items, names, or numerals often written in a certain order
9. to take in your breath suddenly
10. food made from flour and water, such as spaghetti

milk carton

11. a low, sad sound
12. a place for ice-skating
13. a fastening made by tying a rope or string
14. to follow the tracks of someone or something
15. a ring on a chain

aluminum can

16. peaceful, untroubled
17. a channel dug across land
18. hit, throw, or shoot something in a particular direction
19. any living creature that can breathe and move
20. largest or most important

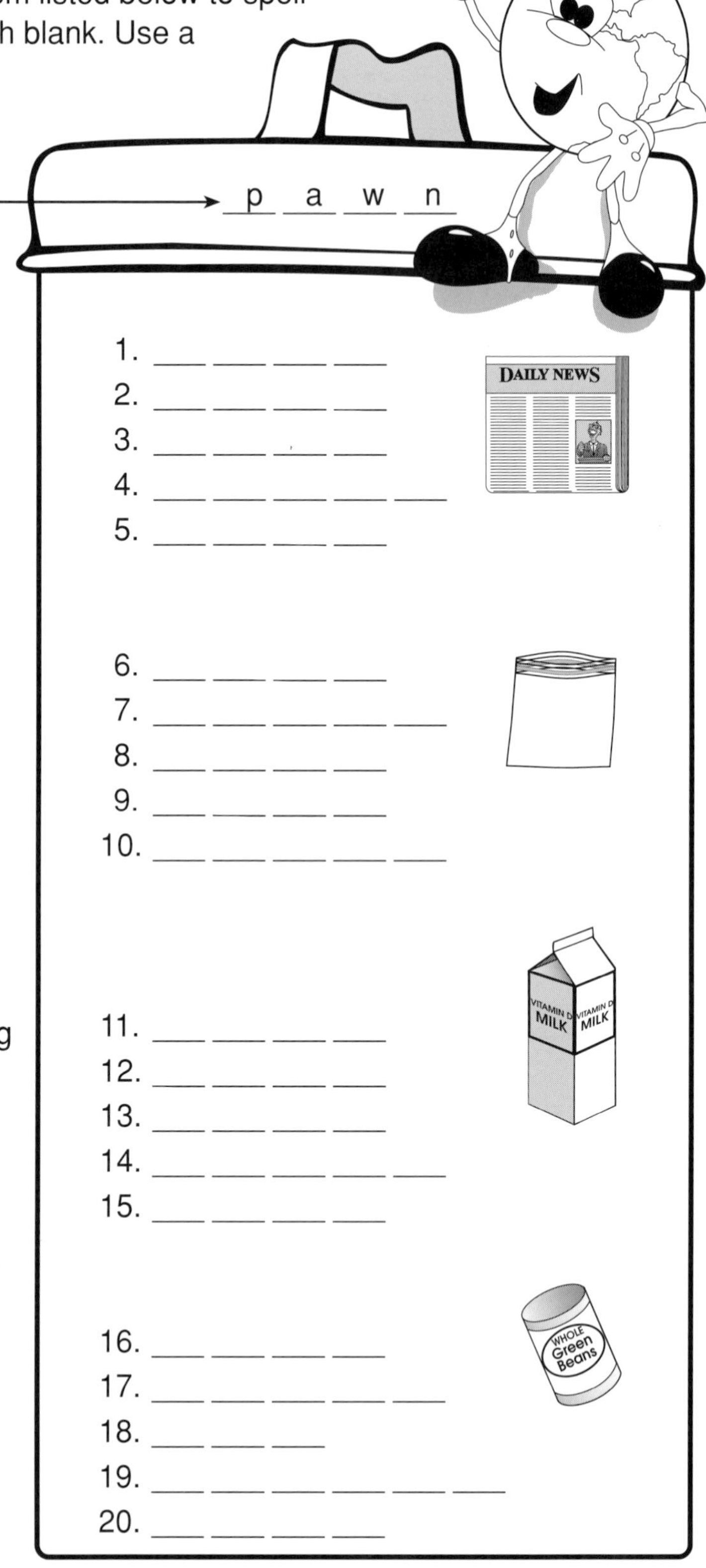

Bonus Box: List five more words using the letters of one recyclable item listed above. Write your words on the back of this sheet.

Name ______________________________ Contract: creative thinking

This Is *Your* Classroom!

What's it like to be a teacher? Below are just a few of the many things teachers do and think about...sometimes every day! To celebrate National Teacher Appreciation Week in May, put yourself in your teacher's shoes for a while. Complete ____ of the following activities by _____.

Your Classroom

The classroom is a home away from home for you and your students! On a sheet of graph paper, design your classroom. Make it comfortable, pleasant, and organized for learning. Include and label all desks, shelves, and computers—everything you and your students need.

Your Rules and Consequences

You have to keep order in the classroom. Make five rules for your students. Next think of some consequences for not following the rules: What happens the first time a rule is broken? The second time? The third? List your rules and consequences on a sheet of paper. Make it neat and colorful.

Your Bulletin Boards

A pleasant classroom has creative, neat bulletin boards. Select a skill or subject that you would like to display on a bulletin board. Then use crayons, markers, construction paper, and any other materials to design your bulletin board on a large sheet of white paper.

Your Rewards and Incentives

Discipline also includes rewards for good behavior and following the rules. Make a list of ten rewards and privileges that you'll provide for your students.

Your Daily Schedule

You've got to have a schedule. Your teaching day begins at 8:30 A.M. and ends at 3:30 P.M. Make a schedule that includes all of the subjects, lunch, recess, and other activities, plus their time blocks. Make sure you have enough time for each activity. (No three-hour recesses!)

Your Original Learning Game

Your students need help with a skill, such as finding verbs in sentences or learning their multiplication facts. You want them to play a game to practice the skill. First decide on a skill. Then create a game that you can use to teach that skill. Be sure to list all of the rules for your game.

Your Parent Letter

A student is having a tough time getting homework completed and turned in on time. Write a letter to this student's parents. Explain the problem and what you think are its reasons. Suggest ways the parents can help their child at home.

Your Writing Assignment

Students will write the rest of their lives! Make up five story starters. For each one, include the first sentence or two. Make them exciting and creative, and include the main idea or problem. Exchange lists with a partner. Choose one story starter and complete the story. Include an illustration with it.

Note to the teacher: Before duplicating this page, fill in the number of activities that you would like for your students to complete and a due date.

Name ______________________

Fractional Flags

On June 14, 1777, the Continental Congress agreed on a design for our country's flag. We celebrate June 14 as Flag Day to remember this event. To honor this day, you have been asked to design four different flags. Shade each of the rectangles below according to its given fractions and colors. Then, on the lines below the designs, explain how you figured out the fractional parts for each color.

Design 1

$\frac{1}{3}$ red, $\frac{2}{3}$ blue

Design 2

$\frac{1}{2}$ red, $\frac{1}{4}$ blue, $\frac{1}{4}$ white

Design 3

$\frac{1}{2}$ red, $\frac{1}{4}$ blue, $\frac{1}{8}$ white, $\frac{1}{8}$ green

Design 4

$\frac{1}{3}$ red, $\frac{1}{4}$ blue, $\frac{1}{4}$ white, $\frac{1}{6}$ green

Bonus Box: John Adams stated "…that the flag of the thirteen United States shall be thirteen stripes, alternate red and white; that the 'Union' be thirteen stars, white in a blue field, representing a new constellation." On the back of this sheet, draw the flag Adams described.

Name ____ End of the year: vocabulary

windup closure inception close terminate halt cease conclusion finish finale outcome debut STOP conclude start wrap up completion last

The End!

The end of another school year is fast approaching. Celebrate by showing off your word power! See how many of the following words you can identify. Each one contains the letter combination *end.* Write one letter in each blank. The first one is done for you.

Can you identify all 25? Now that would be trem**end**ous!

1. to repair — m end
2. to look after — _ end
3. opposite of "borrow" — _ end
4. to cause to go; to deliver — _ end
5. small kitchen appliance — _ _ end _ _ _
6. part of a car or bicycle — _ end _ _ _
7. to last — end _ _ _ _ _
8. to trust or rely on — _ _ _ _ end
9. a seller — _ end _ _ _
10. to drive danger away from — _ _ _ _ end
11. the number divided in a division problem — _ _ _ _ _ _ end
12. to catch a thief — _ _ _ _ _ _ _ _ _ end
13. pal or buddy — _ _ _ _ end
14. delicate; fragile — _ end _ _ _
15. to make right — _ _ end
16. to praise — _ _ _ _ _ end
17. to put in peril — end _ _ _ _ _ _ _
18. to hang; to cause to stop for a while — _ _ _ _ _ end
19. part of a grandfather clock that swings back and forth — _ end _ _ _ _ _
20. bands worn over the shoulders to help hold up pants — _ _ _ _ _ end _ _ _ _
21. awesome; marvelous — _ _ _ _ _ end _ _ _ _
22. to understand — _ _ _ _ _ _ _ _ _ end
23. huge; monstrous — _ _ _ _ _ end _ _ _ _
24. a coin-operated device that sells merchandise — _ end _ _ _ _ _ _ _ _ _ _ _
25. the strong tissue joining the muscles in the calf of the leg to the heel bone — _ _ _ _ _ _ _ _ _ _ _ _ _ end _ _ _

Bonus Box: Read all of the words around the border of this page. Which three are not related to the word *end?*

It's a Sizzlin' Sidewalk Sale!

It seems every store has a sidewalk sale at least once during the summer. Goods are displayed outside with prices that have been greatly reduced.

Each item in a box below is on sale, but only part of the price information is given. Find the missing information and write it in the matching blank. An example of each type of problem has been done for you.

To find a **sale price:**

1. Change discount percent to a decimal or use the discount fraction.
   10% = **.10**
2. reg. price x decimal (or fraction) = savings
   $150.00 x .10 = **$15.00**
3. reg. price – savings = sale price
   $150.00 – $15.00 = **$135.00**

To find a **regular price:**

1. 100% (or 1 if a fraction) – discount
   100% – 25% = **75%**
   (Sale price is 75% of regular price.)
2. sale price ÷ percent of regular price
   $60.00 ÷ 75% =
   $60.00 ÷ .75 = **$80.00**

To find a **discount:**

1. reg. price – sale price = savings
   $90.00 – $54.00 = **$36.00**
2. savings ÷ reg. price = discount
   $36.00 ÷ $90.00 = **0.4**
3. Write the decimal as a percent.
   .4 = .40 = **40%**

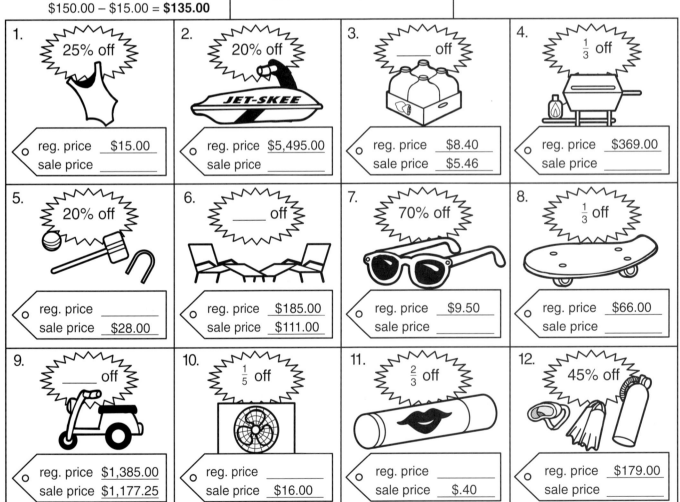

1. 25% off reg. price $15.00 sale price ______	2. 20% off JET-SKEE reg. price $5,495.00 sale price ______	3. ____ off reg. price $8.40 sale price $5.46	4. $\frac{1}{3}$ off reg. price $369.00 sale price ______
5. 20% off reg. price ______ sale price $28.00	6. ____ off reg. price $185.00 sale price $111.00	7. 70% off reg. price $9.50 sale price ______	8. $\frac{1}{3}$ off reg. price $66.00 sale price ______
9. ____ off reg. price $1,385.00 sale price $1,177.25	10. $\frac{1}{5}$ off reg. price ______ sale price $16.00	11. $\frac{2}{3}$ off reg. price ______ sale price $.40	12. 45% off reg. price $179.00 sale price ______

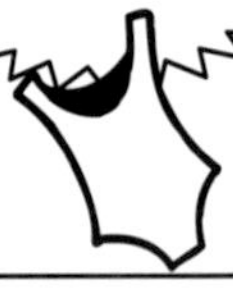

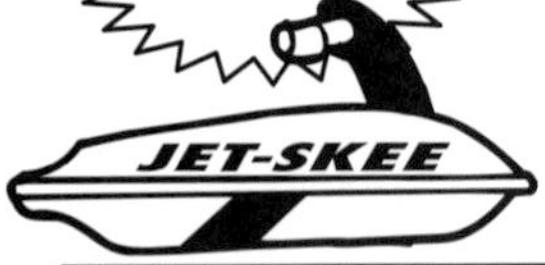

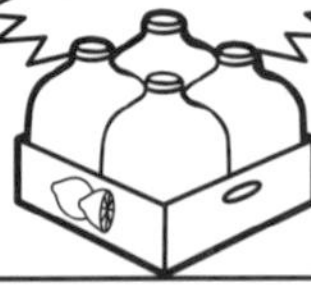

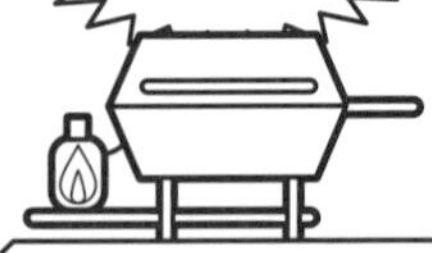

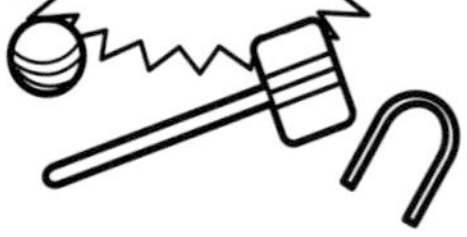

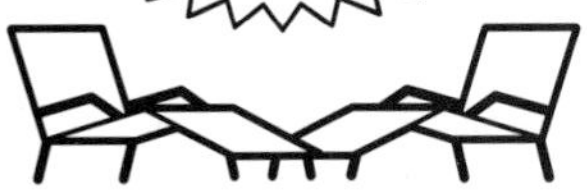

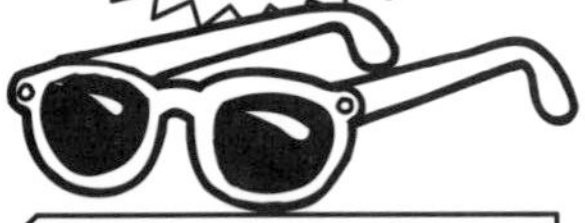

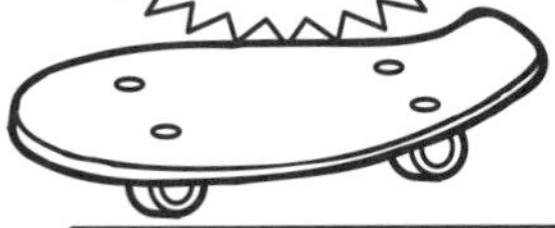

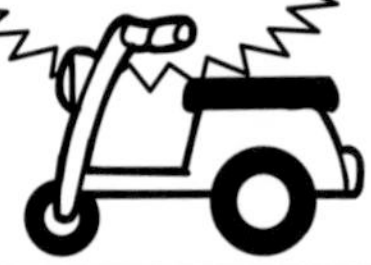

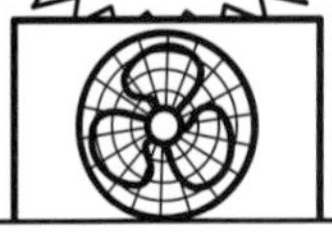

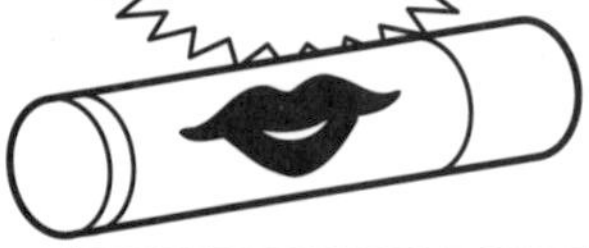

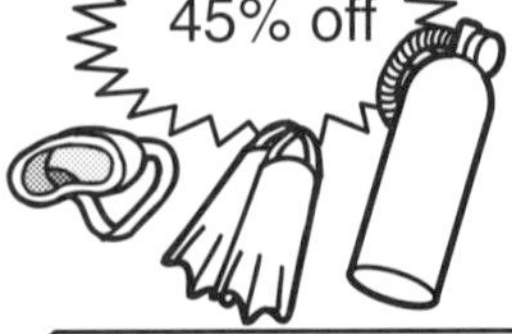

Bonus Box: What is the sale price of the scuba gear (#12) with 6% tax added?

Answer Keys

Page 42
All calculations are based on the dimensions students were asked to draw on the graph paper, not on the actual dimensions of a graham cracker.

1. Each pentagon has a perimeter of 51 cm and an area of 174 sq. cm. The area of the pentagon was found by using the formulas for a square ($A = s^2$) and a triangle ($A = \frac{1}{2}$ bxh).
2. Each square wall has a perimeter of 48 cm and an area of 144 sq. cm.
3. Each rectangular roof has a perimeter of 54 cm and an area of 180 sq. cm.
4. The candies can be classified as follows: a caramel represents a cube, a piece of Toblerone chocolate represents a triangular pyramid (when trimmed), a gumball represents a sphere, a Bugles corn snack represents a cone, a peppermint stick represents a cylinder, and a Jolly Rancher candy represents a rectangular prism.

Page 65
Answers will vary depending on the symbols that each student chooses. Features should be drawn in the approximate locations shown.

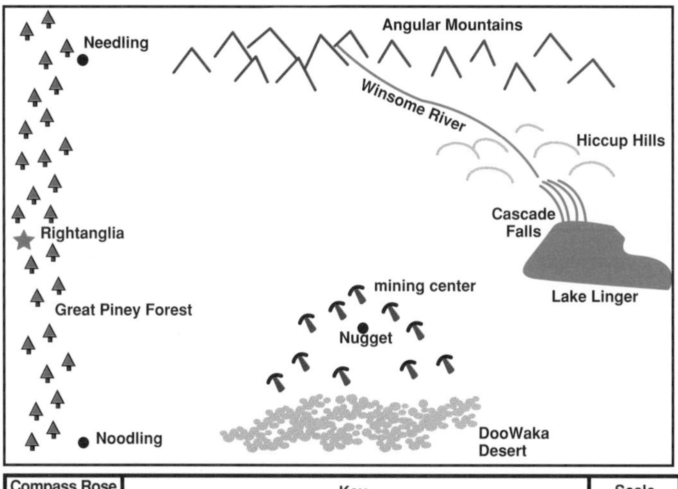

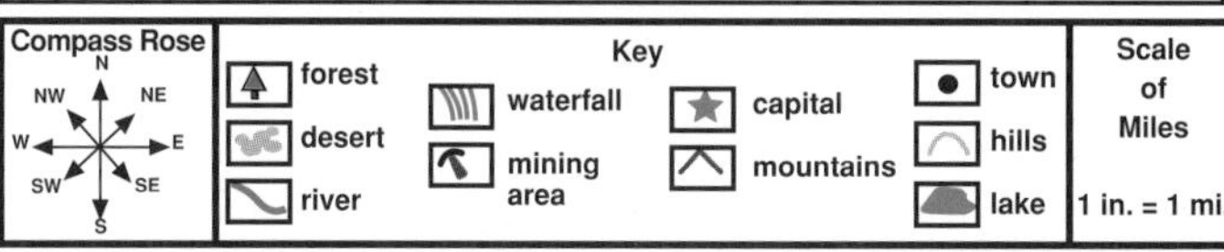

Bonus Box: The area should be approximately 21 sq. mi. (Answers will vary depending on each student's map.)

Page 74
Answers may vary. Suggested answers:
Tornado Safety: 1, 2, 4, 5, 7, 8, 9, 11, 12, 16, 18, 19
Hurricane Safety: 2, 3, 6, 8, 9, 11, 12, 17, 18, 19, 20
Thunderstorm Safety: 8, 9, 11, 12, 13, 14, 17, 19, 20
Blizzard Safety: 8, 10, 11, 12, 15

Page 98
Part I

1. 7 blocks
2. 28 blocks
3. 1
4. 8
5. Answers will vary.

Part III

1. 19 blocks
2. 1:11; 6 blocks
3. 10:08; 21 blocks
4. 2:01; 2:04; or 2:07

Part II

1. 1
2. 2
3. 5
4. 9
5. 5
6. The number of blocks that make up each digit equals that digit: 4 has 4 blocks, 5 has 5 blocks, and 6 has 6 blocks.

Bonus Box: Answers will vary.

Page 102

1. 20 x \$1.89 = \$37.80
2. 20 ÷ 2 = 10 boxes
3. 10 x \$.89 = \$8.90
4. \$37.80 + \$8.90 = \$46.70
5. \$1.00 x 98 = \$98.00
6. \$98.00 – \$46.70 = \$51.30
7. 20 x 5 = 100 cups
8. 150 ÷ 25 = 6 journals
9. 90 ÷ 6 = 15 packs
10. paper: \$1.50 x 15 = \$22.50
    front covers: 90 x \$.09 = \$8.10
    back covers: 90 x \$.05 = \$4.50
    paint pens: \$2.99 x 2 = \$5.98
    TOTAL: \$22.50 + \$8.10 + \$4.50 + \$5.98 = \$41.08
11. 90 x \$1.00 = \$90.00
12. \$90.00 – \$41.08 = \$48.92

Bonus Box: \$51.30 + \$48.92 = \$100.22

Page 121
Accept reasonable answers.

1. Mr. Ages is an older white mouse who was at NIMH with Mr. Frisby and the rats. He is helping the rats carry out their plan.
2. The rats are carrying an electrical cable to tap into a current and bring electricity to their home.
3. Mr. Frisby is well-known because he, like the rats of NIMH, was highly intelligent. While helping the rats put a sleeping powder in Dragon's dish, he was killed.
4. The rats are able to move Mrs. Frisby's home by using a series of pulleys, scaffolding, and logs.
5. The rats' plan is to live on their own—without stealing—in a place called Thorn Valley.
6. NIMH stands for National Institute of Mental Health. The mice and rats were taken to a laboratory at NIMH.
7. Answers will vary.
8. The rats were being injected, trained, and tested to increase their intelligence.
9. The ability to read helped the rats escape from NIMH.
10. The rats convince the exterminators that they are not more of the mechanized rats by making their tunnel-like home appear to be an ordinary rat hole.

Page 164
Puzzle #1: Starting with the middle B in the top row is Miss Pickwell's advice: Books are the keys to learning. The arrows show the direction through the grid.

```
I → N  (B)  K → S
↑   ↓   ↓   ↑   ↓
N   G   O → O   A
↑               ↓
R   T ← S   E ← R
↑   ↓   ↑   ↓
A   O   Y   T → H
↑   ↓   ↑       ↓
E ← L   E ← K ← E
```

Puzzle #2: The body parts that the zookeeper named were arm, ear, eye, gum, hip, jaw, leg, lip, rib, and toe.

Puzzle #3:

40	10	30	0	20
30	0	20	40	10
20	40	10	30	0
10	30	0	20	40
0	20	40	10	30

Puzzle #4:

1. T
2. W
3. I
4. O
5. H
6. T
7. U

DON'T LEAVE HOME WITHOUT IT!
Bonus Box: 4 ÷ 4 = 1 or $\frac{4}{4}$ = 1

Page 165
Code for alphabet:

A =	$.05	N =	$.70
B =	$.10	O =	$.75
C =	$.15	P =	$.80
D =	$.20	Q =	$.85
E =	$.25	R =	$.90
F =	$.30	S =	$.95
G =	$.35	T =	$1.00
H =	$.40	U =	$1.05
I =	$.45	V =	$1.10
J =	$.50	W =	$1.15
K =	$.55	X =	$1.20
L =	$.60	Y =	$1.25
M =	$.65	Z =	$1.30

Students' answers for questions 1–5, 7, and the Bonus Box will vary.

6. Students' predictions about which items are most and least expensive will vary.
   a. pencil: $2.95
   b. crayons: $4.75
   c. scissors: $6.05
   d. glue: $2.25
   e. eraser: $3.30
   f. bookbag: $2.65
   g. calculator: $5.30
   h. sharpener: $5.20

Page 166
Students' answers to the questions will vary.

1. pencil (...dampen cilantro...)
   You would dampen cilantro with salad dressing instead of motor oil.
2. eraser (...water as erosion...)
   Running water can make parts of the earth wear away and change the shape of rocks.
3. locker (...clock erratically...)
   A clock with an irregular tick is not very dependable.
4. crayon (...plastic ray on...)
   An "arm" of a plastic starfish might break off.
5. chalk (...catch Al King...)
   You might be able to catch Al as he's trying to make his kite fly high.
6. staples (...drum's tap lessen...)
   The tapping of a drum could become less frequent if the drummer taps slower.
7. paste (...papa steadily...)
   A person's papa could probably rise calmly and smoothly out of a chair.
8. marker (...mark erroneously...)
   A worksheet could include a mark mistakenly made by the teacher.
9. ruler (...rule resolutely...)
   A rule should firmly remain the same for everyone.
10. sharpener (...melodious harp energize...)
    It is possible for people to feel energized and renewed by listening to pretty music played on a harp.
11. book (...peek-a-boo keenly...)
    A baby is eager to play peek-a-boo with a parent.
12. tape (...tap excitedly...)
    A dog's tail could tap excitedly on the floor when his owner comes into the room.
13. pen (...gape nonchalantly...)
    A person would not stare in a carefree manner if he were about to step on a snake.
14. paper (...dump a person...)
    It would not be acceptable for a taxi driver to dump a person into a large crack in the earth.

Bonus Box: D E N V E R, C O L O R A D O

Page 167

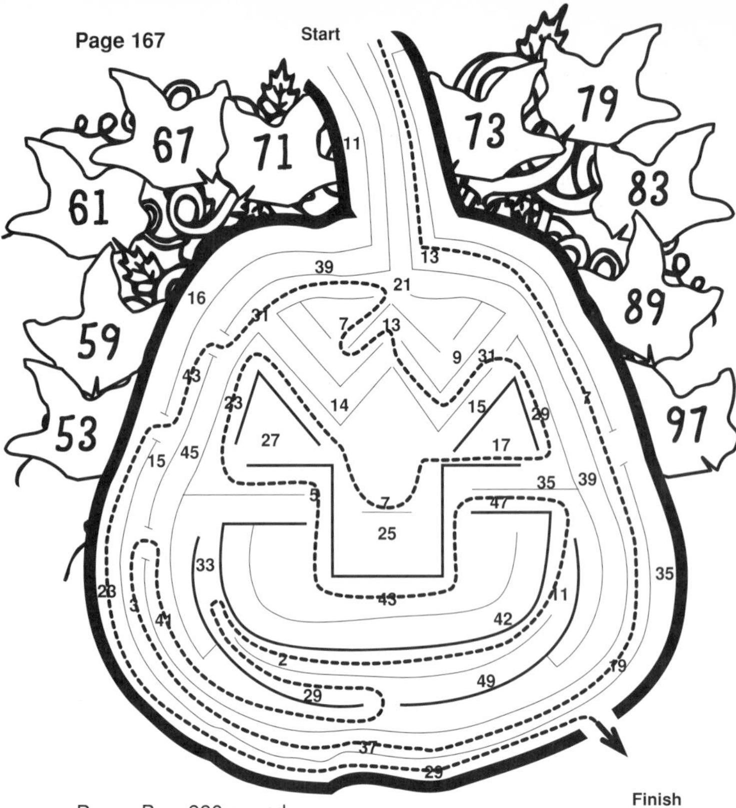

Bonus Box: 990 pounds

Page 168
October: Fact
Month of the Dinosaur: Opinion
National Dessert Month: Fact
National Pizza Month: Fact
National Popcorn Poppin' Month: Fact
Child Health Month: Fact
Computer Learning Month: Opinion
Healthy Lung Month: Opinion
National Communicate With Your Kid Month: Opinion
National Dental Hygiene Month: Fact
National Cookie Month: Opinion
National Roller Skating Month: Opinion
National Stamp Collecting Month: Fact
National Car Care Month: Opinion
Halloween: Fact

Page 169

Kount Drakula (wrong letter)	**Gwen the Ghost (silent letter)**	**Wylie the Werewolf (correct words)**
Nevada	Savannah	Buffalo
Bangor	Massachusetts	Los Angeles
Charlotte	Pittsburgh	Albuquerque
Minnesota	Annapolis	Norfolk
Bismarck	Fort Wayne	Montpelier
Michigan	Rhode Island	Louisiana
Casper	Lincoln	Tulsa
Olympia	Phoenix	Louisville
New Haven	New Hampshire	Tallahassee
San Francisco	Des Moines	Tucson

Bonus Box:

Montpelier, Vermont	Tallahassee, Florida
Annapolis, Maryland	Lincoln, Nebraska
Bismarck, North Dakota	Phoenix, Arizona
Olympia, Washington	Des Moines, Iowa

Page 171

b 1.	h 5.	e 9.
d 2.	k 6.	i 10.
f 3.	c 7.	g 11.
j 4.	l 8.	a 12.

Page 172
Possible answers:
1. tasty, tough
2. frantic, funny
3. creamy, crunchy
4. grumpy, great
5. rubbery, round
6. delicious, delectable
7. marvelous, messy
8. stupendous, sticky
9. plentiful, pleasing
10. historic, heartwarming
11. lightweight, lovely
12. buttery, bountiful
13. drippy, detestable

Page 173

a. 1.6
b. 0.01
c. 0.001
d. 0.006
e. 0.4
f. 0.0012
g. 0.25
h. 2.5
i. 4.2
j. 0.042
k. 0.12
l. 0.0001
m. 0.56
n. 0.025
o. 0.0036
p. 0.25
q. 0.0025
r. 0.27

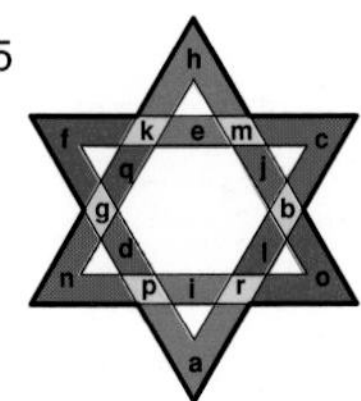

Page 174

bows a. eye**brows**
shop b. bi**shop**
bell c. em**bell**ish
pine d. s**p**l**in**t**e**r
sing e. dres**sing**
star f. re**sta**u**r**ant
card g. **card**inal
trim h. **tri**u**m**ph
host i. **hos**pi**t**al
hide j. c**hi**l**d**r**e**n
snow k. **s**u**n**fl**ow**er
food l. **f**l**ood**ed
sled m. **sl**ipp**ed**
pies n. sup**p**l**ies**
fire o. **fi**gu**r**in**e**
bake p. **b**l**a**n**ke**t
gift q. ma**g**n**if**ican**t**
tree r. **tre**atm**e**nt
toys s. des**t**r**oys**
love t. g**l**o**ve**s

Bonus Box: Answers will vary. Suggested words include arch, cart, cash, cast, char, chat, hair, harm, hiss, mach, mart, mash, mass, mast, math, miss, mist, rash, rich, scam, scar, scat, sham, star, stir, this, tram, trim.

Page 175
3 Book Gift Ideas
Spelled correctly: *Treasure Island, Hatchet, Where the Sidewalk Ends*
Corrected spellings: *Maniac Magee; A Wrinkle in Time; Call It Courage; Island of the Blue Dolphins; Sarah, Plain and Tall*
2 U.S. Cities to Visit
Spelled correctly: Baltimore, MD; Albuquerque, NM
Corrected spellings: Cincinnati, OH; Columbia, SC; Raleigh, NC; Baton Rouge, LA; Sacramento, CA; Bismarck, ND
4 Bodies of Water to Fly Over
Spelled correctly: Lake Tahoe, Great Salt Lake, Gulf of Mexico, Monongahela River
Corrected spellings: Lake Michigan, Saint Lawrence River, Mississippi River, Colorado River
6 Sports Gift Ideas
Spelled correctly: basketball, football helmet, baseball glove, soccer ball, croquet set, roller skates
Corrected spellings: badminton set, ski equipment
5 Foreign Countries to Visit
Spelled correctly: Brazil, Colombia, Zaire, New Zealand, Switzerland
Corrected spellings: Pakistan, Thailand, Australia
7 Musical Gift Ideas
Spelled correctly: violin, trumpet, compact discs, set of drums, trombone, saxophone, stereo system
Corrected spelling: piccolo
8 Clothing Ideas
Spelled correctly: ski jacket, cap, blue jeans, mittens, shirt, sneakers, warm-up pants, sweater
1 More Gift Ideas
Spelled correctly: computer
Corrected spellings: telephone, mall gift certificate, stuffed panda bear, jewelry, camera, miniature golf passes, movie theater tickets

Page 176

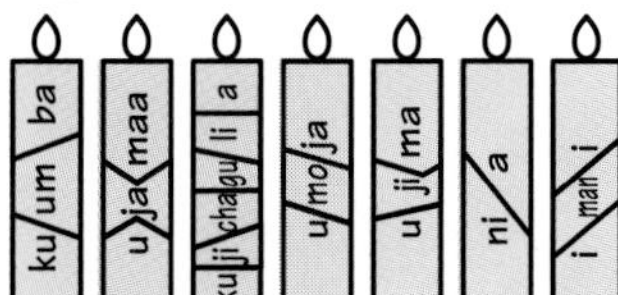

Page 177
1. **good:** nice, useful, excellent
2. **smart:** stylish, intelligent, witty
3. **bypassed:** detoured, skipped, jumped
4. **began:** initiated, started, created
5. **obtained:** caught, earned, acquired
6. **good:** pleasant, helpful, superb
7. **foremost:** good, main, star
8. **maintained:** believed, conserved, serviced
9. **directed:** led, commanded, managed
10. **acclaimed:** famous, great, primary
11. **worked:** performed, strived, satisfied
12. **better:** improve, enhance, exceed
13. **bad:** evil, ill-behaved, inferior
14. **earned:** gained, won, profited
15. **bars:** excludes, slows, prevents

Page 178
1. 7 out of 29 (or 7/29)
2. 5 out of 29 (or 5/29)
3. 5 out of 29 (or 5/29)
4. 8 out of 29 (or 8/29)
5. 4 out of 29 (or 4/29)
6. 13 out of 29 (or 13/29)
7. 12 out of 29 (or 12/29)
8. 12 out of 29 (or 12/29)
9. 17 out of 29 (or 17/29)
10. 19 out of 29 (or 19/29)

11. 7:4
12. 5:8
13. 4:5
14. 5:5 or 1:1
15. 8:7
16. 7:5
17. 5:7
18. 8:5
19. 4:5
20. 5:8

Bonus Box:
1. 7 out of 30 (or 7/30)
2. 5 out of 30 (or 5/30 or 1/6)
3. 5 out of 30 (or 5/30 or 1/6)
4. 9 out of 30 (or 9/30 or 3/10)
5. 4 out of 30 (or 4/30 or 2/15)

Page 179
Adjectives formed *from nouns:*
horrible: horror
biblical: Bible
penniless: penny
visionary: vision
American: America

Adjectives formed *from words that are either nouns or verbs:*
escaped: escape
bustling: bustle
farming: farm
mixed: mix
colored: color
crowded: crowd

Adjectives formed *from verbs*:
fascinating: fascinate
nourishing: nourish
*crippling: cripple
*Students could also list this under "Adjectives formed *from nouns.*"

Bonus Box: unemployed (from the base word *employ*)
Unemployed means "not employed," "not being used."

Page 180

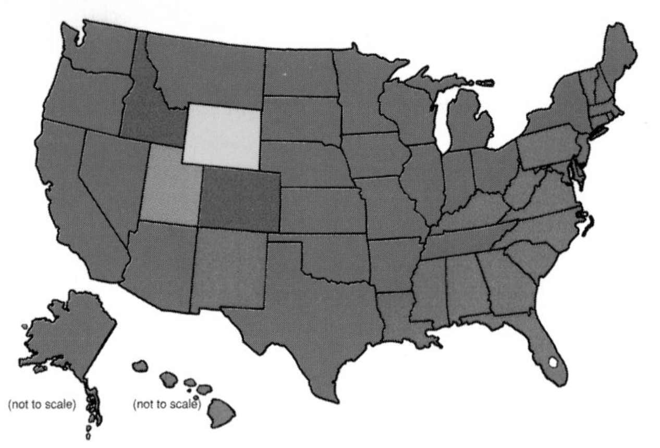

Page 182

1. $0.\overline{5}$
2. $0.\overline{3}$
3. $0.41\overline{6}$
4. $0.\overline{1}$
5. $0.\overline{7}$
6. $0.\overline{3}$
7. $0.\overline{18}$
8. $0.\overline{4}$
9. $0.08\overline{3}$
10. $0.\overline{8}$
11. $0.\overline{6}$
12. $0.\overline{63}$
13. $0.\overline{72}$
14. $0.\overline{27}$
15. $0.\overline{2}$

BILL COSBY IS TOPS!

Page 183

1. total calories: 1,310
   minutes needed to burn
   those calories:
   cycling: 437
   horseback riding: 655
   tennis: 188

2. total calories: 445
   minutes needed to burn
   those calories:
   dancing: 75
   golf: 89
   running: 38

3. total calories: 456
   minutes needed to burn
   those calories:
   swimming: 51
   walking: 114
   dancing: 76

4. total calories: 640
   minutes needed to burn
   those calories:
   cycling: 214
   running: 54
   walking: 160

5. total calories: 1,136
   minutes needed to burn
   those calories:
   golf: 228
   horseback riding: 568
   swimming: 127

6. total calories: 435
   minutes needed to burn
   those calories:
   dancing: 73
   cycling: 145
   tennis: 63

Bonus Box: 770 calories (5 malted-milk eggs = 115; $^{1}/_{2}$ chocolate bunny = 450; 5 jelly beans = 205)

Page 184

1. pane
2. swap
3. wasp
4. spear
5. swan
6. cast
7. blast
8. list
9. gasp
10. pasta
11. moan
12. rink
13. knot
14. trail
15. link
16. calm
17. canal
18. aim
19. animal
20. main

Bonus Box: Accept reasonable answers.
Possible answers:
newspaper: pare, pear, snap, span, spawn, ware, warp, wear, wrap
plastic bag: clasp, clip, gala, glib, last, past, scab, stab, stag
milk carton: clam, clan, rail, rain, tail, track, train, trim
aluminum can: maul, clan, clam, an, man, nun, I'm, inn

Page 186
Students' designs will vary.
Design 1 has 10 red squares and 20 blue.
Design 2 has 20 red squares, 10 blue, and 10 white.
Design 3 has 24 red squares, 12 blue, 6 white, and 6 green.
Design 4 has 20 red squares, 15 blue, 15 white, and 10 green.

Bonus Box:

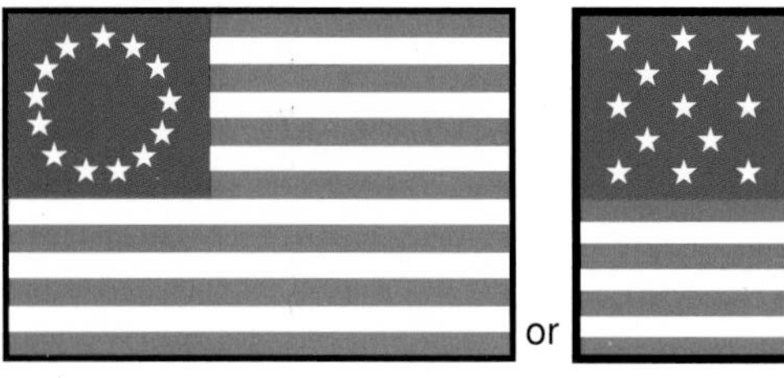

or

Page 187

1. mend
2. tend
3. lend
4. send
5. blender
6. fender
7. endure
8. depend
9. vendor
10. defend
11. dividend
12. apprehend
13. friend
14. tender
15. amend
16. commend
17. endanger
18. suspend
19. pendulum
20. suspenders
21. stupendous
22. comprehend
23. tremendous
24. vending machine
25. Achilles tendon

Bonus Box: debut, start, inception

Page 188

1. sale price \$11.25 (25% = .25; .25 x 15 = 3.75; 15 – 3.75 = 11.25)
2. sale price \$4,396.00 (20% = .20; .20 x 5,495 = 1,099; 5,495 – 1,099 = 4,396)
3. 35% off (8.40 – 5.46 = 2.94; 2.94 ÷ 8.40 = .35; .35 = 35%)
4. sale price \$246.00 ($^{1}/_{3}$ x 369 = 123; 369 – 123 = 246)
5. reg. price \$35.00 (100% – 20% = 80%; 28 ÷ 80%; 28 ÷ .80 = 35)
6. 40% off (185 – 111 = 74; 74 ÷ 185 = .4; .4 = .40 = 40%)
7. sale price \$2.85 (70% = .70; .70 x 9.50 = 6.65; 9.50 – 6.65 = 2.85)
8. sale price \$44.00 ($^{1}/_{3}$ x 66 = 22; 66 – 22 = 44)
9. 15% off (1,385 – 1,177.25 = 207.75; 207.75 ÷ 1,385 = .15; .15 = 15%)
10. reg. price \$20.00 (1 – $^{1}/_{5}$ = $^{4}/_{5}$; 16 ÷ $^{4}/_{5}$; 16 x $^{5}/_{4}$ = 20)
11. reg. price \$1.20 (1 – $^{2}/_{3}$ = $^{1}/_{3}$; .40 ÷ $^{1}/_{3}$; .40 x $^{3}/_{1}$ = 1.20)
12. sale price \$98.45 (45% = .45; .45 x 179 = 80.55; 179 – 80.55 = 98.45)

Bonus Box: total cost \$104.36 (.06 x 98.45 = 5.907; 5.907 = \$5.91; \$98.45 + \$5.91 = \$104.36)